中医药英语阅读教程（上）

主　编：陈　怡　周亚东
副主编：蒋怀周　程　玲
编　者：李　静　韩晶晶
　　　　江　莉

北京师范大学出版集团
BEIJING NORMAL UNIVERSITY PUBLISHING GROUP
安徽大学出版社

图书在版编目(CIP)数据

中医药英语阅读教程.上/陈怡,周亚东主编.—合肥:安徽大学出版社,2018.12
ISBN 978-7-5664-1631-5

Ⅰ.①中… Ⅱ.①陈… ②周… Ⅲ.①中国医药学－英语－阅读教学－高等学校－教材 Ⅳ.①R2

中国版本图书馆 CIP 数据核字(2018)第 136819 号

中医药英语阅读教程(上) 陈 怡 周亚东 主编

出版发行:	北京师范大学出版集团 安 徽 大 学 出 版 社 (安徽省合肥市肥西路 3 号 邮编 230039) www.bnupg.com.cn www.ahupress.com.cn
印　　刷:	安徽省人民印刷有限公司
经　　销:	全国新华书店
开　　本:	184mm×260mm
印　　张:	14.25
字　　数:	330 千字
版　　次:	2018 年 12 月第 1 版
印　　次:	2018 年 12 月第 1 次印刷
定　　价:	39.90 元

ISBN 978-7-5664-1631-5

策划编辑:李 梅 李 雪　　　　　　装帧设计:孟献辉 李 军
责任编辑:葛灵知 李 雪　　　　　　美术编辑:李 军
责任印制:赵明炎

版权所有　侵权必究

反盗版、侵权举报电话:0551－65106311
外埠邮购电话:0551－65107716
本书如有印装质量问题,请与印制管理部联系调换。
印制管理部电话:0551－65106311

前　言

随着中医国际化的深入,英语作为国际化桥梁的重要性已日益凸显,准确实用的英语表达对中医国际化意义重大。医学院校的学生学习中医药英语已势在必行,因为中医要走向世界,首先要打破语言的壁垒。鉴于此,我们组织了部分医学英语教学第一线的骨干教师,结合自身的教学实践,专门为中医药院校的学生编写了这套教材。

本套教材分为上、下两册:上册涵盖了中医药理论、阴阳、五行、气血津液、经络、病因、病机、中医诊断技巧等内容;下册涵盖了中医方剂、针灸和艾灸、内外妇儿的辨证治疗、中医养生与疾病预防、中医简史、中医代表人物及医学著作等内容。

本书共十一个单元,每单元由 Text A, Text B 及 Text C 三篇文章组成,课后设有词汇、阅读、翻译、写作等形式的练习题并在每单元后以不同主题列出常用医学英语词根词缀,便于学生巩固所学内容及拓展医学英语词汇。

《中医药英语阅读教程(上、下)》可供中医院校本科生、研究生作为教材使用,也可作为培训中医药对外交流人员的教材。

编者学识有限,书中错误难免,恳切希望同行和广大读者批评指正。

编　者
2018 年 6 月

Contents

Unit 1 Theory of Traditional Chinese Medicine ········· 1
   Text A An Introduction to Traditional Chinese Medicine ········· 1
   Text B Basic Theories of Traditional Chinese Medicine ········· 6
   Text C Specific and Profound TCM ········· 11

Unit 2 *Yin-Yang* ········· 19
   Text A *Yin* and *Yang*: An Introduction ········· 19
   Text B *Yin* and *Yang*—The Law of Nature ········· 23
   Text C *Yin-Yang* Theory in Traditional Chinese Medicine ········· 29

Unit 3 The Five Elements ········· 36
   Text A The Five-Element Theroy—Natural Philosophy in Ancient China ········· 36
   Text B The Basic Content of Five-Element Theory ········· 41
   Text C Five Elements and *Yin-Yang* Balance ········· 47

Unit 4 Visceral State ········· 55
   Text A The Visceral Theory of TCM ········· 55
   Text B The Relationship Between *Zang* and *Fu* Organs ········· 60
   Text C The Small Intestine ········· 65

Unit 5 *Qi*, Blood and Body Fluid ········· 71
   Text A The Relationship Between Blood and Body Fluid ········· 71
   Text B *Qi*, Blood and Body Fluid of Mutual Causality ········· 75
   Text C *Qigong* Therapy ········· 79

Unit 6 The Channels and Collaterals ········· 86
   Text A The Mystery of Meridian ········· 86

Text B	Meridians and Collaterals—Pathways to Link the Whole Body	91
Text C	Application of the Theory of Channels and Collaterals	95

Unit 7 An Overview of TCM Etiology ... 103
Text A Fire (Heat) ... 103
Text B The Six Climatic Evils ... 108
Text C Etiology ... 112

Unit 8 Disease Mechanism in TCM ... 119
Text A Mechanism of Pathological Changes(1) ... 119
Text B Mechanism of Pathological Changes(2) ... 124
Text C Imbalance Between *Yin* and *Yang* ... 128

Unit 9 Four Diagnostic Techniques ... 135
Text A Diagnostics of Traditional Chinese Medicine ... 135
Text B Diagnosis Methods in TCM ... 140
Text C Listening to Sounds ... 145

Unit 10 Differentiation of Syndromes ... 152
Text A TCM Differential Diagnosis ... 152
Text B Syndrome Differentiation of Spleen Diseases ... 157
Text C Syndrome Differentiation of Fluid Disorder ... 162

Unit 11 Chinese Materia Medica ... 170
Text A Medical Plants ... 170
Text B Magic Chinese Herbs ... 174
Text C The Magic Anti-Tumor Herb—Matrine ... 178

Keys to Exercises ... 185
Glossary ... 207

Unit 1　Theory of Traditional Chinese Medicine

Unit 1　Theory of Traditional Chinese Medicine

 Text A

An Introduction to Traditional Chinese Medicine

Many Chinese people, especially the older generation, are accustomed to going to traditional Chinese doctors① and using traditional Chinese remedies.

Traditional Chinese medicine (TCM) has a history stretching back thousands of years. TCM is an extremely rich discipline, built upon the combined experiences of famous practitioners of past dynasties, and the extensive body of medical writings they produced.

The theories of TCM are quite different from those of Western medicine. TCM considers Nature and Human to form a single whole, and emphasizes the philosophical concept known as "The Unity of Heaven and Human②". Environmental factors such as the four seasons and changes in temperature and weather are believed to influence the human body, with the body and Nature forming an integrated system. For instance, when the weather is humid in the spring, hot in the summer, dry in the fall, or cold in the winter, TCM employs treatments known as "eliminating fire" "expelling dampness" "moistening the body" and "guarding against cold" respectively. All parts and systems of the body are considered to be closely connected and mutually interacted "The outside of the body is *yang*, and the inside is *yin*; the back is *yang*, and the abdomen is *yin*." TCM utilizes the *yin-yang* Theory and the Five-Element Theory, which advocate "administering treatment according to pattern", rather than "treating the head when the head hurts; treating the foot when the foot hurts".③ According to the Five-Element Theory, the liver and gallbladder are Wood, the heart is Fire, the spleen and stomach are Earth, the lungs and intestines are Metal, and the kidneys and bladder are Water. When *yin* and *yang* are out of balance, disease and disorder result. Diagnosis relies on inspecting the complexion, smelling the breath, inquiring about symptoms and feeling the pulse in order to determine the overall condition of the body.

Traditional Chinese remedies consist of natural preparations. Several thousand years of experimentation have determined the specific medicinal properties of numerous herbs, and the specific prescriptions and treatments that should be used for a wide range of conditions. The famous *Compendium of Materia Medica* (*Bencao Gangmu*), written by Li Shizhen during the Ming

Dynasty (1368~1644), contains comprehensive descriptions of thousands of Chinese herbal remedies. Traditional Chinese remedies may either be taken internally or applied externally to promote the recovery of normal functioning, in accordance with the theory of "administering treatment according to pattern". Thus the saying, "Western medicine treats the symptom, Chinese medicine treats the root."④ As more people have become interested in alternative lifestyles in recent years, there has been a corresponding upsurge of interest in⑤ herbal medicine and non-pharmaceutical treatments. Traditional Chinese medicine and remedies have become increasingly popular around the world, and the number of Sino-foreign exchanges⑥ concerning traditional Chinese medicine and remedies has steadily increased. Japan, the United States and Germany have established a number of cooperative projects with China, and the World Health Organization has opened seven traditional Chinese medicine centers in China.

Studies concerning acupuncture, moxibustion and the use of acupuncture for anesthesia and pain relief⑦ have been published in 120 countries and regions around the world. In 1987, the World Acupuncture Association, consisting of over 50,000 members from almost 100 countries and regions, was established in Beijing. In 1991, the International Association of Traditional Chinese Medicine was established in China, with representatives from several dozen countries jointly drafting the "Beijing Proclamation".⑧ To date, China has established medical research and educational exchanges in the field of TCM with more than 100 countries and regions.

(608 words)

New Words

integrated /ˈɪntɪɡreɪtɪd/ a.	综合的，完整的
humid /ˈhjuːmɪd/ a.	潮湿的，湿气重的
expel /ɪkˈspel/ vt.	驱逐，赶走
dampness /ˈdæmpnəs/ n.	潮湿，湿气
moisten /ˈmɔɪsn/ n./v.	润湿
abdomen /ˈæbdəmən/ n.	腹部
gallbladder /ˈɡɔːlblædə/ n.	胆囊
spleen /spliːn/ n.	脾脏，脾
intestine /ɪnˈtestɪn/ n.	肠
bladder /ˈblædə/ n.	膀胱
disorder /dɪsˈɔːdə/ n.	（身心、机能）失调
preparation /ˌprepəˈreɪʃn/ n.	配制剂
jointly /ˈdʒɔɪntlɪ/ ad.	共同地
proclamation /ˌprɒkləˈmeɪʃn/ n.	宣布，声明，公告

Unit 1 Theory of Traditional Chinese Medicine

Expressions

be accustomed to	习惯，适应
stretch back	时间上的延伸、延续
be closely connected	密切相关
out of balance	失衡
rely on	依赖，依靠
inquire about	询问
a wide range of	广泛的，大范围的
either...or...	不论……还是…… 或者……或者……
in accordance with	按照，依照
to date	迄今

Notes

① ...going to traditional Chinese doctors：看中医。
② The Unity of Heaven and Human：天人合一。
③ TCM utilizes the *yin-yang* Theory and the Five-Element Theory, which advocate "administering treatment according to pattern", rather than "treating the head when the head hurts; treating the foot when the foot hurts". 中医运用阴阳和五行理论，提倡"依类型治疗"，而不是"头痛医头，脚痛医脚"。Five-Element Theory：五行理论，包括木、火、土、金、水。
④ Western medicine treats the symptom, Chinese medicine treats the root. 西医治标，中医治本。
⑤ a corresponding upsurge interest in：在……方面的兴趣激增。
⑥ Sino-foreign exchanges：中外交流。Sino-是前缀，表示"中国与……的"，如：Sino-Japanese trade，中日贸易。
⑦ pain relief：减轻、缓解疼痛。
⑧ In 1991, the International Association...drafting the "Beijing Proclamation". 1991年，中医国际协会在北京成立，来自几十个国家的代表联合起草了《北京宣言》。

Exercises

Ⅰ. **Fill in the blanks with the words given below. Change the form when necessary.**

accustom	eliminate	extensive	emphasis
integrate	respectively	mutual	comprehensive
recovery	representative	draft	exchange

1. He soon gets _____ to dormitory life and makes two or three friends there.
2. The union _____ was accused of being a puppet of the management.
3. They sat down and _____ a letter to the local newspaper.
4. We must make _____ analysis of a problem before it can be solved.
5. We must _____ theory with practice.
6. To fight and _____ poverty is a major task facing the world today.
7. The woman was delighted at the _____ of her stolen jewels.
8. The author of this book puts _____ on the importance of the accumulation of cultural knowledge at the meeting.
9. I have benefited a lot from _____ reading.
10. We _____ our opinions about the event at the meeting.
11. Negotiations between unions and management are made more difficult by _____ distrust.
12. My husband and I got pay rises of 8% and 10% _____.

II. Choose the best answer to each of the following questions.

1. What is the difference between the theories of TCM and those of Western medicine?
   A. TCM considers Nature and Human to form a single whole, while Western medicine treats the head when the head hurts and treats the foot when the foot hurts.
   B. Western medicine treats the symptom; Chinese medicine treats the root.
   C. TCM is an extremely rich discipline, built upon the combined experiences of famous practitioners of past dynasties.
   D. Environmental factors are believed to influence the human body according to TCM, but have nothing to do with the Western medicine.

2. How are the factors of season embodied in the practice of TCM?
   A. TCM employs treatments known as "guarding against cold" "expelling dampness" "moistening the body", and "eliminating fire", respectively.
   B. TCM employs treatments known as "eliminating fire" "expelling dampness" "moistening the body", and "guarding against cold" respectively.
   C. TCM employs treatments known as "eliminating fire" "moistening the body" "expelling dampness", and "guarding against cold" respectively.
   D. TCM employs treatments known as "expelling dampness" "eliminating fire" "moistening the body" and "guarding against cold" respectively.

3. Which of the following is true about the *yin-yang* Theory in TCM?
   A. The outside of the body is *yin*, and the inside is *yang*; the back is *yang*, and the abdomen is *yin*.
   B. The outside of the body is *yang*, and the inside is *yin*; the back is *yin*, and the abdomen is *yang*.

C. The outside of the body is *yang*, and the inside is *yin*; the back is *yang*, and the abdomen is *yin*.

D. The outside of the body is *yin*, and the inside is *yang*; the back is *yin*, and the abdomen is *yang*.

4. How do practitioners of TCM diagnose the patients?
   A. Diagnosis relies on inspecting the complexion, smelling the breath, inquiring about symptoms, and feeling the pulse.
   B. Diagnosis relies on inspecting the complexion and some necessary tests.
   C. Diagnosis relies on inspecting the complexion, and feeling the pulse.
   D. Diagnosis relies on feeling the pulse and inquiring about symptoms.

5. Which of the following is NOT mentioned in the development of TCM?
   A. Studies concerning acupuncture, moxibustion and the use of acupuncture for anesthesia.
   B. In 1987, the World Acupuncture Association, consisting of over 50,000 members from almost 100 countries and regions, was established in Beijing.
   C. To date, China has established medical research and educational exchanges in the field of TCM with more than 100 countries and regions.
   D. In 1991, the Asian Association of Traditional Chinese Medicine was established in China.

Ⅲ. Translate the following sentences into English or Chinese.

1. 迄今为止，我们已经收到了一百多份申请书。

2. 协会大部分的收入依靠会员的捐赠。

3. 头痛医头，脚痛医脚。

4. 西医治标，中医治本。

5. 来自几十个国家的代表联合起草了《北京宣言》。

6. TCM utilizes the *yin-yang* Theory and the Five-Element Theory, which advocate "administering treatment according to pattern".

7. TCM emphasizes the philosophical concept known as "The Unity of Heaven and Human".

8. According to the Five-Element Theory, the liver and gallbladder are Wood, the heart is Fire, the spleen and stomach are Earth, the lungs and intestines are Metal, and the kidneys and bladder are Water.

9. Diagnosis relies on inspecting the complexion, smelling the breath, inquiring about symptoms, and feeling the pulse in order to determine the overall condition of the body.

10. To date, China has established medical research and educational exchanges in the field of TCM with more than 100 countries and regions.

Ⅳ. Write a 150-word composition about the basic theories of TCM.

 Text B

Basic Theories of Traditional Chinese Medicine

Traditional Chinese medicine (TCM) has a long history. In remote antiquity, our ancestors created primitive medicine during their struggles against nature. The theories of TCM come mainly from practice and have been continually enriched and expanded through practice.①

TCM has many characteristics both in the understanding of the human body's physiology and pathology and in the diagnosis and treatment of diseases. These characteristics, however, can be summarized in the following two aspects:

The Concept of the Organism as a Whole②

By "organic whole" we mean entirety and unity. TCM attaches great importance to the unity of the human body itself and its relationship with nature, and holds that the human body itself is an organic whole and has very close and inseparable relations with the external natural surroundings. The concept of emphasizing the unity within the body and the unified relations between the body and the outside world is known as that of an organic whole.③

a. The Unity Within the Body

The human body is made up of viscera, bowels, tissues and other organs. Each of them has its own special physiological functions. All these different physiological functions are a component part of the entire life process of the body.④ And this determines the unity within the body. Therefore, the component parts of the human body are inseparable from each other in structure, related, subsidiary and conditional to each other in physiology, and of certain influence upon each other in pathology. These mutual relations and influences are centered around the five viscera (the heart, the liver, the spleen, the lung and the kidney) and come into effect through the channels and collaterals. For instance, the heart is interior-exteriorly related to the small intestine, controls blood circulation, and has its "specific opening" in the tongue proper and so on.

b. The Unity Between the Human Body and Nature

Unit 1　Theory of Traditional Chinese Medicine

　　Man lives in nature and takes nature as his vital conditions for living. In the meantime, he is influenced directly or indirectly by the movements and changes in nature, to which he is bound to make corresponding physiological and pathological responses. For example, as the climate varies with the four seasons in a year, the normal pulse conditions⑤ (including pulse rate, rhythm, volume, tension, etc.) are also varied. The pulse becomes string-like in spring, full in summer, floating in autumn and sunken in winter. This provides a basis for doctors to distinguish abnormal pulse conditions from the normal ones during the clinical diagnosis. The occurrence, development and changes of many diseases are seasonal.

　　Based on the theory of the circulation of *qi* characteristics of TCM, the pathogenesis of the human body is often influenced by the periodic changes of the climate, which take place every 12 years or every 60 years. In recent years, scientists have realized that the law of these periodic changes has something to do with the cycle of sunspots, which is formed every 11 to 12 years.⑥

　　TCM believes that different geographical surroundings produce different effects on the physiology and pathology of the human body.

　　c. The Guiding Function of the Concept of the Organism as a Whole

　　The concept of the organism as a whole not only embodies TCM's understanding of the human body itself and the relationship between it and nature, but also provides the medical workers with a necessary method of thinking in treating diseases. Such a concept penetrates through the entire theory concerning the physiology and pathology of TCM, and of great significance in guiding diagnosis and treatment.⑦

　　Diagnosis and Treatment Based on an Overall Analysis of Signs and Symptoms⑧

　　Generally speaking, the same syndromes are treated in similar ways. Of course, diagnosis and treatment based on an overall analysis and differentiation of symptoms and signs should not remain at the present level or stand still or refuse to make any further progress, but instead, be enriched, renewed, developed and improved continually alongside the advancing of modern natural sciences.

(710 words)

New Words

renew /rɪˈnjuː/	*v.*	更新,恢复
viscera /ˈvɪsərə/	*n.*	内脏,内部的东西
physiological /ˌfɪziˈlɒdʒɪkl/	*a.*	生理学的,生理学上的
subsidiary /səbˈsɪdɪəri/	*n.*	子公司,辅助者,附加物
	a.	辅助的,附带的,隶属的
pulse /pʌls/	*n.*	脉搏,有节奏的跳动
	v.	拍打,跳动,振动

abnormal /æbˈnɔːml/	a.	反常的,例外的,不规则的,变态的
pathogenesis /ˈpæθəˈdʒenɪsɪs/	n.	发病机理
sunspot /ˌsʌnspɒt/	n.	太阳的黑点,雀斑
geographical /ˌdʒiːəˈɡræfɪkl/	a.	地理(学)的

Expressions

in the diagnosis of	在诊断中
be summarized in	被总结为
attach great importance to	认为……很重要
be known as	被看作……
be made up of	由……组成
come into effect	产生作用
in the meantime	同时
be bound to	肯定,必然,注定
provide a basis for	提供基础
distinguish from	辨别,分清
of great significance	非常重要
be bound to	肯定,必然,注定

Notes

① The theories of TCM come mainly from practice and have been continually enriched and expanded through practice. 中医理论主要来源于实践,并通过实践继续丰富和扩充。

② The Concept of the Organism as a Whole：整体观念。

③ The concept of emphasizing the unity within the body and the unified relations between the body and the outside world is known as that of an organic whole. 注重人体本身的统一性以及人体与外部世界的统一关系,这种观念被称为整体观念。

④ All these different physiological functions are a component part of the entire life process of the body. 所有这些不同的生理功能都是人体整个生命活动的组成部分。

⑤ pulse conditions：脉象。健康人脉象应为一次呼吸跳 4 次,寸关尺三部有脉,脉不浮不沉,和缓有力,尺脉沉取应有力。常见病脉有浮脉、沉脉、迟脉、数脉、虚脉、实脉、滑脉、洪脉、细脉、弦脉等。

⑥ In recent years, scientists have realized that the law of these periodic changes has something to do with the cycle of sunspots, which is formed every 11 to 12 years. 近年来,科学家已经认识到,这种周期性变化的规律可能与每 11 年至 12 年形成的太阳黑子的周期有关。has something to do with：与……有关。例如：He has something to do with the college. 他与那所大学有关系。

⑦ Such a concept penetrates through the entire theory concerning the physiology and pathology of TCM, and of great significance in guiding diagnosis and treatment. 这个

Unit 1　Theory of Traditional Chinese Medicine

概念贯穿整个中医生理和病理理论，并且对指导诊断和治疗具有十分重要的意义。

⑧ Diagnosis and Treatment Based on an Overall Analysis of Signs and Symptoms：辨证论治。辨证论治是中医认识疾病和治疗疾病的基本原则。"辨证"就是把四诊（望诊、闻诊、问诊、切诊）所收集的资料、症状和体征进行分析综合，辨清疾病的病因、性质、部位以及邪正之间的关系，将之概括、判断为某种性质的"证"。论治，又称为"施治"，即根据辨证的结果，确定相应的治疗方法。

Exercises

Ⅰ. **Fill in the blanks with the words given below. Change the form when necessary.**

struggle	enrich	expand	bound
corresponding	distinguish	penetrate	concern
symptom	overall	occurrence	surrounding

1. It is more like a made-up story than a real _____.
2. As far as the environmental protection is _____, each country, rich or poor, must play its own part.
3. The written record of our conversation doesn't _____ with what was actually said.
4. Advancing culture is _____ to triumph over declining culture.
5. The two countries agreed to _____ their trade relations in the coming year.
6. The _____ composition of the picture is perfect but some of the details are not so good.
7. The _____ country is a wilderness of sand.
8. Man is engaged in a constant _____ with Nature.
9. People who cannot _____ between colors are said to be color-blind.
10. She could _____ what I was thinking.
11. It is generally thought that traveling abroad can _____ one's knowledge.
12. This demonstration was a(n) _____ of discontent among the students.

Ⅱ. **Choose the best answer to each of the following question or unfinished statements.**

1. TCM has many characteristics in _____.
   A. physiology and anatomy　　　B. the diagnosis and treatment of diseases
   C. pathology and anatomy　　　D. assimilation and storage
2. According to the basic theory of TCM the human body is made up of _____.
   A. small and large intestine, gallbladder, urinary bladder and stomach
   B. heart, liver, spleen, lung and kidney
   C. viscera, bowels, tissues and other organs

D. vessel, skin, muscle, tendon, bone

3. The pulse conditions include _____.
   A. channels and collaterals
   B. *qi* and blood
   C. string
   D. pulse rate, rhythm, volume, tension

4. The pathogenesis of the human body is often influenced by _____.
   A. blood circulation
   B. the circulation of *qi*
   C. the pericardium channel
   D. the periodic changes of the climate

5. Which statement is NOT true according to the passage?
   A. The concept of the organism as a whole only embodies TCM's understanding of the human body itself.
   B. Diagnosis and treatment are based on an overall analysis of symptoms and signs.
   C. The law of these periodic changes has something to do with the cycle of sunspots.
   D. Generally speaking, the same syndromes are treated in similar ways.

Ⅲ. Translate the following sentences into English or Chinese.

1. 中医理论一直在实践过程中丰富和扩展。

2. 人类祖先在与自然做斗争的过程中创造了原始医药。

3. 人体自身是一个有机的整体,与外在的自然环境有非常紧密和不可分割的联系。

4. 人体是由器官、肠、组织和其他组成。

5. 人体的各个组成部分在结构上是不可分割的。

6. Five viscera of human body include the heart, the liver, the spleen, the lung and the kidney.

7. The occurrence, development and changes of many diseases are seasonal.

8. The concept of the organism as a whole provides the medical workers with a necessary method of thinking in treating diseases.

9. In recent years, scientists have realized that the law of these periodic changes has something to do with the cycle of sunspots.

10. The concept of the organism as a whole embodies TCM's understanding of the human body itself and the relationship between it and nature.

Unit 1　Theory of Traditional Chinese Medicine

 Text C

Specific and Profound TCM

Traditional Chinese Medicine (TCM), one of China's splendid cultural heritages, is the science dealing with human physiology, pathology, diagnosis, treatment and prevention of diseases. TCM summed up the experience of the Chinese people in their long struggle against diseases and, under the influence of ancient naive materialism and dialectics, evolved into a unique, integral system of medical theory through long clinical practice. During several thousand years it has made great contributions to the promotion of health, the proliferation and prosperity of the Chinese nation, and the enrichment and development of world medicine as well. The formation of the theoretical system of TCM was greatly influenced by ancient Chinese materialism and dialectics.① The theoretical system takes the physiology and pathology of *zang-fu* organs and meridians as its basis, and treatment by differentiation of syndromes (TDS) as its diagnostic and therapeutic features.

TCM has its own specific understanding both in the physiological functions and pathological changes of the human body and in the diagnosis and treatment of disease. TCM regards the human body itself as an organic whole interconnected by *zang-fu* organs, meridians and collaterals②. And TCM also holds that the human body is closely related to the outside world. In regard to the onset and development of a disease, TCM attaches great importance to the endogenous pathogenic factors, namely③, the seven emotions, but it by no means excludes the exogenous pathogenic factors, namely, the six pathogens. In diagnosis, TCM takes the four diagnostic methods (inspection, auscultation and olfaction, inquiry, pulse-taking and palpation) as its principal techniques, eight principal syndromes as its general guideline, and differentiation of syndrome according to the *zang-fu* theory, differentiation of syndromes according to the six-meridian theory, and differentiation of syndromes according to the theory of *wei*, *qi*, *ying* and *xue*④ as its basic theories of the differentiation of syndromes. It also stresses the prevention and preventive treatment of diseases, and puts forward such therapeutic principles as "treatment aiding at the root cause of disease" and "strengthening vital *qi* and dispelling pathogens, regulating *yin* and *yang*⑤ and treating diseases in accordance with three conditions" (i. e., the climatic and seasonal condition, geographic localities and the patient's constitution).

These characteristics, however, can be generalized as the holistic concept and TDS.

The Holistic Concept

This concept means a general idea of, on the one hand, the unity and integrity within the human body and, on the other, its close relationship with the outer world. The human body is composed of various organs and tissues, each having its own distinct function, which is a component part of the life activities of the whole body. And in TCM the human body is regarded as an organic whole in which its constituent parts are inseparable in structure, interrelated and interdependent in physiology, and mutually influential in pathology. Meanwhile, man lives in nature, and nature provides the conditions indispensable to man's survival. So it follows that the human body is bound to be affected directly or indirectly by the changes of nature, to which the human body, in turn, makes corresponding responses. TCM says, "Physicians have to know the law of nature and geographical conditions when diagnosing and treating diseases."

Treatment by Differentiation of Syndromes

TCM, on the other hand, is characterized by TDS(Treatment by Differentiation of syndromes). Differentiation means comprehensive analysis, while syndrome refers to symptoms and signs. So differentiation of syndromes implies that the patient's symptoms and signs collected by the four diagnostic methods⑥ are analyzed and summarized so as to identify the etiology, nature and location of a disease, and the relation between vital *qi* and pathogens, thereby determining what syndrome the disease belongs to. Treatment refers to selecting the corresponding therapy according to the outcome of differentiating syndromes. Taken as a whole⑦, TDS means diagnosis and treatment based on an overall analysis of symptoms and signs.

(646 words)

New Words

heritage /ˈherɪtɪdʒ/ *n.*	遗产,继承物,传统
influence /ˈɪnfluəns/ *n.*	影响,势力,权势,产生影响的人(事物)
vt.	影响,感化
materialism /məˈtɪərɪəlɪzəm/ *n.*	唯物主义,唯物论,实利主义,物质主义
dialectic /ˌdaɪəˈlektɪk/ *a.*	辩证的,辩证法的
n.	辩证法
integral /ˈɪntɪgrəl/ *a.*	构成整体所必需的
meridian /məˈrɪdɪən/ *n.*	子午圈,子午线,顶点,(权力、成就等的)全盛时期
organic /ɔːˈgænɪk/ *a.*	器官的,器质性的,有机(体)的
interconnect /ˌɪntəkəˈnekt/ *vi.*	互相连接,互相联系
endogenous /enˈdɒdʒənəs/ *a.*	内长的,内生的
auscultation /ˌɔːskəlˈteɪʃn/ *n.*	听诊
olfaction /ɒlˈfækʃn/ *n.*	嗅,嗅觉
inquiry /ɪnˈkwaɪərɪ/ *n.*	打听,询问,调查,查问
palpation /pælˈpeɪʃn/ *n.*	触诊,扪诊
preventive /prɪˈventɪv/ *n.*	预防,防止,预防药

Unit 1　Theory of Traditional Chinese Medicine

a.	预防的，防止的
characteristic /ˌkærɪktəˈrɪstɪk/ *a.*	特有的，典型的
tissue /ˈtɪʃuː/ *n.*	组织，薄纸，棉纸，一套
constituent /kənˈstɪtjuənt/ *n.*	选民，成分，构成部分，要素
corresponding /ˌkɒrəˈspɒndɪŋ/ *a.*	相当的，对应的，符合的，一致的

Expressions

deal with	处理，关于
sum up	总结
struggle against	与……做斗争
under the influence of	在……的影响下
evolve into	演化成为，发展成为
make contributions to	为……做贡献
regard ... as	把……看作
be related to	与……有联系
by no means	决不
put forward	提出
be generalized as	被总结为
be composed of	由……组成的
it follows that	可以得出（……的结论）

Notes

① The formation of the theoretical system of TCM was greatly influenced by ancient Chinese materialism and dialectics. 中医理论系统的形成受到古代中国的唯物论和辩证法的影响很大。materialism and dialectics：唯物论与辩证法。

② meridians and collaterals：经络，研究人体经络系统的生理功能、病理变化以及脏腑的相互关系的学说。它与阴阳、五行、脏腑、气血津液等共同组成了中医学的理论基础。"夫十二经脉者，人之所以生，病之所以成，人之所以治，病之所以起，学之所始，工之所止也。"经络是人体气血运行、经过、联络的通路。

③ namely：即，就是，换句话说。提示词，提示下句话是对前句话的解释说明。

④ *wei*, *qi*, *ying* and *xue*：卫气营血，是构建温病学的基本范畴，中医温病学不仅有着丰富的临床经验，而且有着深刻的理论思维，它是通过自己一套特有的概念范畴及其逻辑体系来展开的。

⑤ regulating *yin* and *yang*：调和阴阳。即阴阳对偶统一、表里的对偶统一、虚实的对偶统一、寒热的对偶统一，在《伤寒论》中有集中体现。

⑥ four diagnostic methods：四诊法，中国古代战国时期的名医扁鹊根据民间流传的经验和他自己多年的医疗实践，总结出来诊断疾病的四种基本方法，即望诊、闻诊、问诊和切诊，总称"四诊"。

⑦ taken as a whole：固定搭配，意为总的来说，通常用于总结和综述观点。

Exercises

Ⅰ. **Fill in the blanks with the words given below. Change the form when necessary.**

heritage	prevention	prosperity	regard
attach	stress	strengthen	compose
interdependent	survival	inquiry	identify

1. The branch of medicine that deals with tumors, including study of their development, diagnosis, treatment, and _____.
2. All nations are _____ in the modern world.
3. The English teacher _____ the importance of reading aloud again and again.
4. Water is _____ of hydrogen and oxygen.
5. The promise of _____ in the United States encouraged many people to immigrate.
6. She is generally _____ as one of the best writers in the country.
7. The miraculous _____ of some people in the air crash was widely reported by the press.
8. A novelist must be able to use the cultural _____ of his nation.
9. How can you _____ the blame for this accident to the taxi-driver?
10. It is a systematic attempt to _____ our competitive ability.
11. They've promised a thorough _____ into the plane crash.
12. She _____ that the man was her attacker.

Ⅱ. **Choose the best answer to each of the following question or unfinished statements.**

1. TCM _____.
   A. was influenced by ancient Taoism
   B. can deal with diagnosis and treatment of the disease
   C. can cure many cancers
   D. stresses the development of the disease

2. The basis of the theoretical system of TCM is _____.
   A. ancient materialism
   B. dialectics
   C. physiology and pathology of *zang-fu* organs and meridians
   D. Both A and B.

3. _____ can be one of the characteristics of TCM.
   A. The Holistic Concept

B. Understanding the physiological functions

   C. Stressing the prevention of the disease

   D. The influence of the materialism

4. The Holistic Concept stresses _____.

   A. the body is composed of various organs

   B. various organs can work independently

   C. human body is bound to be affected by the nature

   D. the human body is regarded as an organic whole in which its constituent parts are inseparable

5. What is the main idea of the text?

   A. TCM is the splendid culture in China.

   B. Compare the differences between TCM and western medicine.

   C. The clear definition of TCM.

   D. The distinct features of TCM.

Ⅲ. Translate the following sentences into English or Chinese.

1. 这些症状可能会进一步发展为威胁生命的疾病。

2. 请你用几句话把你的观点概括一下好吗？

3. 所有这一切均是依据法律执行的。

4. 不久前他提出了一个切实可行的计划.

5. 这篇文章是关于中医基本概念和治疗方法原理的。

6. This is a tumor composed of muscle tissue.

7. China does not pose a grave threat to world food security; in contrary, it may make a great contribution to world food development.

8. TCM holds that the human body is an organic whole.

9. The holistic concept means a general idea of, on the one hand, the unity and integrity within the human body and, on the other, its close relationship with the outer world.

10. TCM has its own specific understanding both in the physiological functions and pathological changes of the human body and in the diagnosis and treatment of disease.

Body System（体区系统）

Root	Meaning	Examples
corpor- somato- -some	body, corpus 体	extracorporeal 体外的 somatopsychic 身心的 ribosome 核蛋白体
capit- cephalo-	head 头	cephalexin 头孢氨苄 cephalic 头部的
facio- prosopo-	face 脸，面孔	facial 面的 prosopagnosia 面容失认，脸盲症 prosopopagus 面部连胎
bucco-	cheek, mala 颊	buccolingual 颊舌的 buccal 颊的，口腔的
mento- genio-	chin 下巴，颏	menton 颏（下）点 mentolabial 颏唇的 geniohyoid 颏舌骨肌 genioplasty 颏成形术
cervico- tracheo-	neck, cervix 颈	cervical 颈的 cervicobrachial 颈臂的 trachelagra 颈痛风 tracheloplasty 宫颈成形术
acro- melo-	limb, extremity 肢	acromegaly 肢端肥大症 melorheostosis 肢骨纹状肥大 meloplasty 肢成形术
omo- scapulo-	shoulder 肩	omohyoid 肩胛舌骨肌 acromion 肩峰 scapulopexy 肩胛固定术 scapulothoracic 肩胛胸的
cubito-	elbow 肘	cubital 肘的，尺骨的 cubitoradial 尺桡的
carpo-	wrist 腕	carpal 腕骨的 carpoptosis 腕下垂 carpometacarpal 腕掌的
brachio-	arm 臂	brachial 臂的，肱的 brachiocephalic 头臂动脉

续表

Root	Meaning	Examples
mano- cheiro-	hand, manus 手	manual 手的 manoptoscope 主视检查器 cheiro-oral syndrome 手口综合征
digito- dactylo-	finger 手指 toe 趾	digital 指（趾）的,数字的 digitoxin 洋地黄毒苷（源于花冠如手指的植物） dactylology 手语 dactylogram 指纹
coxo-	hip 髋	coxarthrosis 髋关节病
femoro- mero-	thigh, femur 股	femoral 股骨的 femoropopliteal 股腘的 merocoxalgia 髋股痛
genu-	knee 膝	genuflect 屈膝
malleo-	ankle 踝	malleolar 踝的 malleotomy 踝切除术,锤骨切开术
ped- pedi- pod- -pod	foot 足	pedal 足的 pedopathy 足病,脚病 podiatry 足病学 arthropod 节肢动物
calcaneo-	heel 足跟	calcaneal 跟骨的
pecto- thoraco- stetho-	chest, breast 胸	angina pectoris 心绞痛 thoracotomy 胸廓切开术 thoracoscopy 胸腔镜检查 stethoscope 听诊器
mammo- masto-	breast 乳房	mammogram 乳房X线照片 mammoplasty 乳房成形术 mastectomy 乳房切除术
mammillo- papillo-	nipple, teat 乳头	mammilliform 乳头状的 papillary 乳头的,乳突的 papilledema 视神经乳头水肿
phreno-	diaphragm 膈	phrenic 膈的

续表

Root	Meaning	Examples
ventro- laparo-	abdomen, tummy 腹	abdominohysterotomy 剖腹子宫切开术 laparoscopy 腹腔镜术
viscero- splanchno-	viscera 内脏	visceroptosis 内脏下垂 splanchnic 内脏的
periton(eo)-	peritoneum 腹膜	peritoneoplasty 腹膜成形术 peritonitis 腹膜炎
omphalo-	navel, umbilicus 脐	omphalocele 脐突出 omphalitis 脐炎
inguino-	groin 腹股沟	inguinal 腹股沟的 inguinoscrotal 腹股沟阴囊的
lumbo-	loin 腰	lumbar 腰的 lumbosacral 腰骶的
pelvi-	basin, pelvis 骨盆	pelvic 骨盆的 pelvimetry 骨盆测量
dorso- opistho-	back 背	dorsomedial 背中线的 dorsal 背的 opisthotonus 角弓反张
caudal-	tail 尾	caudal fin 尾鳍 caudal anesthesia 脊尾麻醉

Unit 2　Yin-Yang

 Text A

Yin and *Yang*: An Introduction

Chinese medical theory is built on a foundation of ancient philosophical thought. Many of these ideas are based on observations of natural phenomena and are the reason why Traditional Chinese Medicine (TCM) has remained a truly holistic approach to health and well being.

The theory of *yin-yang* is one such philosophy. It is said to date back nearly 6,000 years to the third or fourth millennium B. C. and is attributed to[①] an enlightened philosopher named Fuxi (also credited with creating the *I-Ching* or *Book of Changes*). The basic premise of *yin* and *yang* is the notion that the only constant factor in natural phenomena is universal change. In other words, absolutely everything is in a constant state of flux and, therefore, subjects to the laws of change.

It is important to remember that *yin* and *yang* are not static concepts and that they are constantly influencing and determining one another.[②] There is always some measure of *yin* within *yang* and vice versa. To use the analogy of a hillside, during the day the sunlit side of the hill is *yang* within *yang*, while the shaded side is *yin* within *yang*. Conversely, at night the moonlit side of the hill is *yang* within *yin*, while the dark side of the hill is *yin* within *yang*. In this fluid model, it must be understood that neither *yin* nor *yang* can ever exist without the other.

These types of relationships become significant when they impact the body's anatomy and physiology[③] and it is precisely these designations that are used in the diagnosis of imbalances in TCM. For a TCM practitioner, the name of the disease is of secondary importance. The primary key to the proper diagnosis of syndromes is the identification of the condition in terms of *yin* or *yang*. In order to understand what this means, let us examine these concepts in the context of human life.

We can also see this philosophy expressed in everyday life. In respiration, the expansion of inhalation is *yang* while the emptiness which results from exhalation is *yin*. In digestion, the *yin* substance of food is transformed by the metabolic activity[④] of *yang*. It is then converted into *qi* (*yang*) and blood (*yin*). *Qi* and blood interact with one another using this paradigm. *Qi* moves blood, yet blood is thought to be the "mother" or source of *qi*. Within the body *yin* is expressed as the material basis, the tissue and substance without which the transformation of *yang* would not be possible.

Finally, disease and disease progression can be viewed using this paradigm. If the body's *yang* is weak, it will be unable to ward off the invasion of a pathogen.⑤ If the *yin* is weak, there will not be enough nourishment and support for the *yang*, the result will be the same. Expressed in other terms, without the substance, the active immune system is weakened and without activity, the substance becomes vulnerable. Therefore, if *yin* is deficient over time then *yang* also becomes deficient and vice versa. Not only do *yin* and *yang* balance each other, they mutually generate one another.⑥ It is precisely this balance that the TCM practitioner uses various treatment strategies to restore.⑦ The idea is to reestablish the body's innate ability to maintain health and defend itself from disease.

The nature and progression of disease can also be understood using this pattern. When a disease develops rapidly, it is in the acute or *yang* stage. As it progresses and becomes more chronic, thus it enters the *yin* stage. Usually, acute diseases affect the surface or superficial aspects of the body while chronic diseases have already overwhelmed the body's defenses and gone deeper into the interior. In addition, regardless of location or duration, disease can be classified by its affects.⑧ With regard to diagnosis, that which is internal, cold, deficient or chronic is considered *yin*; that which is external, hot, excess or acute is considered *yang*. When conflicting signs are present, it usually points to a more complex condition and the TCM practitioner must evaluate all the symptoms together to determine the appropriate treatment strategy.

In summary, it should be evident that the designations of *yin* and *yang* are universal and extend into every aspect of life. Because of its ubiquity, this theory is a very useful tool for understanding natural phenomena and therefore can be an indispensable diagnostic aid.

(753 words)

New Words

phenomena /fəˈnɒmɪnə/ n.　　　　(phenomenon 的复数)现象,非凡的人,稀有的事,奇迹
analogy /əˈnælədʒɪ/ n.　　　　　类似,相似,类推,类比,比拟
designation /ˌdezɪɡˈneɪʃn/ n.　　指定,命名,称号
organ /ˈɔːɡən/ n.　　　　　　　　器官,元件,机构,机关
identification /aɪˌdentɪfɪˈkeɪʃn/ n.　认同,鉴定,识别,确认
inhalation /ˌɪnhəˈleɪʃn/ n.　　　　吸入,吸入物,吸入剂
exhalation /ˌekshəˈleɪʃn/ n.　　　呼气,散发,蒸发,散发物
metabolic /ˌmetəˈbɒlɪk/ a.　　　　代谢作用的,新陈代谢的
vice versa /ˌvaɪs ˈvɜːsə/ ad.　　　反之亦然
generate /ˈdʒenəreɪt/ v.　　　　　产生,导致,发生

Unit 2　*Yin-Yang*

acute /əˈkjuːt/ *a.*	尖锐的,剧烈的,严重的,敏锐的,[医]急性的
superficial /ˌsuːpəˈfɪʃl/ *a.*	表面的,浅薄的,肤浅的
overwhelm /ˌəʊvəˈwelm/ *v.*	战胜,压倒,征服,覆盖
evaluate /ɪˈvæljʊeɪt/ *v.*	评估,评价
ubiquity /juːˈbɪkwətɪ/ *n.*	到处存在,普遍存在,无所不在
indispensable /ˌɪndɪˈspensəbl/ *a.*	不可缺少的,绝对必要的,不能避免的

Expressions

be built on	建立在……基础上
date back to	追溯到
in terms of	根据,在……方面
convert into	转变成
be classified by	按……分类
point to	指向
with regard to	关于
extend into	扩展到……

Notes

① attribute... to：把……归因于。例如：He attributes his success to the hard work. 他把他的成功归因于努力工作。

② It is important to remember that *yin* and *yang* are not static concepts and that they are constantly influencing and determining one another. 重要的是要记住阴阳不是静止的概念,它们不断地相互影响、相互制约。

③ anatomy and physiology：解剖学与生理学。

④ metabolic activity：新陈代谢活动,其包括物质代谢和能量代谢两个方面。物质代谢是指生物体与外界环境之间物质的交换和生物体内物质的转变过程。能量代谢是指生物体与外界环境之间能量的交换和生物体内能量的转变过程。

⑤ If the body's *yang* is weak, it will be unable to ward off the invasion of a pathogen. 如果阳虚,身体就不能避免病菌的入侵。

⑥ Not only do *yin* and *yang* balance each other, they mutually generate one another. 阴阳不仅相互平衡,而且相互滋生。

⑦ It is precisely this balance that the TCM practitioner uses various treatment strategies to restore. 中医医师使用不同治疗策略正是为了恢复这种平衡。强调句型 It is... that... 例如：It was the goat's eyes that he had seen in the darkness. 他在黑暗中看到的就是这只山羊的眼睛。(强调宾语)

⑧ In addition, regardless of location or duration, disease can be classified by its affects. 此外,撇开发病位置或持续时间,疾病可按其影响进行分类。

Exercises

I. Fill in the blanks with the words given below. Change the form when necessary.

foundation	superficial	constant	conversely
significant	diagnosis	primary	evaluate
digestion	nourish	immune	generate

1. The company has only been open for six months, so it's hard to _____ its success.
2. It is difficult to make a(n) _____ in the early stage of this disease and it is easy to be misdiagnosed.
3. This kind of tea is good to your _____.
4. Failure is the _____ of success.
5. He cannot bear his wife's _____ nagging.
6. You're too _____ to appreciate the great literature works of Shakespeare.
7. We should take vitamins to strengthen our _____ system.
8. You can add the fluid to the powder or, _____, the powder to the fluid.
9. Tourism _____ lots of new job opportunities.
10. Your success today may be _____ for your whole future.
11. The _____ cause of Tom's failure is his wrong attitude toward his study.
12. She had _____ the dream of becoming a great movie star.

II. Choose the best answer to each of the following questions or unfinished statements.

1. Which of the following statements is NOT true?
   A. The theory of *yin-yang* is based on observations of natural phenomena.
   B. The theory of *yin-yang* is similar to the notion of dialectics.
   C. According to the theory everything is in a constant state of flux.
   D. *Yin* and *yang* are static concepts.
2. What's the relationship between *yin* and *yang*?
   A. They cannot determine one another.
   B. Either *yin* or *yang* can ever exist without the other.
   C. Extreme *yin* won't engender *yang*.
   D. Not only do *yin* and *yang* balance each other, they mutually generate one another.
3. For a TCM practitioner, _____ is/are important when diagnosing syndromes.
   A. the name of the disease
   B. the identification of the condition in terms of *yin* or *yang*
   C. anatomy and physiology
   D. *qi* and blood

Unit 2 Yin-Yang

4. Which one is true according to the passage?
   A. During the day the shaded side of the hill is *yang* within *yang*.
   B. At night the moonlit side of the hill is *yin* within *yin*.
   C. In respiration, the expansion of inhalation is *yang*.
   D. When a disease develops rapidly, it is in the acute or *yin* stage.

5. _____ have/has already overwhelmed the body's defenses.
   A. Chronic diseases   B. Acute diseases
   C. The invasion of a pathogen   D. Severe symptoms

Ⅲ. **Translate the following sentences into English or Chinese.**

1. 中医理论是以古代哲学思想为基础的。

2. 阴阳学说代表了古代中国人对于事物运转方式的理解。

3. 阴和阳紧密联系，是互相作用的整体。

4. 如果疾病发展很快，说明它正处在阳阶段或者严重阶段。

5. 急性疾病影响身体表面或浅显的方面。

6. Chronic diseases have already overwhelmed the body's defenses and gone deeper into the interior.

7. The designations of *yin* and *yang* are universal and extend into every aspect of life.

8. The theory of *yin-yang* is a significant tool to understand natural phenomena.

9. The basic premise of *yin* and *yang* is the notion that the only constant factor in natural phenomena is universal change.

10. According to TCM theory, the occurrence of diseases is the imbalance between *yin* and *yang*.

Ⅳ. Write a 150-word composition about the *yin-yang* Theory.

Yin and *Yang*—The Law of Nature

Yin and *yang*, which come from ancient Chinese philosophy, are a general term for two opposites of interrelated things or phenomena in the natural world. At first, their connotations were quite simple, referring to the two opposite sides of an object. The side facing the sun is *yang* and the reverse side is *yin*. In the course of long practice and observation, the ancient Chinese people came to understand that the opposition and wax-wane of *yin* and *yang* are inherent in all things①. *Yi Zhuan* says, "*Yin* and *yang* are what is called Dao (the basic law of the unity of opposites in the universe)," in other words, "Everything in the universe contains *yin* and *yang*." And they further believed that *yin* and *yang* can not only represent two opposite objects but also be used to analyze two opposite aspects existing in a single entity. Generally speaking, things or phenomena which are dynamic, bright, hot, functional, etc., pertain to the category of *yang*②, while those that are static, dark, cold, substantial, etc., pertain to that of *yin*. The theory of *yin-yang* holds that the development and changes of everything in the universe result from the unity of opposites between *yin* and *yang*. *Su Wen*③ says, "*Yin* and *yang* are the law of heaven and earth, the principles of all things, the parents of all changes, the origin of life and death..." It is used to explain physiology and pathology of the body and to guide clinical diagnosis and treatment. The basic content of the theory of *yin-yang* can be summarized as follows.

The Unity of Opposition Between *Yin* and *Yang*

The opposition between *yin* and *yang* means that all things or phenomena in nature have two opposite aspects—*yin* and *yang*. The unity is the outcome of mutual opposition and restriction between *yin* and *yang*. Without opposition, there would be no unity; without mutual opposition, there would be no mutual complement. It is only through this kind of opposition and restriction that the dynamic equilibrium can be established.④ For instance, in the nature world, the motions of celestial bodies⑤, the variations of the four seasons, the alternations of days and nights, as well as sprouting in spring, growing in summer, reaping in autumn and storing in winter, are all the concrete manifestations of the unity of opposites between *yin* and *yang*. TCM believes that the normal physiological functions of the human body result from the opposite and unified relationship between *yin* and *yang*. Both of them are always in a state of dynamic balance. Even under normal physiological conditions of the human body, *yin* and *yang* can not be in a state of absolute balance, but in a state of relative balance. If, for any reason, the relative balance is destroyed, there is bound to be excess or deficiency of *yin* or *yang*, and then a disease will arise. As is stated in *Su Wen*, "*Yin* in excess causing *yang* disease, while *yang* in excess leading to *yin* disease." It is precisely due to the unity of opposites between *yin* and *yang* that all things can develop and change ceaselessly and the natural world is perpetually full of life.

Interdependence Between *Yin* and *Yang*⑥

Yin and *yang* are opposed to and yet, at the same time, depend on each other. Neither can exist in isolation without its opponent's existence. In other words, without *yin* there would be no *yang*, and it's the same the other way round. So either *yin* or *yang* is the prerequisite for the other's existence. And this kind of coexistent relationship is stated in TCM, "solitary *yin* or *yang* failing to live⑦". This interdependence is also reflected in the relationship between substances and functions. The substance corresponds to *yin* and the function, to *yang*. The function is the result of material motion, and nothing in the world is not in a state of motion. Thereby, there is not any substance which can't produce its function and there is also not any function which doesn't originate from the motion of its substance. Therefore, *Su Wen* says, "*Yin* in the interior is the basis for *yang*; while *yang* in the exterior is the activity for *yin*.""*Yin*" refers to the material, basis of functional activity of *yang* and "*yang*" refers to functional activity. The substance and function are interdependent and inseparable. Here is just an imaginable and vivid figure of speech. However, when the interdependent relationships between substances, between functions as well as between substances and functions are abnormal, life activities will be broken, bringing about dissociation of *yin* and *yang*⑧, depletion of essence—*qi* and even an end of one's life.

(783 words)

New Words

interrelated /ˌɪntərɪˈleɪtɪd/	*a.*	相互关联的
connotation /ˌkɒnəˈteɪʃn/	*n.*	内涵意义,隐含意义
represent /ˌreprɪˈzent/	*vt.*	表现,描绘,代表,象征,作为……的代表
dynamic /daɪˈnæmɪk/	*a.*	有活力的,有力的,不断变化的,动力的,动态的
substantial /səbˈstænʃl/	*a.*	坚固的,结实的,大量的,重大的,重要的,实质的,基本的
summarize /ˈsʌməraɪz/	*vt.*	总结,概述
mutual /ˈmjuːtʃuəl/	*a.*	相互的,彼此的,共同的,共有的
restriction /rɪˈstrɪkʃn/	*n.*	约束,限制,管制,限定,法律,规章
variation /ˌveərɪˈeɪʃn/	*n.*	变化,变动(的程度),变奏(曲),变异,变种
concrete /ˈkɒnkriːt/	*a.*	实体的,有形的,确实的,明确的,确定的
precisely /prɪˈsaɪslɪ/	*ad.*	精确地,准确地,恰好
prerequisite /ˌpriːˈrekwəzɪt/	*n.*	先决条件,前提
interdependence /ˌɪntədɪˈpendəns/	*n.*	互相依赖
solitary /ˈsɒlətrɪ/	*a.*	单独的,独居的,唯一的,人迹罕至的,幽静的
correspond /ˌkɒrəˈspɒnd/	*vi.*	相符合,相一致,相当,相类似,通信
originate /əˈrɪdʒɪneɪt/	*v.*	起源于,来自,产生,创造,开创,发明
inseparable /ɪnˈseprəbl/	*a.*	不可分的,分不开的
vivid /ˈvɪvɪd/	*a.*	鲜艳的,生动的,栩栩如生的

Expressions

pertain to   从属,附属

as follows	如下
for instance	比如
result from	由……产生，由……引起
due to	因为
be opposed to	与……相反
depend on	依赖，依靠
in isolation	独自地，单独地
in other words	换言之
the other way round	反过来
correspond to	与……一致，符合
originate from	起源于

Expressions

① ... the opposition and wax-wane of *yin* and *yang* are inherent in all things. 阴阳的对立和互补存在于万事万物。wax-wane：盈亏，文中指阴阳之间必有的、固有的一种互补关系。

② Generally speaking, things or phenomena which are dynamic, bright, hot, functional, etc., pertain to the category of *yang*：一般来说，动态的、明亮的、热的、功能型的物体或者现象都属于阳。pertain to：从属于，有关。

③ *Su Wen*：《素问》。《黄帝内经·素问》简称《素问》，是现存最早的中医理论著作，相传为黄帝创作，大约成书于春秋战国时期。原来9卷，后经王冰增补，改编为24卷，计81篇，定名为《黄帝内经·素问》，所论内容十分丰富，以人与自然统一观、阴阳学说、五行说、脏腑经络学为主线，论述摄生、脏腑、经络、病因、病机、治则、药物以及养生防病等各方面的关系，集医理、医论、医方于一体，保存了《五色》《脉变》《上经》《下经》《太始天元册》等20多种古代医籍，突出阐发了古代的哲学思想，强调了人体内外统一的整体观念，从而成为中医基本理论的渊源。

④ It is only through this kind of opposition and restriction that the dynamic equilibrium can be established. 只有通过阴阳互相对立制约才能达到动态的平衡。dynamic equilibrium：动态平衡。

⑤ celestial bodies：天体，宇宙中各种实体的统称。

⑥ Interdependence Between *Yin* and *Yang*：阴阳互根。阴阳双方均以对方的存在而存在，所以"孤阴"和"独阳"就不能生化和滋长，阴阳互根理论对方药的配伍起着重要的指导作用。

⑦ solitary *yin* or *yang* failing to live：孤阳不生，独阴不长。说明二者是相互依傍、存亡与共的；如果没有阴，也就谈不上有阳。如果有阴无阳，或者有阳无阴，则势必如《黄帝内经》所说："孤阴不生，独阳不长"，则一切都归于静止寂灭了。

⑧ ... bringing about dissociation of *yin* and *yang*：(物质与功能的紊乱) 会引起阴阳的分离。bring about：引起，带来。

Unit 2 *Yin-Yang*

Exercises

I. **Fill in the blanks with the words given below. Change the form when necessary.**

opposite	inherent	represent	analyze
principle	outcome	restriction	manifestation
dynamic	deficiency	excess	originate

1. The swimming club is open to families in the neighborhood without _____.
2. We are looking for _____ persons to be salesmen.
3. The desire for freedom is _____ in all human people.
4. This riot is only one _____ of people's discontent.
5. This essay _____ a considerable improvement on your recent work.
6. Things will go much better if people of the same trade make up the other's _____ from their own surplus.
7. It is essential to adhere to the _____ of equality and mutual benefit in conducting international economic exchanges.
8. All theories _____ from practice and in turn serve practice.
9. Let's _____ the problem and see what went wrong.
10. Public interest concentrates on the _____ of next week's election.
11. Have you seen the house _____ the railway station?
12. The fat boy went on a diet to get rid of his _____ weight.

II. **Choose the best answer to each of the following questions or unfinished statement.**

1. Which of the following statement is NOT true according to the first paragraph?
   A. *Yin* and *yang* cannot be combined in one object.
   B. *Yin* is the opposite of *yang*.
   C. *Yin* and *yang* are interrelated with each other.
   D. When *yin*, is waxing, *yang* will be waning.
2. Which of the following pair can show the opposition relationship between *yin* and *yang*?
   A. Heaven—moon.
   B. Wind—sun.
   C. Fire—water.
   D. Still—quiescence.
3. TCM believes that _____.
   A. *yin* and *yang* is in a state of absolute balance
   B. *yin* and *yang* are always in a state of dynamic balance

C. *yin* and *yang* can keep everything in the balance

D. *yin* in excess is better than *yang* in excess

4. Which understanding is NOT correct according to the interdependence between *yin* and *yang*?

   A. *Yin* and *yang* cannot exist alone in the nature.

   B. Where there is *yin*, there is *yang*.

   C. The abnormal relationship between substance and function would cause dissociation of *yin* and *yang*.

   D. The substance is connected with *yang*, while the function is connected with *yin*.

5. What is the main idea of the text?

   A. *Yin* and *yang* are opposite.

   B. *Yin* and *yang* are always keeping balance.

   C. *Yin* and *yang* are closely connected with each other.

   D. There are opposition and interdependence between *yin* and *yang*.

Ⅲ. Translate the following sentences into English or Chinese.

1. 根据中医理论,疾病的发生是阴阳失调所致。而疾病的治疗就是阴阳的平衡。

2. 阴和阳是贯通整个世界的两个相对立的力量。

3. 阴和阳既相互对立又相互依存。

4. 阴阳总是处于动态的平衡,这是一种相对平衡、而非绝对平衡的状态。

5. 阴阳学说认为宇宙万物的发展和变化都是源自于阴阳的对立和统一。

6. If, for any reason, the relative balance is destroyed, there is bound to be excess or deficiency of *yin* or *yang*, and then a disease will arise.

7. TCM is a science which can be used to explain physiology and pathology of the body and to guide clinical diagnosis and disease prevention.

8. As dialectic thought, the theory of *yin-yang* can be applied in any medical field.

9. TCM believes that the normal physiological functions of the human body result from the opposite and unified relationship between *yin* and *yang*.

10. Either *yin* or *yang* is the prerequisite for the other's existence.

Unit 2 Yin-Yang

 **Text C**

Yin-Yang Theory in Traditional Chinese Medicine

The theory of *yin-yang*, a thought of naive materialism and spontaneous dialectics in ancient China①, believes that the world is material, which is multiplied and developed by *yin-yang*, called *qi*, and metal, wood, water, fire and earth—Five Elements②. The five kinds of elements are interdependent, situated in continuous movement and change. This theory exercises profound influence on ancient materialistic philosophy, for example, ancient astronomy, meteorology, chemistry, mathematics, medicine as well as music.

The theory of *yin-yang* is applied to medical domain to explain origin of mankind, physiological phenomenon, pathological change and to guide clinical prevention, diagnosis, and treatment, which becomes an important part in Chinese medicinal theory and exercises deep influences on the emergence and development of Chinese medicinal science.

The theory of *yin-yang* believes that the world is a material whole including two aspects—*yin* and *yang*, which are interdependent and counterbalance each other. It is a cardinal principle of coming into being, developing, and passing away in nature.③ As *Su Wen: Yin-Yang Yingxiang DaLun* said, "*Yin* and *yang* are doctrines of heaven and earth, guiding principle of everything, parents of variation, foundation of life and death." So the opposition and unity of *yin-yang* is an inherent law for all the changes in nature, and world itself is a result of the opposition and unity of *yin-yang*, two kinds of *qi*. *Yin-yang* is a condensation about two sides of thing and phenomenon which are opposite and interrelated not only in nature, but also in objects.④ So *yin-yang* has university, opposition and division, which includes university of *yin-yang*, division of *yin-yang*, opposition of *yin-yang*, inter-antagonism of *yin-yang*, inter-rooting and inter-utilization of *yin-yang*, inter-counterbalance of *yin-yang* and inter-convertibility of *yin-yang*.

Yin and *yang* always coexist in a dynamic equilibrium in which one waxes while the other wanes.⑤ In other words, waning of *yin* will lead to waxing of *yang* and vice versa. Take the seasonal and climatic variations for example. It gets warm from winter to spring, and hot from spring to summer. This is the process of "*yang* waxing and *yin* waning". Conversely, it gets cool from summer to autumn, and cold from autumn to winter—the process known as "*yin* waxing and *yang* waning". Under normal conditions, the waning-waxing relation of *yin* and *yang* is in a state of relative balance. If this relation goes beyond normal limits, the relative balance of *yin* and *yang* will not be maintained, thus resulting in either excess or deficiency of *yin* or *yang* and the occurrence of disease, so far as to endanger one's life.⑥

In given conditions, either *yin* or *yang* may transform into its opposite⑦, i.e., *yin* may be transformed into *yang* and *yang* into *yin*. If the waning-waxing of *yin* and *yang* is said to be a process of quantitative change, then that of their inter-transformation pertains to a qualitative change based on the quantitative change.⑧ Such a process is mostly a gradual one from quantitative to qualitative change. Pathologically, the *yin* syndromes can be transformed into *yang* syndromes, and vice versa. It must be pointed out that the decisive factor of the mutual transformation is the conditions, including internal and external conditions, without which such transformation will be by no means likely to occur.

The theory of *yin-yang* mainly explains the relationship of interdependence, inter-growth and decline, and inter-transformation between opposite sides in things;⑨ the theory of Five Elements explains property and interrelation in things by the classification of Five Elements and the law of generation, restriction, subjugation and reverse restriction in property of things. In traditional Chinese medicine it is considered that the material bases of both of them are viscera, *qi*, meridian, blood and fluid. Both of them analyze and explain physiological activities of human body, pathological changes, guiding clinical prevention, diagnosis, and treatment from macroscopically natural phenomenon.⑩

(660 words)

New Words

naive /naɪˈiːv/ *a.*	朴素的
multiply /ˈmʌltɪplaɪ/ *v.*	使增加
interdependent /ˌɪntədɪˈpendənt/ *a.*	互相依赖的，互相依存的
situate /ˈsɪtʃʊeɪt/ *v.*	使位于，使处于……地位(位置)
philosophy /fəˈlɒsəfɪ/ *n.*	哲学
astronomy /əˈstrɒnəmɪ/ *n.*	天文学
meteorology /ˌmiːtɪəˈrɒlədʒɪ/ *n.*	气象学
domain /dəˈmeɪn/ *n.*	范围，领域
clinical /ˈklɪnɪkl/ *a.*	临床的
counterbalance /ˌkaʊntəˈbæləns/ *v.*	对……起平衡作用，抵消
condensation /ˌkɒndenˈseɪʃn/ *n.*	凝结，缩合
opposition /ˌɒpəˈzɪʃn/ *n.*	（强烈的）反对，反抗，对抗
pathological /ˌpæθəˈlɒdʒɪkl/ *a.*	病理学的

Expressions

situate sth. in	将……置于其环境中
exersise influence on	对……产生影响
be applied to	应用于
make/give a diagnosis	作出诊断

Unit 2　*Yin-Yang*

come into existence	形成
pass away	消逝
be condensed into	凝结成
result in	导致
go beyond	超越
point out	指出

Expressions

① ... a thought of naive materialism and spontaneous dialectics in ancient China：中国古代一种原始的唯物论和自然辩证法思想。该名词词组作前面 The theory of *yin-yang* and Five Elements（阴阳五行理论）的同位语。

② ... which is multiplied and developed by *yin-yang*, called *qi*, and metal, wood, water, fire and earth—Five Elements：该理论由称作气的阴阳和包括金、木、水、火、土的五行所丰富和发展。该部分作前面 that world is material 的非限制性定语从句。

③ It is a cardinal principle of coming into being, developing, and passing away in nature. 它是自然界形成、发展和消逝的基本准则。其中 coming into being, developing 和 passing away 三个动名词词组作 of 的宾语。

④ *Yin-yang* is a condensation about two sides of thing and phenomenon which are opposite and interrelated not only in nature, but also in objects. 阴阳是自然界与物质中相互对立和相互依存的事物和现象的两方面的概括。这里定语从句 which are opposite and interrelated not only in nature, but also in objects 作前面 two sides of thing and phenomenon 的定语。

⑤ *Yin* and *yang* always coexist in a dynamic equilibrium in which one waxes while the other wanes. 阴阳始终处于动态的平衡中，此消则彼涨。which 引导的是一个状语从句。

⑥ If this relation goes beyond normal limits, the relative balance of *yin* and *yang* will not be maintained, thus resulting in either excess or deficiency of *yin* or *yang* and the occurrence of disease, so far as to endanger one's life. 此消彼长的关系一旦打破，阴阳平衡则无法保持，疾病出现，危及生命。这句阐述了 waning and waxing of *yin* and *yang* 的重要性。

⑦ In given conditions, either *yin* or *yang* may transform into its opposite：在一定条件下，阴阳是可以互相转换的。in given conditions 表明在特定的情况下。

⑧ If the waning-waxing of *yin* and *yang* is said to be a process of quantitative change, then that of their inter-transformation pertains to a qualitative change based on the quantitative change. 阴阳的消长是一种量变的过程，而阴阳的转换则是基于量变基础上的质变。此句表明阴阳可以消长，可以互换，消长是阴阳互换的基础。

⑨ The theory of *yin-yang* mainly explains the relationship of interdependence, inter-growth and decline, and inter-transformation between opposite sides in things. 阴阳理论主要解释了事物

对立面之间相互依存，相互消长以及相互转换的关系。这里 interdependence, inter-growth and decline 和 inter-transformation 并列作介词 of 的宾语。

⑩ Both of them analyze and explain physiological activities of human body, pathological changes, guiding clinical prevention, diagnosis, and treatment from macroscopically natural phenomenon. 二者分析并解释了人类机体生理活动和病理变化，指导了针对肉眼可见的自然现象的临床预防、诊断和治疗。guiding clinical prevention, diagnosis, and treatment from macroscopically natural phenomenon 引导的分词短语作前面句子伴随状语。

Exercises

I. Fill in the blanks with the words given below. Change the form when necessary.

naive	spontaneous	multiply	profound
cardinal	transform	condensation	relative
maintain	endanger	situate	coexist

1. A cloud is a(n) _____ of water vapour.
2. He is so _____ as to believe such a lie.
3. The _____ idea of the Labor Party's political thought is that all people should be equal.
4. We must _____ our efforts to clear up the mystery.
5. Now it is generally accepted that the countries with different social systems can _____ peacefully.
6. The teacher asked me some questions _____ to my paper.
7. Hearing the joke, we burst into _____ laughter.
8. In order to _____ physical well being, a person should eat wholesome food and get sufficient exercise.
9. The board is trying to decide where to _____ the new hospital.
10. His plans were _____ overnight into reality.
11. They listened to the speaker with _____ interest.
12. If you have anything to do with such a scheme you'll _____ your good name and probably lose all your money.

II. Choose the best answer to each of the following questions or unfinished statements.

1. In the first paragraph, *qi* probably means "_____".
   A. materialism   B. dialectics
   C. *yin-yang*   D. Five Elements
2. According to the passage, the theory of *yin-yang* is applied to the following domains

Unit 2 Yin-Yang

EXCEPT _____.
A. astronomy   B. mechanics
C. chemistry   D. music

3. In Paragraph 3, "So the opposition and unity of *yin-yang* is an inherent law for all the changes in nature", here "inherent" probably means _____.
   A. innate   B. acquired   C. received   D. accepted

4. According to the passage, which of the following is NOT true?
   A. Five Elements are interdependent and counterbalanced in continuous movement and change.
   B. The theory of *yin-yang* is the thought of mature materialistic dialectics in ancient China.
   C. *Yin* and *yang* is a cardinal principle of coming into being, developing, and passing away in nature.
   D. *Yin-yang* has unity, opposition and division.

5. Which of the following might best summarize the main idea of the passage?
   A. The theory of *yin-yang*.
   B. Materialism and dialectics in ancient China.
   C. The functions of *yin-yang* Theory.
   D. The relationship between *yin-yang* and Five-Element Theory.

Ⅲ. Translate the following sentences into English or Chinese.

1. 阴阳理论认为世界就是物质。
2. 金、木、水、火、土这五种元素相互依赖，存在于不停的运动和变化中。
3. 阴阳理论对古代的唯物主义哲学产生了深刻的影响。
4. 阴阳理论认为世界是一个物质整体，它包括两部分：阴和阳，这两者既相互依存又对立统一。
5. 阴阳之中有统一、对立和分割。
6. World itself is a result of the opposition and unity of *yin-yang*.
7. *Yin-yang* is a condensation about two sides of thing and phenomenon which are opposite and interrelated.
8. Feeling my pulse, the doctor made a diagnosis that I got a flu.
9. Pathologically, the *yin* syndromes can be transformed into *yang* syndromes, and vice versa.
10. It must be pointed out that the decisive factor of the mutual transformation is the conditions, including internal and external conditions.

Cardiovascular System（心血管系统）

Root	Meaning	Examples
cardio-	heart 心	cardiac catheter 心导管 myocardium 心肌 cardiopuncture 心脏穿刺术 carditis 心脏（肌）炎 cardiac enlargement 心脏增大
atrio-	atrium 心房	atrioventricular block 房室传导阻滞 atrial flutter 心房扑动 atrial 心房的 atrial pressure 心房压 atrioventricular dissociation 房室分离
ventriculo-	ventricle 心室	ventricular fibrillation 室颤 ventricular puncture 脑室穿刺 ventriculography 脑室造影术 ventriculo-atrial conduction 室房传导 ventriculogram 心室图
valv(ul)o- -cuspid	valve 瓣膜	valvuloplasty 瓣膜成形术 valvulitis 心瓣炎 valvulotomy 瓣膜切开术 bicuspid 二尖瓣
vaso- vasculo- angio-	vessel 血管	vascular 血管的 vasodilator 血管舒缩剂 cardiovascular 心血管的 angiotensin 血管紧缩素 angioplasty 血管成形术
arterio-	artery 动脉	arteriosclerosis 动脉硬化 arteriogram 动脉造影照片 arteriosteogenesis 动脉骨化,动脉钙化 arteriopuncture 动脉穿刺术 arteritis 动脉炎
veno- phlebo-	vein 静脉	venous 静脉的 intravenous 静脉内的,静脉注射的 venography 静脉造影术 phlebopexy 静脉固定术 phlebitis 静脉炎

Root	Meaning	Examples
aorto-	aorta 主动脉	aorta stenosis 主动脉狭窄 aortopulmonary 主动脉肺动脉间的 aortic dissection 主动脉夹层 aortic murmur 主动脉瓣杂音 aortitis 主动脉炎
capillar(i)o-	capillary 毛细血管	capillarity 毛细管作用 capillarectasia 毛细血管扩张 capillaroscopy 毛细血管镜检查 capillaropathy 毛细血管病 capillariasis 毛细线虫病
sphygmo-	pulse 脉	sphygmomanometer 血压计
sanqui- hemo- hema- hemato-	blood 血	sanquinopoietic 生血的 hemodialysis 血液透析 hemostasis 止血法 hemabarometer 血比重计 hematuria 血尿, 尿血 hematothermal 温血的

Unit 3   The Five Elements

 Text A

The Five-Element Theory—Natural Philosophy in Ancient China

The five elements refer to wood, fire, earth, metal and water and their motions. The Five-Element Theory resulted from the observations and studies of the natural world by the ancient Chinese people in the course of their lives and productive labor.① Since ancient times, wood, fire, earth, metal and water have been considered as basic substances to constitute the universe and they are also indispensable for life. Zuo's *Interpretation of the Spring and Autumn Annals*② (*Zuo Zhuan*) says, "The five kinds of materials in nature are all used by people. None of them cannot be dispensed with." Another classical work *Shang Shu* states, "Water and fire are used for cooking, metal and wood are used for cultivating and earth gives birth to all things, which are used by people." These five kinds of substances are of the relationships of generation and restriction and are in constant motion and change.③ In TCM the Five-Element Theory, as a theoretical tool, is used to explain and expound different kinds of medical problems by analogizing and deducing their properties and interrelations. It is also used to guide clinical diagnosis and treatment. The theory, like the theory of *yin-yang*, has become an important component of the theoretical system of TCM.

In ancient China, the Five-Element Theory was unceasingly developed and gradually became perfected. In time, it came to recognize that everything in nature might be respectively attributed to one of the five elements. For instance, wood has the nature of growing freely and unfolding. So, anything that is similar to the characteristics is attributed to the category of wood.④ Fire has the nature of flaring up. Thereby the things similar to the nature of fire are classified into the attribute of fire. Earth has the nature of giving birth to all things. Thus, those that possess the nature of earth are attributed to earth. Metal has the nature of purifying and descending.⑤ Hence, those with the nature of metal can be attributed to metal category. Water has the nature of moistening and flowing downwards. For this reason, the things that have moistening, downward movement and coldness correspond to water.

Among the five-elements, there exist the relationships of generation, restriction,

Unit 3 The Five Elements

subjugation and counter-restriction, and mutual affection between mother-organ and child-organ. ⑥ Generation implies that one kind of thing can promote, aid or bring forth another, i.e., wood generates fire, fire generates earth, earth generates metal, metal generates water, and water, in turn, generates wood. Each of the five elements contains the dual nature—"being generated" and "generating". ⑦ This relationship of the five elements is called the "mother-child" relationship. The element that generates is called the "mother", while the element that is generated is called the "child". Take wood for example, because wood produces fire, it is the mother of fire; but it is produced by water, so it's water's child.

Restriction means bringing under control or restraint. The order of restriction goes as follows: wood restricts earth, earth does water, water does fire, fire does metal, and metal, in turn, does wood. Any one of the five elements has two aspects—being restricted and restricting. For example, the element restricting wood is metal, and the element that is restricted by wood is earth.

Generation and restriction have the correlations inseparable in the five elements. And they oppose each other and yet also complement each other. Without generation, there would be no growth or development of things; without inter-restriction there would be no balance or coordination during development and change, and excessive growth would bring about harm. ⑧ For example, on the one hand, wood generates fire, and, on the other hand⑨, it restrains earth; while earth, in turn, generates metal and restricts water. Precisely, because generation resides in restriction and restriction resides in generation, the natural world and life processes are full of vitality. Thus, the relative balance maintained between generation and restriction ensures normal growth and development of things. ⑩

(690 words)

New Words

motion /ˈməʊʃn/	n.	运动,动作
	v.	打手势,摆动
constitute /ˈkɒnstɪtjuːt/	v.	制定,组成,构成
dispense /dɪˈspens/	v.	分发,分配,免除,省掉
generation /ˌdʒenəˈreɪʃn/	n.	一代,一世,产生
theoretical /ˌθɪəˈretɪkl/	a.	理论上的
expound /ɪkˈspaʊnd/	v.	解释,详细述说
analogize /əˈnælədʒaɪz/	v.	以类推来说明,类推
deduce /dɪˈdjuːs/	v.	推论;演绎
component /kəmˈpəʊnənt/	n.	组成整件部分的单件,构成要素,成分
respectively /rɪˈspektɪvlɪ/	ad.	分别地,各自地

purify /ˈpjʊərɪfaɪ/ v.　　　　　　　使纯净，提纯，净化
descend /dɪˈsend/ v.　　　　　　　下降，屈尊
subjugation /ˌsʌbdʒʊˈɡeɪʃn/ n.　　　镇压，征服，平息
correlation /ˌkɒrəˈleɪʃn/ n.　　　　　相互关系，关联
complement /ˈkɒmplɪmənt/ n.　　　补足物，余角，补语
　　　　　　　　　　　v.　　　　　补充，补足
coordination /kəʊˌɔːdɪˈneɪʃn/ n.　　协调，调和

Expressions

in the course of	在……的过程中
be considered as	被看做……
be indispensable for	对……是不可或缺的
for instance	举例来说
under restraint	在……控制下
be restricted by	由……控制
bring about	带来
in turn	轮流
reside in	居住在

Notes

① The Five-Element Theory resulted from the observations and studies of the natural world by the ancient Chinese people in the course of their lives and productive labor. 五行学说源于中国古代人民在生活和生产过程中对自然界的观察和研究。

② *Zuo's Interpretation of the Spring and Autumn Annals* (*Zuo Zhuan*)：《左传》又称《春秋左氏传》或《左氏春秋》，是记载春秋时期各诸侯国的政治、经济、军事、外交、文化等方面情况的一部编年体史书。《史记》和《汉书·艺文志》都认为它是孔子的同代人鲁国史官左丘明所作。

③ These five kinds of substances are of the relationships of generation and restriction and are in constant motion and change. 这五种物质有着相生相克的关系，并处于不断的运动和变化之中。

④ So, anything that is similar to the characteristics is attributed to the category of wood. 因此，任何有类似特性的物质都归属于木。that 引导的是定语从句修饰 anything。

⑤ Metal has the nature of purifying and descending. 金具有净化和沉降属性。

⑥ Among the five elements, there exist the relationships of generation, restriction, subjugation and counter-restriction, and mutual affection between mother-organ and child-organ. 五行之间存在着生、克、乘、侮的关系和相互影响的母子关系。

⑦ Each of the five elements contains the dual nature—"being generated" and "generating". 五行中的任何一行都有"生我"和"我生"的双重性质。

Unit 3 The Five Elements

⑧ Without generation, there would be no growth or development of things; without inter-restriction there would be no balance or coordination during development and change, and excessive growth would bring about harm. 没有生就没有事物的成长和发展；没有克就没有在发展中的协调和平衡，过度生长会造成危害。

⑨ on the one hand...on the other hand：一方面……另一方面……例如：On the one hand, she taught English; on the other hand, she learned Chinese. 她一方面教英语，一方面学习汉语。

⑩ Thus, the relative balance maintained between generation and restriction ensures normal growth and development of things. 因此，生、克之间维持相对平衡是事物生长和发展的保证。

Exercises

I. Fill in the blanks with the words given below. Change the form when necessary.

motion	substance	constitute	generation
deduce	component	purify	descend
complement	respectively	restriction	moisten

1. Secretary of State Hillary Clinton—speaking at a news conference in Monterrey, Mexico—said the civilian _____ is essential.
2. They were asked to perform ten different movements, including moving the wrist in a circular _____ and moving their elbows.
3. Nor does it _____ all of what we're going to have to do to turn our economy around.
4. There is different ideas on the topic between the elder _____ and younger ones.
5. Anyway, what physicists do is that they put bodies in various circumstances(环境) and they _____ various forces.
6. These divine beings(伟大的神灵) _____ to earth and mate with (与……结合)female humans.
7. Her eyes _____ as she listens to the sad story.
8. He wrote it to be performed by Bridgewater's three children: the Lady Alice, who obviously played the Lady, and Bridgewater's two sons and they play the Elder Brother and the second brother, _____.
9. The court says the _____ on political speech violates free speech rights guaranteed (保证) by the Constitution(宪法).
10. And I think there is all sorts of different ways to learn that outside the classroom that _____ the classroom.
11. When I realized that I was writing plays, I read a lot more plays for style and for _____

and for technique.

12. These plants should _____ the house completely.

Ⅱ. Choose the best answer to each of the following questions or unfinished statements.

1. The Five-Element Theory resulted from _____.
   A. the observations and studies of the natural world
   B. *Zuo's Interpretation of the Spring and Autumn Annals*
   C. *the Yellow Emperor's Inner Classic*
   D. *the Canon of Difficult Issues*

2. What have been considered as basic substances to constitute the universe in ancient times?
   A. Wood, fire, earth, air and water.
   B. Wood, fire, earth, metal and water.
   C. Wood, water, fire, earth and motion.
   D. Atoms.

3. Which statement is NOT true?
   A. Wood has the nature of growing freely and unfolding.
   B. Water has the nature of purifying and descending.
   C. Fire has the nature of flaring up.
   D. Earth has the nature of giving birth to all things.

4. Generation implies that _____.
   A. one kind of thing can control another
   B. one kind of thing is controlled by another
   C. one kind of thing can promote another
   D. one kind of thing can restrict another

5. What's the relationship between generation and restriction?
   A. They oppose each other.
   B. They complement each other.
   C. Generation has nothing to do with restriction.
   D. They oppose and yet also complement each other.

Ⅲ. Translate the following sentences into English or Chinese.

1. 五行学说来源于古代中国人民在生活过程中对自然界进行的观察和研究。
2. 从古时候起，金、木、水、火、土就被看作组成宇宙的基本物质。
3. 五行学说和阴阳学说一样，成为了中医理论系统的重要组成部分之一。
4. 木曰曲直，自由生长，向外扩展。
5. 土，主含万物。

Unit 3　The Five Elements

6. Generation and restriction have the correlations inseparable in the five elements.
7. Since ancient times, wood, fire, earth, metal and water have been considered as basic substances to constitute the universe and they are also indispensable for life.
8. Metal has the nature of purifying and descending.
9. Water has the nature of moistening and flowing downwards.
10. Any one of the five elements has two aspects—being restricted and restricting.

Ⅳ. Write a 150-word composition to introduce the theory of five elements briefly.

Text B

The Basic Content of Five-Element Theory

Similar to the theory of *yin-yang*, the theory of Five Elements—wood, fire, earth, metal and water—was an ancient philosophical concept used to explain the composition and phenomena of the physical universe①. In traditional Chinese medicine, the theory of five elements is used to interpret the relationship between the physiology and pathology of the human body and the natural environment. According to the theory, the interdependence and mutual restraint of the five elements explain the complex connection between material objects as well as the unity between the human body and the natural world②.

In traditional Chinese medicine, the visceral organs, as well as other organs and tissues, have similar properties to the five elements③; they interact physiologically and pathologically as the five elements do. Through similarity comparison, different phenomena are attributed to the categories of the five elements. Based on the characteristics, forms, and functions of different phenomena, the complex links between physiology and pathology as well as the interconnection between the human body and the natural world are explained④.

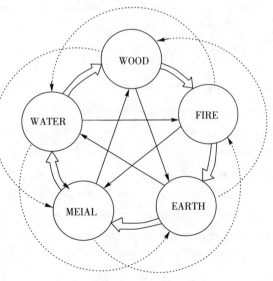

The five elements emerged from an observation of the various groups of dynamic processes, functions and characteristics observed in the natural world⑤. The aspects involved in each of the five elements are as follows:

Fire: draught, heat, flaring, ascendance, movement, etc.⑥
Wood: germination, extension, softness, harmony, flexibility, etc.
Metal: strength, firmness, killing, cutting, cleaning up, etc.
Earth: growing, changing, nourishing, producing, etc.
Water: moisture, cold, descending, flowing, etc.

Between the five elements there exists close relationships that can be classified as mutual promoting and mutual restraining under physiological conditions, and mutual encroaching and mutual violating under pathological conditions⑦. By mutually promoting and restraining, functions of the various systems are coordinated and homeostasis maintained.⑧ By encroaching and violating, pathological changes can be explained and complications predicted.

—	Wood	Fire	Earth	Metal	Water
Flavors(味)	sour	bitter	sweet	pungent	salty
Zang	liver	heart	spleen	lung	kidney
Fu	gallbladder	s. intestine	stomach	l. intestine	urinary
Senses(觉)	eye	tongue	mouth	nose	ear
Tissue	tendon(腱)	vessel(脉)	muscle	hair/skin	bone
Directions	east	south	center	west	north
Changes	germinate(发育/孕育)	grow	transform	reap(收获/割)	store
Color	green	red	yellow	white	black

The order of mutual promoting among the five elements is that wood promotes fire, fire promotes earth, earth promotes metal, metal promotes water, and water generates wood.⑨ In this way each of the five elements has this type of mutual promoting relationship with the other, thus promoting is circular and endless. According to the order of mutual restraining, however, wood restrains earth, metal restrains wood, etc. Each of the five elements also shares this restraining relationship with the other. Mutual promoting and mutual restraining are two aspects that cannot be separated. If there is no promoting, then there is no birth and growth. If there is no restraining, then there is no change and development for maintaining normal harmonious relations. Thus the movement and change of all things exists through their mutual promoting and restraining relationships. These relationships are the basis of the circulation of natural elements.

Encroaching and violating are the pathological conditions of the normal mutual promoting and restraining relationships.⑩ Encroaching denotes that the restraining of one of the five elements to another surpasses the normal level, while violating means that one of the five elements restrains the other opposite to the normal mutual restraining order.

(724 words)

New Words

philosophical	/ˌfɪləˈsɒfɪkl/ a.	哲学的(等于 philosophic),冷静的
property	/ˈprɒpətɪ/ n.	财产,性质,性能,所有权
attribute	/əˈtrɪbjuːt/ vt.	把……归于,归属
category	/ˈkætəgərɪ/ n.	种类,分类,范畴
interconnection	/ˌɪntəkəˈnekʃn/ n.	互相连络
draught	/drɑːft/ n.	气流,汇票,草稿
ascendance	/əˈsendəns/ n.	上升,权势,支配地位
germination	/ˌdʒɜːmɪˈneɪʃn/ n.	发生,发芽,伟晶作用
harmony	/ˈhɑːmənɪ/ n.	协调,融洽,调和,和睦
nourish	/ˈnʌrɪʃ/ vt.	滋养,养育,抚养
moisture	/ˈmɔɪstʃə/ n.	潮湿,水分,湿气
tendon	/ˈtendən/ n.	腱
vessel	/ˈvesl/ n.	容器,器皿,船,舰,脉管,血管
restrain	/rɪˈstreɪn/ vt.	抑制,控制,限定,约束
encroach	/ɪnˈkrəʊtʃ/ vi.	(暗中或逐步)侵占,占用(on/upon)
violate	/ˈvaɪəleɪt/ vt.	违反,侵犯,妨碍;亵渎
surpass	/səˈpɑːs/ vt.	胜过,优于,超越,非……所能办到或理解

Expressions

similar to	与……相似
according to	根据
as well as	以及,和
be based on	根据
emerge from	产生于,来源于
various groups of	各种各样的
involved in	涉及
be classified as	划分为
opposite to	与……相对应

Notes

① ... the theory of Five Elements—wood, fire, earth, metal and water—was an ancient philosophical concept used to explain the composition and phenomena of the physical universe. 木、火、土、金、水的五行理论是一个用来解释物理宇宙的组成和现象的古代哲

学概念。

② ... the interdependence and mutual restraint of the five elements explain the complex connection between material objects as well as the unity between the human body and the natural world. 五种元素之间的相互依赖、相互制约解释了物体与物体之间的复杂关系以及人与自然的和谐统一。

③ ... the visceral organs, as well as other organs and tissues, have similar properties to the five elements. 内脏器官以及其他器官和组织有着与这五种元素相似的属性。as well as other organs and tissues 在句中作插入语。

④ ... the complex links between physiology and pathology as well as the interconnection between the human body and the natural world are explained. 由此可以说明生理和病理之间的复杂联系以及人体和自然界的相互关系。as well as：以及。

⑤ ... the various groups of dynamic processes, functions and characteristics observed in the natural world. 在大自然中所观察到的各种各样的动态过程、功能和特征。

⑥ **Fire**：draught, heat, flaring, ascendance, movement, etc. 火包括：气、热量、光、上升、运动等。

⑦ ... mutual promoting and mutual restraining under physiological conditions, and mutual encroaching and mutual violating under pathological conditions. 生理条件下的相互促进、相互制约,和病理条件下的相互侵蚀和相互干扰。

⑧ By mutually promoting and restraining, functions of the various systems are coordinated and homeostasis maintained. 通过相互促进和抑制,各种系统的功能得到了动态的协调和平衡。by doing... 通过做……

⑨ The order of mutual promoting among the five elements is that wood promotes fire, fire promotes earth, earth promotes metal, metal promotes water, and water generates wood. 五行之间相互促进的顺序是：木促生火、火促生土、土促生金、金促生水,水促生木。

⑩ Encroaching and violating are the pathological conditions of the normal mutual promoting and restraining relationships. 侵蚀及干扰是正常相生相克关系的病变。

Exercises

Ⅰ. Fill in the blanks with the words given below. Change the form when necessary.

merge	tendon	pungent	kidney
violate	encroach	surpass	moisture
philosophical	pathology	interconnection	dynamic

1. Students who _____ the terms of their visa—for example, by working off-campus without permission—could be sent home.

Unit 3　The Five Elements

2. We felt that we were not prepared to create a situation that, in fact, could begin to _____ on the field of play.
3. We wanted to quickly catch up and _____ everyone in terms of search quality for Chinese users.
4. After the potato plants appear, organic mulch can be spread around to hold _____, help suppress weed growth and cool the soil.
5. The members discussed _____ ideas and began writing about them.
6. He later returned to the University of Minnesota to study plant _____.
7. I found that this _____ between the manmade and the natural world was most powerful.
8. On some level, forgetfulness would just ease the grievousness of this miserable new psychological _____ with which they are tormented.
9. We will rebuild, we will recover, and our country will _____ stronger than before.
10. A _____ consists of parallel fibres.
11. A youngster who develops diabetes in his teens may need a(n) _____ transplant by the time he's thirty.
12. She's rank, ill-tempered, _____ in all senses.

II. Choose the best answer to each of the following questions or unfinished statements.

1. The theory of five elements was an ancient _____.
   A. natural concept used to explain the problems of the world
   B. chemical concept used to explain the composition and phenomena of the physical universe
   C. political concept used to explain the ancient policy
   D. philosophical concept used to explain the physical universe
2. Which statement is true?
   A. The five elements of the universe are air, tree, water, earth, fire.
   B. The five elements are stable and fixed.
   C. The five elements are in constant move and change.
   D. The five elements are not in constant move and change.
3. Which statement is NOT true?
   A. Wood refers to germination, extension, softness, harmony, flexibility, etc.
   B. Fire includes draught, heat, flaring, nourishing, producing, etc.
   C. Earth is about growing, changing, nourishing, producing, etc.
   D. Water is about moisture, cold, descending, flowing, etc.
4. The correct order of mutual promoting among the five elements is _____.
   A. wood promotes fire, fire promotes earth, earth promotes metal, metal promotes water, and water generates wood
   B. wood promotes fire, fire promotes earth, metal promotes earth, metal promotes

water, and water generates wood

C. wood promotes fire, fire promotes earth, earth promotes metal, metal promotes water, wood generates water

D. fire promotes wood, fire promotes earth, earth promotes metal, metal promotes water, wood generates water

5. The sentence "The movement and change of all things exists through their mutual promoting and restraining relationships" means "_____".

A. All things will not move or change because they restrain each other

B. All things existing in the universe move and change by promoting and restraining each other

C. All things will not promote because they always restrain each other

D. All things will not restrain each other because they always promote each other

Ⅲ. Translate the following sentences into English or Chinese.

1. 与阴阳理论相似,中医五行说是我国古代用来解释宇宙万物的哲学概念。
2. 中医五行说阐明了人体和自然环境之间的生理及病理关系。
3. 相依相克说明了人体和自然之间物质的以及统一的复杂关系。
4. 中医理论说内脏以及人体的其他器官和组织有着与五大元素相似的性质。
5. 所有事物的变化和发展都是由于彼此之间相生相克的关系。

6. The order of mutual promoting among the five elements is that wood promotes fire, fire promotes earth, earth promotes metal, metal promotes water, and water generates wood.

7. Mutual Encroaching and violating are the pathological conditions of the normal mutual promoting and restraining relationships.

8. Each of the five elements also shares this restraining relationship with the other.

9. By mutually promoting and restraining, functions of the various systems are coordinated and homeostasis(动态平衡) maintained.

10. Mutual promoting and mutual restraining are two aspects that cannot be separated.

Unit 3 The Five Elements

 Text C

Five Elements and *Yin-Yang* Balance

The ancient Chinese *yin-yang* scholars[①] believed that there are two natural, complementary and contradictory forces in our universe. The scholars named them as *yin* and *yang*. *Yin* represents the female, negative, darkness, softness, moisture, night-time, even numbers and docile aspects of things. *Yang* represents the male, positive, brightness, hardness, dryness, day-time, odd numbers and dominant aspects. *Yin* and *yang* are continually in the state of flux and always looking for the BALANCE point. One moves, the other responses. Therefore, ancient scholars treated this natural phenomenon as a natural universal law.[②] These scholars also believed that our universe consisted of five basic elements, which are Metal, Water, Wood, Fire and Earth (Soil).[③] Everything, including humans, in the universe (between Heaven and Earth) must have a relationship with these five elements. So they tried to apply the five elements not only to every physical thing in the world, but also to the Colors, Directions, Seasons and Sounds.[④] They even applied to the Years, Months, Days, Hours, Minutes and Seconds of the Chinese Calendar.

Now, people are able to know their five-element weights from their birth date and time. Based on the combination of these five-element weights plus the concept of the natural phenomenon, they can tell the rise and fall of human destiny (fate) cycle[⑤].

FIVE ELEMENTS does not only mean metal, water, wood, fire and soil. The "element" in Chinese also means MOVEMENT, CHANGEABLE and DEVELOPMENT. These elements have their *yin* and *yang* sides too. They are moving, waning, waxing and changing all the time.[⑥] Just like *yin* and *yang*, the movements of five elements are slow and stable when they are in a kind of balance. If they are out of balance, then the movements are unstable and unpredictable[⑦]. When a person is in a stable environment, he should live peacefully. When a person is in an unpredictable environment, he is easily out of control. A person will feel lucky when everything is under control. A person will feel bad luck when everything is out of control. If you want to be a lucky person, you have to move to an environment to bring your five elements into balance.

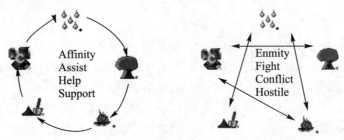

In the fortune-telling system, we want to use metal, water, wood, fire and earth as the five elements to explain everything. Metal stands for mineral, gold, jewelry, iron, rock or something hard. Water stands for liquid or something cold. Wood stands for tree or something to do with wood. Fire stands for sun, fire, heat, light or something hot. Earth stands for soil, dust or ground.⑧ There are affinity and enmity relationships between five elements.

The affinity relationship means supporting, helping, producing, etc.

* Water can help tree (Wood) grow.
* Wood can help Fire to burn.
* Fire can help to produce dust (Earth).
* Earth can help mineral (Metal) to form.
* Metal can hold Water.

We can say that:

* Water is the supporting element of Wood. Wood can release the power of Water.
* Wood is the supporting element of Fire. Fire can release the power of Wood.
* Fire is the supporting element of Earth. Earth can release the power of Fire.
* Earth is the supporting element of Metal. Metal can release the power of Earth.
* Metal is the supporting element of Water. Water can release the power of Metal.

The enmity relationship means fighting, conflicting, rejecting, etc.

* Water can extinguish Fire, but Fire might evaporate Water.⑨
* Wood can break the ground (Earth), but Earth can bury Wood too.
* Fire can melt Metal, but Metal might not melt before Fire is extinguished.
* Earth can absorb Water, but Water can cover the land (Earth).
* Metal can cut Wood, but Metal might become dull before breaking Wood.

We can say that:

* Water and Fire are enemies. Water overwhelms the movement of Fire.
* Wood and Earth are enemies. Wood overwhelms the movement of Earth.
* Fire and Metal are enemies. Fire overwhelms the movement of Metal.
* Earth and Water are enemies. Earth overwhelms the movement of Water.
* Metal and Wood are enemies. Metal overwhelms the movement of Wood.

(730 words)

New Words

complementary /ˌkɒmplɪˈmentrɪ/ a.　　补足的,补充的
contradictory /ˌkɒntrəˈdɪktərɪ/ a.　　矛盾的,反驳的,反对的,抗辩的
docile /ˈdəusaɪl/ a.　　温顺的,驯服的,容易教的
flux /flʌks/ n.　　流量,流出,变迁,不稳定
negative /ˈnegətɪv/ a.　　消极的,否定的,负的,阴性的
dominant /ˈdɒmɪnənt/ a.　　支配的,统治的,占优势的,显性的

Unit 3 The Five Elements

calendar /ˈkælɪndə/ n.　　　　　　　　日历,历法,日程表
combination /ˌkɒmbɪˈneɪʃn/ n.　　　　结合,化合,联合,组合
unpredictable /ˌʌnprɪˈdɪktəbl/ a.　　出乎意料的,不可预知的
affinity /əˈfɪnətɪ/ n.　　　　　　　　吸引力,姻亲关系,密切关系,类同
enmity /ˈenmətɪ/ n.　　　　　　　　　敌意,憎恨
release /rɪˈliːs/ vt.　　　　　　　　释放,发布,允许发表
hostile /ˈhɒstaɪl/ a.　　　　　　　　敌对的,敌方的,怀敌意的
wane /weɪn/ vi.　　　　　　　　　　　衰落,亏缺,退潮,消逝
evaporate /ɪˈvæpəreɪt/ v.　　　　　　蒸发,脱水,消失
scholar /ˈskɒlə/ n.　　　　　　　　　学者,奖学金获得者
odd /ɒd/ a.　　　　　　　　　　　　　奇数的,古怪的,临时的,剩余的,零散的
destiny /ˈdestənɪ/ n.　　　　　　　　命运,定数,天命
female /ˈfiːmeɪl/ a.　　　　　　　　女性的,雌性的,柔弱的,柔和的

Expressions

name... as　　　　　　　　　　　　　把……命名为……
look for　　　　　　　　　　　　　　寻找
treat... as...　　　　　　　　　　　把……当作……来对待
consist of　　　　　　　　　　　　　由……组成
apply... to...　　　　　　　　　　　把……应用于……
not only... (but) also...　　　　　不但……而且……
stand for　　　　　　　　　　　　　　代表
do with　　　　　　　　　　　　　　　与……相关
use... as...　　　　　　　　　　　　把……当作……来用
out of control　　　　　　　　　　　失去控制,无法控制

Notes

① *yin-yang* scholars：指研究中医阴阳理论的学者。
② Therefore, ancient scholars treated this natural phenomenon as a natural universal law. 因此,古代学者把这种自然现象看作一种自然界的普遍规律。
③ These scholars also believed that our universe consisted of five basic elements, which are Metal, Water, Wood, Fire and Earth (Soil). 这些学者认为宇宙是由金、水、木、火和土这五行组成的。这里的 which 为关系代词,引导非限制性的定语从句,解释 five basic elements。
④ So they tried to apply the five elements not only to every physical thing in the world, but also to the Colors, Directions, Seasons and Sounds. 因此,他们不仅将五行应用到世间每个物质上,还应用于色彩、方向季节和声音。这里的 not only... but also... 连接的是两个并列的宾语 to every physical thing in the world; to the Colors, Directions,

Seasons and Sounds。

⑤ ... they can tell the rise and fall of human destiny (fate) cycle. 这里的 the rise and fall 意思是（命运的）起起落落。

⑥ They are moving, waning, waxing and changing all the time. 他们一直在移动、减弱、增强和变化着。moving, waning, waxing 和 changing 四个现在分词并列在句中作表语。all the time：一直，自始至终。

⑦ unstable and unpredictable：not stable and not predictable，前缀 un- 表示 not。

⑧ Water stands for liquid or something cold. Wood stands for tree or something to do with wood. Fire stands for Sun, fire, heat, light or something hot. Earth stands for soil, dust or ground. 这一部分包含了几个排比句，解释了五大元素之间相生相克的原理。

⑨ Water can extinguish Fire, but Fire might evaporate Water. 水可以灭火，但火也可以蒸发水。

Exercises

Ⅰ. **Fill in the blanks with the words given below. Change the form when necessary.**

female	destiny	evaporate	hostile
release	affinity	complementary	contradictory
negative	dominant	unpredictable	calendar

1. She took pictures of couples and families and even of _____ twins—sisters born at the same time.

2. The ethical message here is that humans are in control of their _____ and the action of every individual affects and influences the fate of society.

3. Pieter Hoff says the nice thing about the siphons is that, once collected, the water is not able to _____ anymore.

4. In other words, you can win people to your side more easily with gentle persuasion than by _____ actions.

5. Research has shown that just three rows of trees near poultry houses can reduce the _____ of dust and ammonia.

6. When Suna particularly said to me "I really want to be best", it was just such an instant _____.

7. We need, absolutely, to focus on the restructuring of our own public resources towards agriculture, and then the resources coming from the international community will be a _____ form of resource.

8. Was the story hard to follow? Was it self-_____ and in what ways? Anything?

9. Bullying(欺负，恐吓)is defined as _____ behavior repeated over time against the same person.

10. And you know we have a very _____ traffic share over there, so it's really a very good spot to be in.

11. The first is that while God's promise is sure, the manner and the timing of its fulfillment is quite _____ .

12. If you ask what is today's lunar date, we will come up with a(n)_____ of it.

Ⅱ. **Choose the best answer to each of the following questions or unfinished statements.**

1. Which statement is true according to the passage?
   A. The ancient Chinese *yin-yang* scholars believed that there are two natural, complementary and contradictory forces in our universe, that is the five elements.
   B. The ancient Chinese *yin-yang* scholars believed that there are two natural, complementary and contradictory forces in our universe, and they also believe that there are five elements in our universe.
   C. The ancient Chinese *yin-yang* scholars believed that there are two natural, complementary and contradictory forces in our universe, that is not the five elements.
   D. *Yang* represents the female, negative, darkness, softness, moisture, night-time, even numbers and docile aspects of things.

2. The main idea of the first paragraph is that _____ .
   A. The ancient Chinese scholars believed *yin-yang* and five-elements were in balance
   B. The ancient Chinese scholars believed *yin-yang* was the only natural law of our universe
   C. The ancient Chinese scholars believed that *yin-yang* equaled to five-elements
   D. The ancient Chinese scholars believed that *yin* stands for the moon, and the *yang* stands for the sun

3. According to the passage, the word "affinity" in Para. 4 refers to _____
   A. assisting, aiding, growing, producing, etc.
   B. regulating, holding, absorbing, dying, etc.
   C. fighting, conflicting, assisting, helping, dying, etc.
   D. fighting, conflicting, hostile, contradictory, etc.

4. Which statement is NOT true according to the passage?
   A. *Yin* represents the female, negative, darkness, softness, moisture, night-time.
   B. *Yang* represents the male, positive, brightness, hardness, dryness, day-time, odd numbers and dominant aspects.
   C. *Yin* and *yang* are continually in the state of flux and always looking for the BALANCE point.

D. Fire can extinguish Water, but Water might evaporate Fire.
5. Which statement is true?
    A. Water and Fire are enemies. Water overwhelms the movement of Fire.
    B. Wood and Earth are enemies. Earth overwhelms the movement of Wood.
    C. Fire and Metal are enemies. Metal overwhelms the movement of Fire.
    D. Earth and Water are enemies. Water overwhelms the movement of Earth.

Ⅲ. Translate the following sentences into English or Chinese.

1. 在我们的宇宙里有两种相互补充和相互冲突的东西。
2. 阴代表着雌性、否定、柔软、潮湿和黑暗。
3. 古代学者把自然界的现象看做是宇宙运行之规律。
4. 五行也意味着运动、变化和发展。
5. 五行也有着各自的阴和阳的两面性。
6. These scholars also believed that our universe consisted of five basic elements, which are Metal, Water, Wood, Fire and Earth (Soil).
7. Everything, including humans, in the universe (between Heaven and Earth) must have a relationship with these five elements.
8. So they tried to apply the five elements not only to every physical thing in the world, but also to the Colors, Directions, Seasons and Sounds.
9. They even applied the theory to the Years, Months, Days, Hours, Minutes and Seconds of the Chinese Calendar.
10. If you want to be a lucky person, you have to move to an environment to bring your five elements into balance.

Respiratory System（呼吸系统）

Root	Meaning	Examples
-spiro- pneumo- pneumato- -pnea	breath 呼吸	expiratory 呼气的 respiratory distress syndrome 呼吸窘迫综合征 median peak inspiratory flow 平均吸入流峰值 spirometry 呼吸测量法 pneumatic 气体的，呼吸的 pneumatosis 积气症 apnea 呼吸暂停 dyspnea 呼吸困难
naso- rhino-	nose 鼻	nasal mucosa 鼻黏膜 nasopharyngeal 鼻咽的 rhinitis 鼻炎 rhinovirus 鼻病毒 rhinal 鼻的
laryngo-	throat 喉	laryngeal cancer 喉癌 laryngorhinology 鼻喉科学 laryngitis 喉炎 laryngalgia 喉痛 laryngomalacia 喉软骨软化病
glotto-	glottis 声门	glottic 声门的 glottogram 声门图 glottography 声门描记（法） glottic carcinoma 声门癌
tracheo-	trachea, windpipe 气管	tracheostomy 气管造口术 tracheobronchitis 气管支气管炎 tracheofissure 气管裂开术 tracheotomy 气管切开术
broncho- bronchiolo-	bronchus 支气管	bronchoalveolar 支气管肺泡的 bronchocele 支气管囊肿 bronchopneumonia 支气管肺炎，小叶性肺炎 peribronchitis 支气管周炎 bronchoplasty 支气管成形术 bronchiolitis 细支气管炎

续表

Root	Meaning	Examples
pulmo(no)- pneumono-	lung 肺	pulmonology 肺科学 pulometry 肺量测定法 pulmonologist 肺脏学家 pneumonectasia 肺气肿 pneumorrhagia 肺出血 pneumococcus 肺炎球菌
alveolo-	air sacs, alveolus 肺泡	bronchoalveolitis 支气管肺泡炎 interalveolar 牙槽间的，肺泡间的 alveolar macrophage 肺泡巨噬细胞 alveolar hyperventilation 肺泡通气过度 alveolar hypoventilation 肺泡通气不足
pleuro-	pleura 胸膜	pleurisy 胸膜炎 interpleural 胸膜间的 extrapleural 胸膜外的 pleuralgia 胸膜痛 pleurocentesis 胸膜穿刺术 pleurotomy 胸膜切开术 pleural cavity 胸腔

Unit 4　Visceral State

　Text A

The Visceral Theory of TCM

Along with the improvement of our life, more and more people are concerned about TCM though Western medicine's equipment has been considerably changed. Especially, TCM is applied to keep healthy and cure complex sickness, because it is greatly different from Western medicine in method and viewing. The visceral theory① of TCM has the important position in TCM.

So what is the visceral theory of TCM? The visceral theory studies the physiological functions and pathological changes of the viscera.② This theory is based on *zang-fu* (viscera), a general term for internal organs. TCM classifies the internal organs of the body into three kinds: the five *zang*, the six *fu* and the extraordinary organs that include the brain, marrow, bone, vessel and uterus. The heart, lungs, spleen, liver and kidneys are together known as the five *zang* organs, whose common physiological function is producing and storing essence—*qi*.③ They store but not eliminate essence—*qi*.

The heart is located in the thorax and guarded externally by the pericardium. Its physiological function is governing blood and the vessels, and giving motive power for blood circulation. The heart also governs spiritual activities, and opens to tongue, manifests on the face.

The lungs are situated in the thorax. They are related to the throat and open to the nose. The major of the lungs include governing *qi*, controlling respiration, dispersing and descending, and smoothing water passages, governs the skin and hair.

The spleen is located in the middle—*jiao*. Its major physiological functions include governing transformation and transportation, controlling blood, and ascending essence. It dominates the muscles and limbs, opens to mouth, manifests on the lips.

The liver is located in the hypochondrium. It is responsible for regulating the smooth flow of *qi* and the storage of blood, and dominates the tendons. The liver opens to the eyes and manifests on the nails.

The kidneys are located in the lumbar region. The kidneys store vital essence, manufacture marrow, dominate bone, and are the source for growth, development and reproduction. They also govern ears, and manifest in the hair.

TCM refers to the gallbladder, the stomach, the large intestine, the small intestine, the urinary bladder and the triple energizer④ to the six *fu* organs, which have the common physiological functions of receiving, transforming, and transporting food and water⑤.

The mainly physiological functions of the gallbladder are to store and discharge of bile which helps digestion of food and liquid.

The major physiological functions of the stomach include receiving and digesting food and fluids.

The small intestine's mainly physiological functions are transforming chyme and separating the clear from the turbid.

The large intestine receives waste materials sent down from the small intestine. After the remained water it still contains is absorbed, stool is formed and finally it discharges the stool through the anus.

The major functions of urinary bladder include storing and discharging urine.

The *san-jiao* is a collective term including the upper-*jiao*, middle-*jiao* and lower-*jiao*.⑥ The major functions of the *san-jiao* are controlling *qi* of body, and also are passageway of digesting drink and food, and of fluid metabolism.

It should be pointed out that according to the theory of visceral manifestation, the name of the *zang-fu* organs, correspond to those of the modern human anatomy and refer to the substantial internal organs. However, in the physiology and pathology, the knowledge of TCM differs greatly from that of Western medicine, which has been learnt a lot from the above.⑦

Harmony between the functions of the five *zang* organs is a key link for maintaining stability of the internal system of the body. Equilibrium between the external and internal environments is maintained through the connection between the viscera and various tissues and organs, and the relation between the five *zang* organs and emotions.

(669 words)

New Words

extraordinary /ɪkˈstrɔːdnrɪ/	*a.*	非常的,特别的
uterus /ˈjuːtərəs/	*n.*	子宫
thorax /ˈθɔːræks/	*n.*	胸,胸部,胸廓
pericardium /ˌperɪˈkɑːdɪəm/	*n.*	心囊,心包膜
dominate /ˈdɒmɪneɪt/	*v.*	支配,控制,统治
hypochondrium /ˌhaɪpəˈkɒndrɪəm/	*n.*	忧郁症,疑病症,季肋部
lumbar /ˈlʌmbə/	*n.*	腰,腰椎

discharge /dɪsˈtʃɑːdʒ/ n.	排泄
chyme /kaɪm/ n.	食糜
turbid /ˈtɜːbɪd/ a.	混浊的,混乱的,浓密的
absorb /əbˈsɔːb/ v.	吸收,使全神贯注,汲取,理解
anus /ˈeɪnəs/ n.	肛门
metabolism /məˈtæbəlɪzəm/ n.	新陈代谢
equilibrium /ˌiːkwɪˈlɪbrɪəm/ n.	平衡,均衡,平静

Expressions

classify... into	给……分类
locate in	位于
manifest on	显示出
be situated in	位于
differ from	与……不同
separate from	分离,分开
learn from	向……学习

Notes

① the visceral theory: 藏象理论,是研究脏腑形体官窍的形态结构、生理活动规律及其相互关系的学说。

② The visceral theory studies the physiological functions and pathological changes of the viscera. 藏象理论研究的是脏腑的生理功能和病理变化。

③ The heart, lungs, spleen, liver and kidneys are together known as the five *zang*, whose common physiological function is producing and storing essence—*qi*. 心、肺、脾、肝和肾被称为五脏,它们的共同特点是具有产生、贮藏精气的功能。

④ triple energizer: 三焦。三焦是中医藏象学说中一个特有的名词,是上焦、中焦和下焦的合称,即将躯干划分为3个部位,横膈以上为上焦,包括心、肺;横膈以下至脐为中焦,包括脾、胃;脐以下为下焦,包括肝、肾、大肠、小肠、膀胱。

⑤ ...which have the common physiological function of receiving, transforming, and transporting food and water. 它们的共同特点是具有受盛和传化水谷的功能。

⑥ The *san-jiao* is a collective term including the upper-*jiao*, middle-*jiao* and lower-*jiao*. 三焦是一个集合名词,包括上焦、中焦和下焦。

⑦ However, in the physiology and pathology, the knowledge of TCM differs greatly from that of Western medicine, which has been learnt a lot from the above. 然而,在生理学和病理学方面,中医和西医有着很大的区别,从上文我们已了解很多。

Exercises

I. Fill in the blanks with the words given below. Change the form when necessary.

extraordinary	vessel	eliminate	dominate
intestine	discharge	absorb	turbid
harmony	correspond	emotion	transform

1. But the forces and heat that _____ meteors into meteorites can create beauty as well.
2. The trends for the advance are still _____.
3. It seeks distinction, the desire to be first in the race of life and lead us to seek to _____ others.
4. We can virtually _____ transmission of HIV from mother to child. The Global Fund was established as a financial tool.
5. Here, a concept is to introduce a gene that causes the process of new blood _____ growth.
6. His unusual childhood and _____ actions tell about people who believed there were no limits to what they could do.
7. But it can also harm the inside of the stomach and small _____.
8. After his army _____, no law school in his native Tennessee would admit him because of his color.
9. They noted that the grass can _____ and control the spread of harmful wastewaters, like those from pig farms.
10. She told me about all the traveling she'd done and how she discovered ways to expand her mind and learn how to live in _____.
11. If I could find the unique set of proteins that _____ to those genes I could define chemically what the cell is.
12. We must not be enemies. Though _____ may have damaged them, it must not break our ties of love.

II. Choose the best answer to each of the following questions or unfinished statements.

1. What does the visceral theory study?
   A. It studies health and cure complex sickness.
   B. It studies the physiological functions and pathological changes of the viscera.
   C. It studies harmony between the functions of the five *zang*.
   D. It studies equilibrium between the external and internal environments.
2. TCM classifies the internal organs of the body into three kinds: _____.
   A. the five *zang*, the six *fu*
   B. the brain, marrow, bone, vessel, and uterus

C. the heart, lungs, spleen, liver and kidneys

   D. the five *zang*, the six *fu* and the extraordinary organs

3. What are the major functions of spleen?

   A. Governing blood and the vessels.

   B. Regulating the smooth flow of *qi*, storage of blood.

   C. Helping digestion of food and liquid.

   D. Governing transformation and transportation, controlling blood, and ascending essence.

4. Which statement is NOT true according to the passage?

   A. The six *fu* have the common physiological function of receiving, transforming, and transporting food and water.

   B. The functions of the small intestine are transforming chyme and separating the clear from the turbid.

   C. The *san-jiao* discharge of bile, which helps digestion of food and liquid.

   D. The liver opens to the eyes and manifests on the nails.

5. The major functions of urinary bladder include _____.

   A. storing and discharging urine　　B. discharging the stool

   C. separating the clear from the turbid　D. smoothing water passages

Ⅲ. Translate the following sentences into English or Chinese.

1. 中医和西医在方法和观点上有很大的不同。

2. 脏腑是中医藏象理论的基础，它是内在器官的统称。

3. 心脏的生理机能是支配血液、血管并给血液循环提供动力。

4. 心脏支配着人的精神活动。

5. 肺脏位于胸腔内。

6. The spleen is located in the middle-*jiao*.

7. The liver is responsible for regulating the smooth flow of *qi*, storage of blood.

8. The major physiological functions of the stomach include receiving and digesting food and fluids.

9. TCM classifies the internal organs of the body into three kinds: the five *zang*, the six *fu* and the extraordinary organs that include the brain, marrow, bone, vessel, and uterus.

10. The large intestine receives waste materials sent down from the small intestine.

Ⅳ. Write a 150-word composition about the relationship between the liver and the kidney.

 Text B

The Relationship Between *Zang* and *Fu* Organs

The relationship among the *zang-fu* organs is quite a complicated matter. Thanks to TCM's concise and brilliant summarization, it may just as well be briefed in a broad outline. In TCM, the *zang* organs pertain to *yin* and are thought of as interior, while the *fu* organs to *yang* and, naturally enough, as exterior. The interior-exterior relationship between them is formed by the connections of their meridians. This relationship can be clearly seen in the interrelations between the heart and the small intestine, the lung and the large intestine, the spleen and the stomach, the liver and the gallbladder and the kidney and the urinary bladder.①

The heart and the small intestine are connected by the heart meridian and the small intestine meridian to form an exterior-interior relationship. The excessive heart-fire tends to go into the small intestine, resulting in oliguria, burning pains during urination, etc. Conversely, the excessive heat in the small intestine may go upward along the meridian to the heart and cause internal hyperactivity of heart-fire, leading to dysphoria, crimson tongue, oral ulceration and so on.

The lung and the large intestine form an exterior-interior relationship by mutual connections of their meridians. When the lung functions normally, the large intestine does well. Conversely, when the descending function of the lung *qi* does not work well, it will affect the function of the large intestine in transportation, causing difficult bowel movements. On the other hand, loose stools and the stoppage of *fu-qi* may affect the descent of lung-*qi*, giving rise to asthmatic cough and chest distress②.

Both the stomach and the spleen lie in the middle energizer and are connected by their meridians to form an exterior-interior relationship. The stomach governs the reception, while the spleen governs the transportation and transformation. If pathogenic damp attacks the spleen, it will injure the transporting and transforming functions of the spleen and affect the reception and the descending action of the stomach, resulting in poor appetite, vomiting, nausea and gastric distention. So the spleen and the stomach share out the work and cooperate with each other to jointly accomplish the task of the digestion, absorption and distribution of food. On the contrary, intemperance of food intake (improper diet) and dyspeptic retention of the stomach will bring about both the dysfunction of the stomach in descent but that of the spleen's transportation and transformation, causing such symptoms as abdominal distention, diarrhea.

The gallbladder is attached to the liver, and they are connected by their meridians to form an exterior-interior relationship. Bile derives from surplus *qi* of the liver. It is stored and excreted by the gallbladder located under the liver. Only when the liver performs its function successfully can bile be secreted, stored and excreted normally. ③ On the other hand, when bile is excreted properly, the liver can give full play to its function in regulating the normal flow of *qi*. Conversely, when bile fails to be excreted normally, the liver function will be affected, too. Therefore, the liver and gallbladder are closely related physiologically and pathologically.

The kidney and urinary bladder, like the other *zang-fu* organs, form an exterior-interior relationship through their meridians. The kidneys control opening and closing, while the urinary bladder governs storing and excreting urine. Both are related to water metablism. When kidney *qi* is sufficient and its astringency is right, the urinary bladder will open and close regularly, thus maintaining normal water metabolism. In case kidney *qi* is deficient, there will be the disturbance of its *qi* transformation and astrictive action, causing the irregular opening and closing of the urinary bladder. ④

In short, although the *zang* and *fu* organs have different physiological functions, there is a close relationship between them in maintaining the normal functions of the body, and it is the meridian-collateral system that makes them internally-externally interconnected⑤. Without the interconnecting pathways of the meridians and collaterals, each of the *zang-fu* organs would become an isolated and static organ and unable to perform its functional activities.

(696 words)

New Words

complicated	/ˈkɒmplɪkeɪtɪd/ *a.*	复杂的
concise	/kənˈsaɪs/ *a.*	简洁的,简明的
summarization	/ˌsʌməriˈzeɪʃən/ *n.*	摘要,概要
meridian	/məˈrɪdɪən/ *n.*	经络
interrelation	/ˈɪntərɪˈleɪʃn/ *n.*	相互关系
oliguria	/ɒlɪˈgjʊərɪə/ *n.*	尿过少,少尿(症)
dysphoria	/dɪsˈfɔːrɪə/ *n.*	焦虑,烦躁不安
crimson	/ˈkrɪmzn/ *n.*	深红色
	v.	变得绯红,成熟,染成深红色
ulceration	/ˌʌlsəˈreɪʃn/ *n.*	溃疡,腐败
stool	/stuːl/ *n.*	大便
distress	/dɪˈstres/ *n.*	悲痛,不幸,穷困
	v.	使悲痛,使苦恼,使贫困
appetite	/ˈæpɪtaɪt/ *n.*	爱好,食欲,欲望
nausea	/ˈnɔːzɪə/ *n.*	反胃,恶心,晕船
gastric	/ˈgæstrɪk/ *a.*	胃的
distention	/dɪsˈtenʃən/ *n.*	膨胀,扩张

intemperance /ɪnˈtempərəns/	*n.*	放纵,酗酒,过度
dyspeptic /dɪsˈpeptɪk/	*n.*	消化不良的人
	a.	消化不良的,胃弱的
bile /baɪl/	*n.*	胆汁,愤怒,坏脾气
surplus /ˈsɜːpləs/	*n.*	剩余,盈余
	a.	过剩的
excrete /ekˈskriːt/	*v.*	排泄,分泌
astringency /əˈstrɪndʒənsɪ/	*n.*	收敛性,严厉,严峻

Expressions

thanks to	由于,多亏
be briefed in	总结为
pertain to	关于,属于
tend to	有……的趋势
go upward	向上
lie in	在于
share out	分配,均分
cooperate with	与……合作
on the contrary	相反的是
be attached to	依附于
derive from	得到,得来
in short	简言之

Notes

① This relationship can be clearly seen in the interrelations between the heart and the small intestine, the lung and the large intestine, the spleen and the stomach, the liver and the gallbladder and the kidney and the urinary bladder. 在心脏和小肠、肺和大肠、脾和胃、肝和胆囊以及肾脏和膀胱的相互关系中,能清楚地体现这种关系。

② give rise to asthmatic cough and chest distress：引起喘咳和胸闷。例如：Her disappearance gave rise to the wildest rumors. 她失踪一事引起了各种流言蜚语。

③ Only when the liver performs its function successfully can bile be secreted, stored and excreted normally. 只有当肝成功地履行其职能,胆汁才能正常地分泌、储存和排泄。当 only 放在句首时,句中谓语使用部分倒装。

④ In case kidney *qi* is deficient, there will be the disturbance of its *qi* transformation and astrictive action, causing the irregular opening and closing of the urinary bladder. 如肾气不足,可使肾气化无常,固摄无权,导致膀胱开合失度。

⑤ ... it is the meridian-collateral system that makes them internally-externally interconnected：正是经络系统使得他们内外相互关联。此句为强调句型。

Unit 4 Visceral State

Exercises

I. Fill in the blanks with the words given below. Change the form when necessary.

summarization	concise	dyspeptic	distress
complicated	surplus	appetite	bile
distention	dysphoria	intemperance	stool

1. —It's not a good time. There are some, uh, _____ things happening right now.
   —Well, whatever they are, you can fix them.
2. If you have a(n) _____, and that's a desirable thing to do, you can sell it.
3. An ear and a(n) _____ for these sounds of sense is the first qualification of a writer, be it of prose(散文) or verse(诗歌).
4. —Oh, good god. you're not going to tell me a bedtime story, are you?
   —My stomach's almost out of _____.
5. There's a lot of imagery of swelling(肿胀), of distortion(变形) and _____ of the body that some critics point to her biography to explain.
6. And yet every time I read those two words, I find myself overwhelmed with _____.
7. As we know, notes are the _____, the core content, our understanding and the abbreviations of the books.
8. This is my _____, short, summary version of literacy policy, which is part of information policy processing.
9. See the pictures, read the pictures until you get _____.
10. They pledged more resources to the IMF to help countries in _____ and promised to avoid restrictions on trade.
11. Health does not consist with _____.
12. When Thoreau sits on his little _____ outside his cabin at Walden Pond and he hears the train go by over the ridge, and he puts his hands over his ears—he doesn't want to hear it—he's representing something.

II. Choose the best answer to each of the following questions or unfinished statements.

1. The interior-exterior relationship can be clearly seen in the interrelations between _____.
   A. the spleen and the urinary bladder   B. the heart and the large intestine
   C. the liver and the gallbladder   D. the kidney and the stomach
2. The excessive heart-fire may lead to _____.
   A. oliguria   B. oral ulceration
   C. dysphoria   D. crimson tongue

3. The spleen governs _____.
   A. reception
   B. storing and excreting urine
   C. opening and closing
   D. transportation and transformation
4. What organs are related to water metablism?
   A. The heart and the small intestine.
   B. The spleen and the stomach.
   C. The kidney and the urinary bladder.
   D. The liver and the gallbladder.
5. Which statement is NOT true according to the passage?
   A. The interior-exterior relationship between them is formed by the connections of their meridians.
   B. If the function of lung *qi* does not work well, it will affect the function of the small intestine.
   C. If pathogenic damp attacks the spleen, it will result in gastric distention.
   D. When bile fails to be excreted normally, the liver function will be affected.

Ⅲ. Translate the following sentences into English or Chinese.

1. 在中医上，脏器附属于阴，是内在。
2. 脏和腑的内在和外在联系由相互连接的经络形成。
3. 心脏和小肠由心脏经络和小肠经络连接形成内外在关联。
4. 当肺运转正常时，大肠同样运转正常。
5. 相反，当肺气的下行功能不顺畅时，就会影响大肠的传输功能。
6. Thanks to TCM's concise and brilliant summarization, it may just as well be briefed in a broad outline.
7. In TCM, the *zang* organs pertain to *yin* and are thought of as interior, while the *fu* organs to *yang* and, naturally enough, as exterior.
8. The stomach governs the reception, while the spleen governs the transportation and transformation.
9. When bile is excreted properly, the liver can give full play to its function in regulating the normal flow of *qi*.
10. The urinary bladder governs storing and excreting urine.

Unit 4　Visceral State

 Text C

The Small Intestine

The small intestine is located in the middle of the abdomen, connected with the stomach at the pylorus in the upper and the large intestine at ileocecal junction in the lower.① The physiological function of the small intestine is to receive the chyle and separate the lucid from the turbid. The small intestine receives the chyme from the stomach② and keeps for a certain period of time in order to further digest it.

The lucid refers to food nutrients and the turbid refers to the waste of food.③ After further digestion and absorption of the nutrients and part of the water, the small intestine transmits the waste to the large intestine. This process is called "to separate the lucid from the turbid" in TCM.④ In fact, to receive the chyme and to separate the lucid from the turbid are two aspects in the digesting and absorbing process⑤. There is a close relationship between these two aspects. The former is the condition of the latter and the latter is the result of the former.⑥

TCM emphasizes the functions of the five *zang* organs, so the digesting function of the small intestine is attributed to the transporting and transforming function of the spleen. That is why clinically diseases or disorder of the small intestine in digestion and absorption, such as anorexia, abdominal distension and loose stool, are differentiated as "dysfunction of the spleen" and treated from the aspect of the spleen.

The function of the small intestine to absorb water decides the quantity of urine. If the small intestine absorbs water normally and if the water fully absorbed and distributed to all parts of the body, the stool will appear in normal form and the urination will be smooth. If the small intestine is abnormal in absorbing water and the water is kept in the intestines and moves downward with the waste, then the stool will be sloppy and the urine will become scanty. Such a condition is usually differentiated as "dysfunction of the spleen". If the small intestine absorbs too much water, the urine will become profuse and the stool will become retained. Such a condition is called "constipation due to spleen deficiency and scanty fluid"⑦, indicating the relationship between the small intestine and the spleen. Clinically diarrhea in some cases is treated by the therapy "for promoting urination to consolidate the stool"⑧, focusing on promoting urination to reinforce the function of the small intestine to absorb water. The syndrome of "constipation due to spleen deficiency and scanty fluid" can be treated by slowing down the descending activity⑨ to reduce the speed of the small intestine in absorbing water.

(446 words)

New Words

pylorus /paɪˈlɔːrəs/	*n.*	幽门
ileocecal /ˌɪlɪəʊˈsiːkəl/	*a.*	回盲肠的
junction /ˈdʒʌŋkʃn/	*n.*	结合，连接
lucid /ˈluːsɪd/	*a.*	清楚的，透明的
chime /tʃaɪm/	*n.*	一致，和谐
digest /daɪˈdʒest/	*vt.*	消化
nutrient /ˈnjuːtrɪənt/	*n.*	营养物
clinically /ˈklɪnɪklɪ/	*ad.*	临床上地
anorexia /ˌænəˈreksɪə/	*n.*	神经性厌食症
sloppy /ˈslɒpɪ/	*a.*	稀薄
scanty /ˈskæntɪ/	*a.*	缺乏
diarrhea /ˌdaɪəˈrɪə/	*n.*	腹泻

Expressions

transmit to	把……传送到
be differentiated as	把……区别为……
distribute to	分发给……
slow down	（使）慢下来

Notes

① The small intestine is located in the middle of the abdomen, connected with the stomach at the pylorus in the upper and the large intestine at ileocecal junction in the lower. 这句话向读者介绍了小肠的位置，connected 引导的过去分词短语作状语。

② receive the chyme from the stomach：这里是指小肠接收胃里留下的物质，保持一段时间，然后再将其向下排除。

③ The lucid refers to food nutrients and the turbid refers to the waste of food. 此句对 lucid 和 turbid 两词进行了深入的解释，它们在句中的意思分别是营养物质和废物。

④ This process is called "to separate the lucid from the turbid" in TCM. 这一方法在中医里叫做"清浊分离"。

⑤ the digesting and absorbing process：人体消化和吸收的过程。

⑥ The former is the condition of the latter and the latter is the result of the former. The former... the latter：指上文中提到的消化和吸收过程，这里充分体现了中医的辨证理论，即万事万物的相互作用性。

⑦ "constipation due to spleen deficiency and scanty fluid"：医学上常说的由于脾虚造成的便秘，后面的现在分词短语作为后置定语，对其作进一步说明。

⑧ "for promoting urination to consolidate the stool"：为增加排尿量以使大便变实。

⑨ slowing down the descending activity：减缓食物向下流动的速度，使之在肠内停留时间

Unit 4　Visceral State

增加,这是中医理论中治疗由于脾虚引起的便秘的一种方法。

Exercises

I. Fill in the blanks with the words given below. Change the form when necessary.

nutrient	digest	lucid	chime
sloppy	urine	diarrhea	anorexia
abdomen	scanty	attribute	transmit

1. At the time, most safety belts in cars crossed the body over the _____.
2. I am making light of it and I think it's somewhat justified, because the evidence is just so _____.
3. It is moving in the right direction, and they _____ it to good security and reconstruction efforts.
4. Mister Kao discovered how to _____, or send, light signals over long distances through optical glass fibers.
5. Professor Drinkwater says farmers need to think about ways to solve some of the causes of _____ loss from agriculture.
6. These monks(僧侣) sleep, eat, _____ and pray every day.
7. Toward the end of his life while he was still 100% _____, it was more difficult for him to be mobile and to go into organizations.
8. Fleur, leaning out of her window, heard the hall clock's muffled(发出低沉的声音) _____ of twelve.
9. Her research methodology is _____, she's unjustifiably arrogant(盲目自大).
10. A tube is placed inside the body to collect _____, so the patient does not have to get out of bed.
11. This leads to an increase in diseases like _____, the second leading cause of death in children under five.
12. Drivers in Italy are getting an up-close(直观地) look at the dangers of _____.

II. Choose the best answer to each of the following questions or unfinished statement.

1. Where in the body do the small intestine and the large intestine meet, according to the passage?
   A. In the middle of the abdomen.　　B. In the upper abdomen.
   C. In the lower abdomen.　　D. In the spleen.
2. Which of the following statement is true?
   A. The lucid refers to the waste of food and the turbid refers to food nutrients.

B. The function of the small intestine to absorb water decides the quantity of stool.

C. There is a close relationship between to receive the chyme and to separate the lucid from the turbid.

D. Clinically constipation in some cases is treated by the therapy "for promoting urination to consolidate the stool".

3. What can be the best word to replace "profuse" in the last paragraph?

   A. Abundant.   B. Little.   C. Light.   D. Dense.

4. If a patient who has got diarrhea, his or her _____.

   A. small intestine is abnormal in absorbing water

   B. small intestine absorbs water normally

   C. urination will be smooth

   D. urine will become profuse

5. According to the passage, what is the right thing to do to treat constipation due to spleen deficiency and scanty fluid?

   A. Drink a lot of water.   B. Avoid eating any food.

   C. Eat food which is easy to be digested.   D. Food which contains little water.

Ⅲ. Translate the following sentences into English or Chinese.

1. 小肠位于腹部中间。

2. 小肠的生理功能是接受胃传送来的食糜分清泌浊。

3. "清"是指食物中的精华部分,"浊"是指食物的残渣糟粕。

4. 小肠把食物的残渣糟粕传送到大肠。

5. 小肠的消化功能归属于脾胃纳运功能。

6. After further digestion and absorption of the nutrients and part of the water, the small intestine transmits the waste to the large intestine.

7. The lucid refers to food nutrients and the turbid refers to the waste of food.

8. The function of the small intestine to absorb water decides the quantity of urine.

9. If the small intestine absorbs too much water, the urine will become profuse and the stool will become retained.

10. All this conversation slows down the action of the play.

Digestive System（消化系统）

Root	Meaning	Examples
gest- pepsio-	digestion 消化	maldigestion 消化不良 pepsinogen 胃蛋白酶原 dyspepsia 消化不良
pharyngo-	throat 咽	pharyngitis 咽炎 pharyngolaryngeal 咽喉的 pharyngorrhagia 咽出血 pharyngostenosis 咽狭窄
esophago-	esophagus 食管	esophagogastric 食管胃的 esophagism 食管痉挛 esophagitis 食管炎 esophagoptosis 食道脱垂
gastro-	stomach 胃	gastrointestinal 胃肠的 gastritis 胃炎 gastropexy 胃固定术 gastrorrhagia 胃出血
entero-	intestine, bowel, gut 肠	enterotoxin 肠毒素 enteral 肠的 enterospasm 肠痉挛 enteritis 肠炎
duodeno-	duodenum 十二指肠	duodenoscopy 十二指肠镜检查 duodenitis 事儿直肠炎 duodenal ulcer 十二指肠溃疡
jejuno-	jejunum 空肠	jejunostomy 空肠造口术
ileo-	ileum 回肠	ileocolostomy 回肠结肠吻合术 ileocolitis 回结肠炎 ileostomy 回肠造口术
colon- col-	colon 结肠	colonoscopy 结肠镜检查 colic 结肠的，绞痛的 colonfiberscopy 结肠纤维镜检查 colitis 结肠炎
ceco- typhlo-	blind gut, caecum 盲肠	cecal 盲肠的 typhlitis 盲肠炎 cecal diverticulum 盲肠憩室

续表

Root	Meaning	Examples
appendio-	appendix 阑尾	appendicitis 阑尾炎 appendectomy 阑尾切除术
sigmoido-	sigmoid 乙状结肠	sigmoidoscopy 乙状结肠镜检查 sigmoidopexy 乙状结肠固定术 sigmoiditis 乙状结肠炎
recto- procto(co)-	rectum 直肠	rectovaginal 直肠阴道的 rectal 直肠的 proctocolectomy 直肠结肠切除术 proctosigmoiditis 直肠乙状结肠炎
ano-	anus 肛门	anorectal 肛门直肠的 anal 肛门的
hepato-	liver 肝	hepatitis 肝炎 hepaticostomy 肝管造口术 heparin 肝素
cholecysto-	gall bladder 胆囊	cholecystitis 胆囊炎 cholecystectomy 胆囊切除术
pancreato-	pancreas 胰腺	pancreatoduodenectomy 胰十二指肠切除术 pancreatolith 胰石 pancreatitis 胰腺炎

Unit 5　*Qi*, Blood and Body Fluid

 Text A

The Relationship Between Blood and Body Fluid

　　Both blood and body fluid are liquid substances and function to nourish and moisten the viscera and the body. Compared with *qi*, both blood and body fluid pertain to *yin*.① Physiologically, blood and body fluid depend on and transform into each other. Pathologically, blood and body fluid affect each other.②

　　Blood is made up of body fluid and the nutrient. After the transformation by the spleen and stomach, body fluid is transported first to the vessels and then flows with blood to the whole body. Part of body fluid extravasates from the vessels and flows outside the vessels to moisten and nourish the viscera and the body. At the same time, part of body fluid flowing outside the vessels enters the vessels again to participate in the production of blood.③ In fact, body fluid inside and outside the vessels frequently transforms and supplements each other. Normally, there is a dynamic balance maintained between them under pathological condition. If great quantity of body fluid is consumed, or if great amount of body fluid comes out of the vessels, it will lead to insufficiency of blood inside the vessels. On the contrary, if too much body fluid outside the vessels enters the vessels because of massive hemorrhage, it will lead to insufficiency of body fluid. As a result, a morbid state of scanty fluid and dryness of blood is caused due to insufficiency of body fluid and blood.④

　　Sweat, transformed from body fluid, is closely related to blood. Blood deficiency, usually followed by insufficiency of body fluid, cannot be treated simply by diaphoresis because profuse sweating consumes body fluid and further aggravates the deficiency of blood⑤. On the other hand, profuse sweating and scanty body fluid, often accompanied by insufficiency of blood⑥, cannot be simply treated by blood-breaking therapy because excessive bleeding exhausts the blood and further aggravates the scanty state of body fluid. That is why it is said in *Ling Shu*⑦ that "the patients with massive bleeding cannot be treated by diaphoresis, while the patients with profuse sweating should not be treated by bloodletting therapy."

　　Blood and body fluid not only depend on and transform into each other, but also share the same origin. That is to say that both of them come from the food nutrients.⑧ Such a relationship between blood and body fluid is generalized as "body fluid and blood sharing the same origin⑨" in TCM.

(412 words)

New Words

fluid /ˈfluːɪd/ n.	液体，流体
substance /ˈsʌbstəns/ n.	物质
pertain /pəˈteɪn/ vi.	属于，附属(to)
transform /trænsˈfɔːm/ vt.	转变，使变态，使改变性质
extravasate /eksˈtrævəˌseɪt/ vt.	使(血液等)由脉管中渗出
participate /pɑːˈtɪsɪpeɪt/ vi.	参与，参加
supplement /ˈsʌplɪmənt/ vt.	补充，增补
hemorrhage /ˈhemərɪdʒ/ n.	[医]出血
morbid /ˈmɔːbɪd/ a.	病态的，不健康的
diaphoresis /ˌdaɪəfəˈriːsɪs/ n.	发汗，出汗
profuse /prəˈfjuːs/ a.	极多的，充足的
aggravate /ˈæɡrəveɪt/ vt.	加重，加剧

Expressions

transform into	变成
be made up of	由……组成
participate in	参加
under... condition	在…条件下
as a result	结果，因此
be related to	和……相关

Notes

① Compared with *qi*, both blood and body fluid pertain to *yin*. 与气相比，血液与体液属阴。compared with sth.：与……相比，在句子里作状语。

② Physiologically, blood and body fluid depend on and transform into each other. Pathologically, blood and body fluid affect each other. 这一句分别从生理角度和病理角度来分析血液和体液的关系。Physiologically 和 Pathologically，两个副词的使用相当于 in terms of physiology/pathology。

③ At the same time, part of body fluid flowing outside the vessels enters the vessels again to participate in the production of blood. 本句中的 flowing outside the vessels 是现在分词短语作后置定语，在这里相当于一个定语从句，修饰前面的 part of body fluid。

Unit 5 *Qi*, Blood and Body Fluid

④ As a result, a morbid state of scanty fluid and dryness of blood is caused due to insufficiency of body fluid and blood. due to：形容词短语作原因状语，这里意思类似于 because of；morbid state of scanty fluid and dryness of blood：由于体液稀少与贫血而导致的病态。

⑤ ... because profuse sweating consumes body fluid and further aggravates the deficiency of blood. 因为过多的发汗会耗费身体里的体液，并加剧血液的匮乏。所以贫血是不能用发汗的方法来治疗的。

⑥ ... often accompanied by insufficiency of blood：过去分词短语作后置定语。

⑦ *Ling Shu*：《灵枢经》，又称《灵枢》《针经》《九针》，是现存最早的中医理论著作之一，约成书于战国时期。共九卷，八十一篇，与《素问》九卷合称《黄帝内经》，在针灸学上有着绝对权威。明代马莳编《灵枢注证发微》，是历史上诠注《灵枢》的第一人。

⑧ That is to say that both of them come from the food nutrients. 在中医理论看来，人体血液和体液是同源之水，它们都来自于食物的养分。

⑨ ... body fluid and blood sharing the same origin：体液和血液的精髓是相同的。

Exercises

Ⅰ. **Fill in the blanks with the words given below. Change the form when necessary.**

substance	nourish	moisten	supplement
transform	dynamic	pathological	morbid
participate	scanty	profuse	aggravate

1. They needed good food to _____ their bodies.
2. Heroin is an illegal _____.
3. To _____ and rub a part of the body with lotion can be helpful with relieving stress.
4. A steam engine _____ heat into power.
5. She _____ her diet with eggs and fresh fruit from the farm.
6. Every doctor in the hospital is expected to _____ in the competition.
7. He is diagnosed as being caught a(n) _____ disease.
8. The kid has unfortunately developed a(n) _____ fear of the dark.
9. It's _____ to dwell on cemeteries and such like.
10. There is _____ evidence to support their accusations.
11. The patient was _____ in her thanks.
12. Ice water _____ my toothache.

Ⅱ. **Choose the best answer to each of the following questions.**

1. Which of the following statements is NOT true?
    A. Blood and body fluid are liquid substances.

B. Blood and body fluid function to nourish and moisten the viscera and the body.

C. Blood and body fluid pertain to *yang*.

D. In terms of pathology, blood and body fluid affect each other.

2. Having come out of stomach, where does body fluid reach?

   A. Small intestine.   B. The vessels.
   C. The viscera.   D. The large intestine.

3. What causes a morbid state of scanty fluid according to the passage?

   A. Great quantity of body fluid consumed.   B. Sweating.
   C. Crying.   D. Starving.

4. Why can't the patients with massive bleeding be treated by diaphoresis?

   A. Because diaphoresis may be accompanied with excessive bleeding.

   B. Because excessive bleeding exhausts the blood and further aggravates the scanty state of body fluid.

   C. Because profuse sweating consumes body fluid and further aggravates the deficiency of blood.

   D. None of the above.

5. What is the origin of both blood and body fluid?

   A. Water.   B. The food nutrients.
   C. Sweat.   D. Milk.

Ⅲ. Translate the following sentences into English or Chinese.

1. 血液是由体液和营气组成的。

2. 血管内外的体液之间通常会保持一种机能上的平衡。

3. 由体液转化而来的汗液与血液密切相关。

4. 他解释说他的跛脚是意外造成的。

5. 另一方面，天然气仍比其他能源便宜。

6. She supplements her diet with vitamin tablets.

7. Blood and body fluid depend on and transform into each other.

8. He aggravated his condition by leaving hospital too soon.

9. That is to say, if you examine yourself, feeling no shame, that is nothing to be worried and fear.

10. Neural networks are able to generalize and are resistant to noise.

Ⅳ. Write a 150-word composition, briefly introducing what do body fluids, *qi* and blood have to do with human health?

Unit 5   *Qi*, Blood and Body Fluid

 **Text B**

Qi, Blood and Body Fluid of Mutual Causality

Despite their differences in nature, form and function, *qi*, blood and body fluid have something in common with each other. They are the basic materials that constitute the human body and maintain life activities; they all derive from cereal essence①; they, physiologically, depend on each other for existence and restrain and utilize each other; they, pathologically, act upon each other and have causality between them.

Qi and blood are closely related. *Qi* is the "commander" of blood, and blood is the "mother" of *qi*. As the commander of blood, for one thing, *qi* is the motive power for blood formation, or rather, it produces blood. Blood is formed from mutative *qi* and body fluid, both of which come from food and water. All these cannot be separated from the functions of *qi*. Blood circulation depends on the propelling function of heart-*qi*.② For another, *qi* controls blood and keep it flowing in the blood vessels without extravasation. This function of *qi* is performed by spleen-*qi*. When *qi* is deficient, it fails to control blood, thus leading to hemorrhage.③ Blood is referred to as the mother of *qi* because on the one hand, blood is a carrier of *qi*; and on the other, blood provides adequate nutrients for *qi*. Therefore, it is impossible for *qi* to exist without its "mother", blood.

The relationship between *qi* and body fluid is rather similar to that between *qi* and blood. This is shown in the following four aspects. First, *qi* produces body fluid. The formation, distribution and excretion of body fluid depend upon all the movements of *qi* and its warming, promoting and controlling functions. The existence of *qi* in the body not only depends upon blood, but on body fluid which is formed from food essence by the functions of the stomach and spleen. So, whether body fluid is adequate or inadequate depends upon the conditions of spleen-*qi* and stomach-*qi*. Second, *qi* promotes the transportation of body fluid. The movements of *qi* are the motivity for the transportation, and distribution of body fluid, and the excretion of sweat and urine. Therefore, in case of deficiency of *qi* or dysfunction of *qi*, disturbance of body fluid in transportation, distribution and excretion will occur, thereby leading to the stagnation④ of body fluid. Third, *qi* controls body fluid. *Qi* may control the excretion of body fluid and maintain the balance of the metabolism of body fluid. In case *qi* fails to control the excretion of body fluid some of body fluid will run off. Fourth, body fluid is a carrier of *qi* (*Qi* resides in body fluid, which serves as a carrier of *qi*). That is, body fluid carries *qi*. *Qi* cannot exist without body fluid. This is the reason why the loss of body fluid often damages *qi*. If *qi* fails to attach to body fluid, *qi*-deficiency and even *qi* prostration will ensue. So the medical book *Synopsis of Prescriptions of the Golden Cabinet*⑤ says, "No one has perfect *qi* after hidrosis, vomiting etc." Examples in point are: hidrosis, polyuria, enormous vomiting and diarrhea cause great loss of body fluid, which, in turn, gives rise to *qi* collapse. Blood and body fluid are liquids and, what's more, they both perform the nourishing and moistening functions. Body fluid will become and important component of blood when infiltrating into the blood vessels. As blood and body fluid originate from the essence of food and water, they are known as "body fluid and blood are derived from a common source". Recurrent or severe bleeding may do damage to body fluid, resulting in thirst, scanty urine and dry skin. And severe consumption or loss of body fluid will affect the source of blood, leading to the exhaustion of both blood and body fluid. For this reason, it is not advisable to use diaphoretics for haemorrhagic patients, and the methods of breaking blood or pricking blood should be avoided in treating patients with the inadequate of body fluid and hidrosis. *Miraculous Pivot* states, "The patients lost blood should avoid perspiring; while the patients lost perspiration should avoid losing blood."⑥ And "the first contraindication refers to emaciated patients⑦; the second to patients lost blood; the third to patients after severe perspiration; the fourth to patients after severe diarrheal and the fifth to patients of postpartum hemorrhage. Purgation is contraindicated in all these cases.⑧"

To sum up, the close and complicated relationships between the three are often shown in physiology and pathology, and are of great importance⑨ in Treatment by Differentiation of Syndromes (TDS).

(756 words)

New Words

derive /dɪˈraɪv/ *vt.*   获得，导出(from)
cereal /ˈsɪərɪəl/ *a.*   谷类的
physiologically /ˌfɪzɪəˈlɒdʒɪklɪ/ *ad.*   生理学上地
mutative /ˈmjuːtətɪv/ *a.*   突变的
circulation /ˌsɜːkjəˈleɪʃn/ *n.*   循环
propel /prəˈpel/ *vt.*   推动
extravasation /eksˌtrævəˈseɪʃn/ *n.*   [医]外渗(沉)
deficient /dɪˈfɪʃnt/ *a.*   缺乏，不足
dysfunction /dɪsˈfʌŋkʃn/ *n.*   [医]机能障碍，机能不良
disturbance /dɪsˈtɜːbəns/ *n.*   障碍，失调
stagnation /stæɡˈneɪʃn/ *n.*   停滞，不流动，萧条
excretion /ɪkˈskriːʃn/ *n.*   排泄，分泌
prostration /prɒˈstreɪʃn/ *n.*   [医]虚脱，虚弱
hidrosis /hɪˈdrəʊsɪs/ *n.*   [医]汗病，多汗病
polyuria /ˌpɒlɪˈjʊərɪə/ *n.*   [医]多尿症
infiltrate /ˈɪnfɪltreɪt/ *vt.*   渗透，吸入

Unit 5 *Qi*, Blood and Body Fluid

diaphoretics /ˌdaɪəfəˈretɪks/ *n*.	发汗剂
emaciate /ɪˈmeɪʃieɪt/ *vt*.	使憔悴，使瘦弱
postpartum /ˌpəʊstˈpɑːtəm/ *a*.	产后的
purgation /pɜːˈgeɪʃən/ *n*.	清洗，净化

Expressions

have something in common	有共同之处
for one thing	首先，举个例子说
run off	流掉
attach to	使依恋，把……放在
do damage to	破坏

Notes

① They all derive from cereal essence. 它们均来自谷物精华。cereal essence：谷物精华。derive from：从……获得；来自，起源于。

② Blood circulation depends on the propelling function of heart-*qi*. 心气和心阳都是心脏功能活动的一部分，其共同作用的结果是维持和促进心脏的搏动。

③ When *qi* is deficient, it fails to control blood, thus leading to hemorrhage. 气虚不能摄血可导致出血。*qi* is deficient：气虚，又译作 deficiency of vital energy，泛指身体虚弱、面色苍白、呼吸短促、四肢乏力、头晕、动则汗出、语声低微等。包括元气、宗气、卫气的虚损，以及气的推动、温煦、防御、固摄和气化功能的减退，从而导致机体的某些功能活动低下或衰退，抗病能力下降等衰弱的现象。多由先天禀赋不足，或后天失养，或劳伤过度而耗损（"劳则气耗"），或久病不复，或肺脾肾等脏腑功能减退，气的生化不足等所致。

④ stagnation：淤积。

⑤ *Synopsis of Prescriptions of the Golden Cabinet*：《金匮要略》，东汉张仲景著，中医经典古籍之一，也是我国现存最早的一部诊治杂病的专著。古今医家对此书推崇备至，称之为方书之祖，医方之经、治疗杂病的典范。书名"金匮"，言其重要和珍贵之意，"要略"，言其简明扼要之意，表明本书内容精要，价值珍贵，应当慎重保藏和应用。

⑥ *Miraculous Pivot* states," The patients lost blood should avoid perspiring; while the patients lost perspiration should avoid losing blood."《灵枢》指出："夺血者无汗，夺汗者无血。"*Miraculous Pivot*：《灵枢》，又称《灵枢经》，现存最早的中医理论，成书于战国时期。

⑦ the first contraindication refers to emaciated patients：形肉已夺，是一夺也。

⑧ Purgation is contraindicated in all these cases.《灵枢》指出："大夺血之后，是二夺也；大出汗之后，是三夺也；大泄之后，是四夺也；新产及大血之后，是五夺也。此皆不可泻。"

⑨ be of great importance：be of＋*n*. 相当于该名词的形容词，这种用法比较正式，常用于书面语中。例如：This activity is of great importance to the people of the two countries.

Exercises

I. Fill in the blanks with the words given below. Change the form when necessary.

derive	propel	deficient	nutrient
disturbance	stagnation	infiltrate	emaciate
purgation	hemorrhage	physiologically	cereal

1. Our bodies _____ an abundance of hematin from food.
2. Mothers' breast milk contains essential _____ for babies.
3. How to lose weight can be experienced _____ period?
4. He was _____ by long illness.
5. The heart-*qi* is the fundamental motive power to _____ blood circulation.
6. Iron is an indispensable trace element which is easily _____ in human body.
7. Temporary mental _____ and muscular incoordination can be caused by excessive consumption of alcohol.
8. Parathyroid carcinomas _____ surrounding structures in the neck.
9. The pathological report demonstrated an omental _____.
10. Wheat may have been the first _____ to be cultivated.
11. _____, the fear response is linked to activity in the amygdala of the limbic system.
12. The results indicate that *luohanshen* has a positive effect on _____ in constipated mice but has no effect in normal mice.

II. Choose the best answer to each of the following questions or unfinished statements.

1. *Qi*, blood and body fluid have something in common with each other. Which of the following is NOT included?
   A. They are the basic materials that constitute the human body.
   B. They help maintain life activities.
   C. They all derive from cereal essence.
   D. They do not depend on other materials.

2. When *qi* is deficient, it can NOT control over blood, then _____ occurs.
   A. high blood pressure   B. hemorrhage   C. color blindness   D. fever

3. According to TCM, in order to has perfect *qi*, people need to take care of their _____.
   A. stomach   B. liver   C. spleen   D. both A and C.

4. According to the writer, what is the reason why the loss of body fluid often damages *qi*?
   A. Because the relationship between qi and body fluid is rather similar to that between *qi* and blood.
   B. Because body fluid carries *qi*, *qi* cannot exist without body fluid.
   C. Because body fluid is formed from food essence by the functions.

D. None of the above.

5. As far as TCM is concerned, recurrent or severe bleeding may cause the following symptoms EXCEPT _____.
   A. thirst
   B. dry skin
   C. exhaustion of both blood and body fluid
   D. scanty urine

Ⅲ. Translate the following sentences into English or Chinese.

1. 尽管气血、津液之间在性质、形式和功能上有所不同,但他们之间有很多共同之处。
2. 它们是构成人体、维持生命活动的基本物质。
3. 血液是由变化的气和体液构成。
4. 血液循环取决于心脏气血的推进功能。
5. 血液为气提供足够的营养物质。

6. The relationship between *qi* and body fluid is rather similar to that between *qi* and blood.
7. The formation, distribution and excretion of body fluid depend upon all the movements of *qi*.
8. Blood and body fluid perform the nourishing and moistening functions.
9. In addition, growth hormone can attach to binding proteins.
10. Its outbreak reason mainly can sum up endopathic(内部的) cause and exopathic(外部的) cause.

 Text C

Qigong Therapy

The Concept of *Qi*

Similar to the theory of *yin-yang*, *qi* was derived from ancient Chinese philosophy, which believes everything is related. In traditional Chinese medicine, *qi* is treated as the fundamental substance of the human body, and its movements explain various life processes. *Qi* in its physiological sense constitutes, replenishes and nourishes the human body. *Qi* is often called vital energy because it is believed to be the motive energy derived from the essential substance for various vital processes.

Qi is often classified according to what it acts on. For example, the heart-*qi* refers to the force with which the heart works and the blood circulates, so it regulates the cardiac function; the stomach-*qi* refers to the force with which the stomach functions, so it regulates the gastric function. The *qi* that maintains normal function for resistance against disease is called *zhengqi*, which means genuine energy or body resistance. The *qi* that warms the body and maintains normal body temperature is called *yang qi*, which is similar to the heat energy. Metabolism of materials and energy also depends on the action of *qi*, including metabolism of blood, fluids and other essential materials.

Qi is formed from the inhaled oxygen, the dietary nutrients, and the inborn primordial *qi* stored in the kidney, which may be genetically related.① *Qi* circulates along meridians and collaterals②. A healthy body requires normal circulations of *qi*. Health problems occur if the flow of *qi* is stagnated. The circulation of *qi* is also closely related to mental conditions. Emotional instability③ may cause the stagnation of *qi*. For example, anger may lead to dizziness, headache, distress in the hypochondriac regions, or distention in the stomach with impairment of appetite.④ On the other hand, the exercise of mind can help the circulation of *qi*, which is the purpose *qigong* exercise.

General Methods of *Qigong*

Qigong is an exercise to regulate the mind and breathing in order to control or promote the flow of *qi*.⑤ Since *qi* plays such an important role in the vital processes of the human body, the regulation of *qi* flow is therefore be used to preserve health and treat disease. Medical *qigong*, the *qi* exercise practiced to prevent and treat disease, is different from general physical exercise⑥. While physical exercise is aimed at building up health or restoring physical functioning by enhancing strength, medical *qigong* is focused on the mobilization of functional potentialities by regulating the mind.⑦ In other words, physical exercise is purely somatic, while *qigong* exercise is generally psycho-somatic⑧. Another important difference between physical exercise and *qigong* is that physical exercise expends energy by tensing the muscles and accelerating the heart beat and respirations, while *qigong* works to ease, smooth and regulate breathing to store up or accumulate energy in the body⑨.

Medical *qigong* can be divided into two main categories: internal *qigong*, which is practiced by the patients themselves to preserve and promote their own health, and external *qigong*, which is performed by a *qigong* master on a person with health problems. Practicing internal *qigong* requires regulation of the mind, body and respiration. There are many kinds of internal *qigong*, some with motion and others without. *Qigong* can be practiced while sitting still, standing upright, or lying on the back or side. The basic requirement is to stay comfortable and relaxed.⑩

(576 words)

Unit 5   *Qi*, Blood and Body Fluid

New Words

replenish /rɪˈplenɪʃ/ *vt.*   再斟(装)满(with),添足,加强,补充,再充电
inhale /ɪnˈheɪl/ *vt.*   吸入(空气、水蒸气等),把……吸进肺里
primordial /praɪˈɔːdɪəl/ *a.*   原始的,初生(发)的,(从)原始时代存在的,基本的,根本的
genetically /dʒəˈnetɪklɪ/ *ad.*   基因地,遗传上地,从遗传学角度,从基因方面
circulate /ˈsɜːkjəleɪt/ *vt.*   使(血液等)循环,使流通,散布,传播
instability /ˌɪnstəˈbɪlətɪ/ *n.*   不稳定性,不坚决,反复无常,[化]不稳定度(性)
dizziness /ˈdɪzɪnəs/ *n.*   头昏眼花
hypochondriac /ˌhaɪpəˈkɒndrɪæk/ *a.*   忧郁症的,患疑难症的
impairment /ɪmˈpeəmənt/ *n.*   故障,缺陷,损害,损伤
mobilization /ˌməʊbɪlaɪˈzeɪʃn/ *n.*   流通
somatic /səʊˈmætɪk/ *a.*   身体的,肉体的
respiration /ˌrespəˈreɪʃn/ *n.*   呼吸,[生理]呼吸作用,生物的氧化作用
accumulate /əˈkjuːmjəleɪt/ *vt.*   积累,存储,蓄积(财产等),堆积
requirement /rɪˈkwaɪəmənt/ *n.*   需求,要求,必要条件

Expressions

be according to   依照
act on   对……起作用,按……行动,作用于
store up   储藏
sit still   静坐
stand upright   站直
lie on one's back/side   仰卧/侧卧

Notes

① *Qi* is formed from the inhaled oxygen, the dietary nutrients, and the inborn primordial *qi* stored in the kidney, which may be genetically related. 气是由吸入的氧气和膳食营养素形成的,可能与基因有关,与生俱来的原始的气储存在肾中。

② meridians and collaterals:经络。

③ emotional instability:情绪不稳定。

④ For example, anger may lead to dizziness, headache, distress in the hypochondriac regions or distention in the stomach with impairment of appetite. 例如,愤怒可能会导致头晕、头痛、季肋区的压力或腹胀,而损害胃口。

⑤ *Qigong* is an exercise to regulate the mind and breathing in order to control or promote the flow of *qi*. 气功是一种通过调节心理、顺畅呼吸等来控制并改善气流的活动。

⑥ general physical exercise:一般体育锻炼。

⑦ While physical exercise is aimed at building up health or restoring physical functioning by enhancing strength, medical *qigong* is focused on the mobilization of functional potentialities by regulating the mind. 体育锻炼目的是通过增强力量来锻炼身体、积蓄体能,而医疗气功主要是通过调节心理将精力集中在运气上。

⑧ ... physical exercise is purely somatic, while *qigong* exercise is generally psychosomatic 体育锻炼是纯身体运动,而气功是身心兼具的运动。

⑨ ... physical exercise expends energy by tensing the muscles and accelerating the heart beat and respirations, while *qigong* works to ease, smooth and regulate breathing to store up or accumulate energy in the body. 体育运动通过锻炼肌肉和加速心跳和呼吸来消耗能量,而气功则放松、舒缓和调节呼吸并积聚和存储体内的能量。

⑩ The basic requirement is to stay comfortable and relaxed. 最基本的要求就是保持舒适和放松。

Exercises

I. Fill in the blanks with the words given below. Change the form when necessary.

replenish	inhale	primordial	circulate
instability	dizziness	impairment	mobilization
somatic	respiration	accumulate	category

1. The crackling sound can be heard on auscultation when patients with respiratory diseases _____.
2. Coconut oil, bee pollen and glycerin nourish your skin and help _____ its natural moisture.
3. The blood which _____ in our blood-vessel is a mixture of several substances.
4. Lack of oxygen at birth can result in mental _____.
5. Would adding communication and social _____ help produce better outcomes?
6. Life seems to have originated in the _____ oceans that covered the earth four billion years ago.
7. To some extent, this _____ is a result of gross overorganizing.
8. _____ effects are those which cause damage to the individual.
9. The warning signs of the illness are respiratory problems and _____.
10. These questions may be included in the same _____.
11. Nitrogen compounds in particular tend to _____ in groundwater.
12. I'll perform artificial _____ on the patient.

II. Choose the best answer to each of the following questions or unfinished statements.

1. How many parts does the passage deal with?

Unit 5 Qi, Blood and Body Fluid

  A. Two.　　　　B. Three.　　　　C. Four.　　　　D. Five.
2. What is *qi* according to the passage?
   A. *Qi* is *zhengqi* and *yangqi*.
   B. *Qi* is the inhaled oxygen.
   C. *Qi* is the fundamental substance of human body.
   D. *Qi* is the regulation in human body.
3. *Qi* is often classified into the heart-*qi* and the stomach-*qi* _____.
   A. according to its form
   B. according to what it acts on
   C. according to the rule whether it is inhaled or exhaled
   D. Both A and B.
4. Internal *qigong* is _____.
   A. performed by a *qigong* master on a person with health problems
   B. performed by the patients themselves as well as a *qigong* master
   C. performed by the patients themselves to preserve and promote their own health
   D. not necessarily good to one's health
5. *Qigong* can be practiced while _____.
   A. sitting still, standing upright or lying on the abdomen
   B. sitting still, running fast or lying on the back
   C. sitting still, jogging or lying on the side
   D. sitting still, standing upright or lying on the back or side

Ⅲ. Translate the following sentences into English or Chinese.

1. 与阴阳理论一样,气也来源于古老的中国哲学。
2. 气的运动解释了各种各样的生命运动过程。
3. 气通常被称为重要的能量。
4. 健康的身体需要正常的气流循环。
5. 气在人体的运动过程中起着重要的作用。

6. *Qi* is often classified according to what it acts on.
7. Medical *qigong* can be divided into two main categories.
8. *Qigong* can be practiced while sitting, standing, or lying.
9. During the summer months some small animals usually store up nuts to eat during the winter.
10. They enable your child to take some weight through their legs and to stand upright.

Stomatognathic System（口颌系统）

Root	Meaning	Examples
oro- stomato-	mouth, orifice 口	oropharyngeal 口咽的 oroantral fistula 口腔上颌窦瘘 stomatitis 口炎 stomatocytosis 口形红细胞增多
labio- cheilo-	lip, labium 唇	labiodental 唇齿的 labioversion 唇向错位 cheilorrhaphy 唇裂修复术 cheilitis 唇炎
palato- urano-	palate, palatum 腭	palatal 腭的 palatoschisis 腭裂 uranorrhaphy 腭裂缝术 uranoplasty 腭成形术
uvulo- staphylo-	uvula 悬雍垂	uvulopalatopharyngoplasty 悬雍垂腭咽成形术 staphyloptosis 悬雍垂下垂 staphyledema 悬雍垂水肿 staphylitis 悬雍垂炎
tonsillio- amygdalo-	tonsil, amygdala 扁桃体	tonsillectomy 扁桃体切除术 tonsillitis 扁桃体炎 amygdalotomy 扁桃体部分切除术 amygdaloid 扁桃体样的
bucco-	cheek, mala 颊	buccal 颊的 buccolingual 颊舌的 buccoangular impaction 颊向阻生
mento- genio-	chin 颏	menton 颏下点 mentolabial 颏唇的 genioplasty 颏成形术
linguo- glosso-	tongue, lingua 舌	linguosalivary 舌唾液腺的 linguoversion 舌向错位 glossopharyngeal 舌咽的, 舌咽神经的 glossodynia 舌痛

续表

Root	Meaning	Examples
gnatho-	jaw 颌	gnathion 颌下点 orthognathic 正颌学的 gnathankylosis 颌关节强直 gnathodynia 颌痛
maxillo-	upper jaw, maxilla 上颌骨	maxillofacial 上颌面 maxillectomy 上颌骨切除术 maxillofacial prosthesis 颌面缺损修复
mandibulo-	lower jaw, mandibular 下颌	mandibulectomy 下颌骨切除术 mandible 下颌骨 mandibular cyst 颌骨囊肿
gingivo-	gum, gingivae 齿龈	gingivitis 龈炎 gingivoplasty 龈成形术 gingivostomatitis 龈口炎
dento- odonto-	tooth 牙	dental 牙齿的 dentalgia 牙痛 odontoblast 成牙本质细胞 odontocele 齿囊肿
cemento-	cementum 牙骨质	cementogenesis 牙骨质发生 cementitis 牙骨质炎 cementoid 类牙骨质 cementoma 牙骨质瘤
pulpo-	pulp 牙髓	pulpitis 牙髓炎 pulpotomy 牙髓切断术
amelo-	enamel 釉质	ameloblastoma 成釉细胞瘤 ameloblastic fibrosarcoma 成釉细胞纤维肉瘤

Unit 6　The Channels and Collaterals

 Text A

The Mystery of Meridian

The term meridian (*jing-luo*) originated in TCM. *Jing* means the route or path, and *luo* means the network. Just as roads and waterways link every city and village, the meridian which is distributed throughout the body connects all the *zang-fu* organs, tissues and other organs.① It is a channel system along which *qi* and the blood circulate and through which *zang-fu*, limbs and joints are connected and the exterior, interior, superior and inferior parts of the body communicate with one another.②

The meridian system consists of meridians (*jing*) and collaterals (*luo*) as well as 12 tendon systems and 12 skin regions.③ The meridians are divided into 12 main meridians and 8 extraordinary meridians, while the collaterals can be further divided into 15 collaterals and numerous fine collaterals and superficial collaterals④. The 12 main meridians are the principal course for *qi* and the blood to circulate along. The 8 extraordinary meridians, on the other hand, have the functions of governing, connecting and regulating 12 main meridians. The 12 branch meridians are the meridian branches parting from 12 main meridians with the function of enhancing the cooperation between each exteriorly-interiorly-related pair of the 12 main meridians.⑤ The 15 collaterals are the general term for the large collaterals that branch out from 12 main meridians, *renmai*, *dumai* and the spleen⑥, and their functions are to strengthen the connection between two interiorly-exteriorly-related meridians in the body surface and to help *qi* and the blood to permeate. The superficial collaterals are the collaterals that can be seen though the skin.⑦ The fine collaterals refer to numerous tiny collaterals. The 12 tendon systems are the part of the meridian system through which the 12 main meridians connect with muscles and joints and link the four limbs and the bones so as to control the movements of joints.⑧ The 12 skin regions are the areas of the body surface where the functional activities of the 12 main meridians are manifested.

Twelve main meridians are symmetrically distributed on both sides of the body; each main meridian travels along either the medial or the dorsal aspect of the arms or legs and belongs to one of the *zang-fu* organs. Because of these features, the name of each main

Unit 6　The Channels and Collaterals

meridian includes three parts: hand or foot, *yin* or *yang*, and *zang* or *fu*. The meridians that pass through the arm are called hand meridians, those meridians travelling through the leg are named foot meridians. *Yin* meridians, each of which belongs to one of the *zang* organs, refer to those meridians that go along the medial side of the arms or legs, while *yang* meridians are the ones that run along the dorsal side of the limbs and belong to one of the *fu* organs each.

　　The 12 main meridians are the general term for Hand three-*yin*, Foot three-*yin*, Hand three-*yang* and Foot three-*yang* meridians.⑨ The Hand three-*yin* meridians are the lung meridian of Hand-*taiyin*, the pericardium meridian of Hand-*jueyin* and the heart meridian of Hand-*shaoyin*. The Hand three-*yang* meridians refer to the large intestine meridian of Hand-*yangming*, the triple energizers meridian of Hand-*shaoyang* and the small intestine meridian of Hand-*taiyang*. The Foot three-*yang* meridians consist of the stomach meridian of Foot-*yangming*, the gall bladder meridian of Foot-*shaoyang* and the urinary bladder meridian of Foot-*taiyang*, while the Foot three-*yin* meridians are made up of the spleen meridian of Foot-*taiyin*, the kidney meridian of Foot-*shaoyin* and the liver meridian of Foot-*jueyin*. The direction of the 12 main meridians and their connection with one another is following certain rules. Hand *yin* meridians start from the chest and go to the fingertips, where they connect with Hand *yang* meridians. Hand *yang* meridians begin at the fingertips and travel to the face and/or head, connecting with Foot *yang* meridians. The Foot *yang* meridians run from face and head down to the tips of toes, where Foot *yin* meridians start. The Foot *yin* meridians course from toes up to the abdomen and chest, link up with Hand *yin* meridians. Thus the circulation course of the meridians forms an endless cycle with *yin* and *yang* meridians following one another.⑩

(783 words)

New Words

collateral /kəˈlætərəl/ *n.*　　　　　　络脉
　　　　　　　　　　a.　　　　　　并行的,旁系的,附随的
tendon system /ˈtendənˈsɪstəm/　　　[医]经筋
enhance /ɪnˈhɑːns/ *v.*　　　　　　　提高,增加,加强
muscle /ˈmʌsl/ *n.*　　　　　　　　　肌肉
joint /dʒɔɪnt/ *n.*　　　　　　　　　 关节
limb /lɪm/ *n.*　　　　　　　　　　　肢
manifest /ˈmænɪfest/ *v.*　　　　　　表明,显示
symmetrically /sɪˈmetrɪklɪ/ *ad.*　　　对称性地,对称地,平衡地
distributed /disˈtrɪbjuːtɪd/ *a.*　　　　分布式的
gall bladder /ɡɔːlˈblædə/ *n.*　　　　 胆囊

Expressions

communicate with	交流
be divided into	被分成
function as	起……作用
belong to	属于
skin regions	皮部
12 main meridians	十二经脉
8 extraordinary meridians	奇经八脉
fine collaterals	孙络
superficial collaterals	浮络
12 branch meridians	十二经别

Notes

① Just as roads and waterways link every city and village, the meridian which is distributed throughout the body connects all the *zang-fu* organs, tissues and other organs. 正如道路和水路连接每一座城市和村庄,遍及全身的经络连接了所有的脏腑器官、组织和其他器官。这里 just as 引导的是比较状语从句。

② It is a channel system along which *qi* and the blood circulate and through which *zang-fu*, limbs and joints are connected and the exterior, interior, superior and inferior parts of the body communicate with one another. 气血沿着这一通道,体系循环往复,通过这一通道,脏腑、四肢和关节连接成一个整体,并且各器官以及身体内外彼此连接通畅。这里 along which *qi* and the blood circulate 和 through which *zang-fu*, limbs and joints are connected and the exterior, interior, superior and inferior parts of the body communicate with one another 并列作 channel system 的定语。

③ The meridian system consists of meridians(*jing*) and collaterals(*luo*) as well as 12 tendon systems and 12 skin regions. 人体的经络系统包括经和络以及12条经筋和12个皮部。这里 as well as 相当于介词的用法,后面跟名词或名词短语。

④ ... while the collaterals can be further divided into 15 collaterals and numerous fine collaterals and superficial collaterals: 同时络还将进一步分成15条络脉,众多孙络和浮络。这里 while 引导的从句作时间状语,表示并列同时发生。

⑤ The 12 branch meridians are the meridian branches parting from 12 main meridians with the function of enhancing the cooperation between each exteriorly-interiorly-related pair of the 12 main meridians. 十二经别是从12条主要经络中分出的经络支脉,其功能在于加强内外联系的12条主要经络之间的沟通与协调。这里 with the function of enhancing the cooperation between each exteriorly-interiorly-related pair of the 12 main meridians 作伴随状语,补充说明前面的内容。

⑥ The 15 collaterals are the general term for the large collaterals that branch out from 12 main meridians, *renmai*, *dumai*, and the spleen: 十五络脉是从12条主要的经脉、任脉、

Unit 6　The Channels and Collaterals

督脉和脾之大脉的统称。这里 branch out from 表示从……中分出。

⑦ The superficial collaterals are the collaterals that can be seen though the skin. 浮络是从皮肤表面看出来的络脉。这里 that can be seen though the skin 作 superficial collaterals 的定语。

⑧ The 12 tendon systems are the part of the meridian system through which the 12 main meridians connect with muscles and joints and link the four limbs and the bones so as to control the movements of joints. 十二经筋是经络系统的一部分，通过它 12 条主要的经脉与肌肉和关节、四肢与骨头相连来控制关节的运动。这里 through 的定语从句修饰 meridian system。

⑨ The 12 main meridians are the general term for Hand three-*yin*, Foot three-*yin* Hand three-*yang* and *foot three-yang* meridians. 12 条主要的经脉是对手三阴经、足三阴经、手三阳经和足三阳经的统称。

⑩ Thus, the circulation course of the meridians forms an endless cycle with *yin* and *yang* meridians following one another. 因此经络的循环过程形成了阴阳经彼此间无止境的往复运动。

Exercises

I. **Fill in the blanks with the words given below. Change the form when necessary.**

enhance	superficial	manifest	distribute
circulation	symmetrical	originate	principal
feature	joint	muscle	extraordinary

1. It is said that the abdominal massage could help _____ the digestive system.
2. Their work was to collect information and _____ publication against AIDS.
3. However if a problem arises in one of the last three issues it will _____ itself in some form on an illness.
4. Farcy: a chronic form of glanders that affects chiefly the skin and _____ lymph vessels.
5. One thing that makes men and women attractive to each other is having a(n) _____ body.
6. Many cases of seasickness _____ in indigestion.
7. In complete combustion is the _____ source of man-made carcinogens.
8. It contributes to _____ of lymphocytes and other immunologic factors.
9. Transient immobilization and starvation add to this impost on the skeletal _____ mass.
10. Faultless he was in form and _____, and he had no blemish save his white hair.

11. I dislocated my left elbow _____.
12. The brain needs _____ stability.

Ⅱ. **Choose the best answer to each of the following questions or unfinished statements.**

1. According to Paragraph 1, which of the following is NOT true?
   A. Meridian is distributed throughout the body.
   B. Meridian is a channel system along which *qi* and the blood circulate.
   C. Each parts of the body communicate with one another along *zang-fu*.
   D. Meridian connects all the *zang-fu* organs, tissues and other organs.
2. The meridian system consists of the following EXCEPT _____.
   A. *jing-luo*   B. *yin-yang*
   C. tendon systems   D. skin regions
3. What is the function of 12 main meridians?
   A. They are the principal course for *qi* and the blood to circulate along.
   B. governing, connecting and regulating 12 main meridians.
   C. Each parts of the body communicate with one another along *zang-fu*.
   D. Meridian connects all the *zang-fu* organs, tissues and other organs.
4. The name of each main meridian includes the following parts EXCEPT _____.
   A. hand or foot   B. *yin* or *yang*
   C. *zang* or *fu*   D. *jing* or *luo*
5. The Hand three-*yin* meridians include _____.
   A. the lung meridian of hand *taiyin*, the pericardium meridian of hand *jueyin* and the heart meridian of hand shaoyin
   B. the large intestine meridian of hand *yangming*, the triple energizers meridian of hand *shaoyang* and the small intestine meridian of hand *taiyang*
   C. the stomach meridian of foot *yangming*, the gall-bladder meridian of foot *shaoyang* and the urinary bladder meridian of foot *taiyang*
   D. the spleen meridian of foot *taiyin*, the kidney meridian of foot *shaoyin* and the liver meridian of foot *jueyin*

Ⅲ. **Translate the following sentences into English or Chinese.**

1. 经络起源于中医。
2. 经络被分为十二经脉和奇经八脉。
3. 孙络是指很多细小的络脉。
4. 十二经脉对称分布在身体的两侧。
5. 每一条经脉的名字包括三个部分：手或足，阴或阳，以及脏或腑。
6. The direction of the 12 main meridians and their connection with one another is

Unit 6　The Channels and Collaterals

following certain rules.
7. The Foot *yang* meridians run from face and head down to the tips of toes.
8. The 12 skin regions are the areas of the body surface where the functional activities of the 12 main meridians are manifested.
9. The arcuate arteries entered the wall of the uterus and branch out to form three vascular layers: muco-muscular layer, large vascular layer and serous membrane layer.
10. Impulses and actions originate from both higher self and lower self.

Ⅳ. Write a 150-word composition about what can be done with the theory of the channels and collaterals in order to modernize acupuncture and moxibustion.

 Text B

Meridians and Collaterals—Pathways to Link the Whole Body

The meridian-collateral theory is concerned with the physiological functions and the pathological changes of the meridian-collateral system, and their relationships with *zang-fu* organs.① It is an important component of the theoretical system of TCM. And it is considered as a theoretical basis of all clinical subjects of TCM, especially that of acupuncture, moxibustion, *tuina* and *qigong*. Besides, it guides the clinical practice of other branches of TCM.

The meridians and collaterals are pathways along which *qi* and blood circulate through the whole body.② The meridians are the major trunks of the meridian-collateral system and run longitudinally within the body, while the collaterals are the branches of the meridians and are distributed over the whole body.③ Hence, the meridians and collaterals, connecting the *zang-fu* organs with extremities, the upper with the lower and the internal with the external portions of the body, make all the body's organs and tissues an organic whole.

The meridian-collateral system consists of meridians and collaterals as well as their subsidiary parts. This system, internally, links the *zang-fu* organs and, externally, joins the tendons, muscles and skin.

The meridians are classified into three categories: the regular meridians, the extra meridians and the divergent meridians.④ There are twelve regular meridians, namely the three *yin* meridians as well as the three *yang* meridians of the hands and feet.⑤ They are known collectively as "the twelve regular meridians", which are the main passages for *qi* and blood circulation and start and terminate at given seats, run along fixed routes and meet indefinite orders. They are directly connected with the relevant *zang-fu* organs. The eight extra meridians are composed of *du*, *ren*, *chong*, *dai*, *yinqiao*, *yangqiao*, *yinwei* and *yangwei* meridians.⑥ They are interrelated with the twelve regular meridians and perform the functions of dominating, connecting and adjusting the twelve regular meridians. And they are not directly related to the internal organs. In addition, the twelve divergent meridians are the extensions of the twelve meridians. They originate from the limbs, run deeper into the *zang-fu* organs and emerge from the shallow neck. Their action is to enhance the links between every pair of meridians exteriorly-interiorly related in the twelve meridians and complement the organs and bodily areas to which the regular meridians can not get.

The collaterals are the branches of the meridians. They are divided into three groups: divergent collaterals, superficial collaterals and tertiary collaterals.⑦ The divergent collaterals are the larger and main collaterals. The divergent collaterals originate from the twelve meridians as well as *du* and *ren* meridians respectively. Together with large splenic collateral, they are altogether "fifteen divergent collaterals."⑧ Their chief task is to strengthen the links between every pair of meridians exteriorly-interiorly related on the body surface. The superficial collaterals are ones that run through the surface layer of the human body and often emerge on the surface.⑨ And the tertiary collaterals refer to the smallest and the thinnest ones of the whole body.

In addition, there are the subsidiary parts of the meridian system, including the twelve skin zones and twelve musculature zones. Therefore, they are the parts that connect the twelve meridians with the superficial portions and the muscular portions of the body respectively.⑩

(553 words)

New Words

branch /brɑːntʃ/	*n.*	树枝,支流,分店
	v.	分支,分割
circulate /ˈsɜːkjəleɪt/	*v.*	循环,传阅,传播,流通
longitudinally /ˌlɒndʒɪˈtjuːdɪnəlɪ/	*ad.*	经向,纵向,经度上,长度上
extremity /ɪkˈstremətɪ/	*n.*	极端,困境,极点
portion /ˈpɔːʃn/	*n.*	部分,一份,命运,定数
	v.	把……分成多份
divergent /daɪˈvɜːdʒənt/	*a.*	分歧的,扩散的
terminate /ˈtɜːmɪneɪt/	*v.*	使终止,使结束,结束,满期,终止
splenic /ˈsplenɪk/	*a.*	脾脏的,脾的
musculature /ˈmʌskjələtʃə/	*n.*	肌肉组织

Unit 6 The Channels and Collaterals

muscular /ˈmʌskjələ/ *a*.　　　　　强壮的，有力的，肌肉发达的

Expressions

be concerned with	关心，关切
be classified into	分类为……
be interrelated with	与……有内在联系
originate from	源于，来自于
be divided into	分为
together with	和……一起
run through	穿过

Notes

① The meridian-collateral theory is concerned with the physiological functions and the pathological changes of the meridian-collateral system, and their relationships with *zang-fu* organs. 经络理论是有关经络系统的生理功能和病理变化以及和脏腑之间关系的理论。

② The meridians and collaterals are pathways along which *qi* and blood circulate through the whole body. 经络是气血循行全身的通道。

③ The meridians are the major trunks of the meridian-collateral system and run longitudinally within the body, while the collaterals are the branches of the meridians and are distributed over the whole body. 经是经络系统的主干，纵行于人体，而络是经的分支，呈网状分布于全身。

④ The meridians are classified into three categories：the regular meridians, the extra meridians and the divergent meridians. 经可以分为三类：正经、奇经和经别。

⑤ There are twelve regular meridians, namely, the three *yin* meridians as well as the three *yang* meridians of the hands and feet. 有十二正经即手足三阴三阳经。

⑥ The eight extra meridians are composed of *du*, *ren*, *chong*, *dai*, *yinqiao*, *yangqiao*, *yinwei* and *yangwei* meridians. 奇经八脉由督、任、冲、带、阴跷、阳跷、阴维和阳维脉组成。be composed of：由……构成，由……组成。例如：Nuclei are composed of protons and neutrons. 原子核是由质子和中子构成的。

⑦ They are divided into three groups：divergent collaterals, superficial collaterals and tertiary collaterals. 它们可分为三类：别络、浮络和孙络。

⑧ Together with large splenic collateral, they are altogether "fifteen divergent collaterals". 它们和脾之大络统称为"十五别络"。

⑨ The superficial collaterals are ones that run through the surface layer of the human body, and often emerge on the surface. 浮络循行于人体的表层并常显露于体表。

⑩ Therefore, they are the parts that connect the twelve meridians with the superficial portions and the muscular portions of the body respectively. 因此，它们是分别连接十

二经络与人体浅表和肌肉的部分。

Exercises

I . **Fill in the blanks with the words given below. Change the form when necessary.**

branch	extremity	portion	tissue
organic	subsidiary	divergent	terminate
dominate	enhance	superficial	muscular

1. Do you know the percentage of the damaged _____?
2. The tumor extends into soft _____.
3. To cultivate _____ thinking is an important part of cultivating creativity.
4. In the practicing history of human education, there are two kinds of _____ forms existing in child education: lack-freedom and over-freedom.
5. Bacteria can decompose _____ matter.
6. The hospital has decided to close down its Chicago _____.
7. They use the surgical method to _____ pregnancy.
8. I tried to discuss this and some _____ questions.
9. _____ scratches can be easily removed.
10. Eucalyptus oil is good for easing _____ pains.
11. The team has _____ international football for years.
12. Fiber will _____ the peristaltic movement of gastrointestinal tract.

II . **Choose the best answer to each of the following questions or unfinished statements.**

1. The meridian-collateral system consists of _____.
   A. meridians B. collaterals
   C. meridians and collaterals D. organs and tissues
2. Which one of the following is true with the meridian-collateral system?
   A. This system externally links the *zang-fu* organs.
   B. This system internally joins the tendons muscles and skin.
   C. The collaterals are the trunks of the meridians.
   D. The meridians are the major trunks of the meridian-collateral system.
3. What circulate through the whole body along the meridians and collaterals?
   A. Body fluid. B. *Qi* and blood.
   C. Liquid substances. D. Water.
4. Which one of the following does NOT belong to the eight extra meridians?
   A. The divergent meridians. B. *Ren* meridians.

C. *Chong* meridians.   D. *Dai* meridians.

5. The twelve divergent meridians are the extensions of _____.
   A. the eight extra meridians   B. the divergent collaterals
   C. the superficial collaterals   D. the twelve meridians

Ⅲ. **Translate the following sentences into English or Chinese.**

1. 经络理论指导着中医临床应用。

2. 经是经络系统的主干。

3. 络是经的分支，遍布身体的各个部分。

4. 经络使身体的器官和组织形成了一个有机的整体。

5. 别络是更大的主要络脉。

6. The twelve divergent meridians are the extensions of the twelve meridians.

7. The tertiary collaterals refer to the smallest and the thinnest ones of the whole body.

8. The superficial collaterals run through the surface layer of the human body.

9. It is pointed that the filtration bed can be composed of different size of filtration particles making it more ideal for coal slurry（泥浆）filtration.

10. In addition, early rising is also good to our health.

Text C

Application of the Theory of Channels and Collaterals

1. Explaining Pathological Changes

The channels and collaterals have a direct bearing on the occurrence and progress of diseases.① If a channel is in functional disorder, it is apt to be attacked by exogenous factors; then the exogenous factors will further intrude into the internal organs along the channels.②

The channels and collaterals are not only the route along which exogenous factors intrude into the internal organs from the body surface, but also the way through which the pathological changes between the viscera, and between the internal organs and tissues of the body surface affect one another.③ For instance, just as the Liver Channel of Foot-*jueyin* runs by the stomach and pours into the lung, so liver disease may affect the stomach or lung; owing to the fact that the Kidney Channel of Foot-*shaoyin* enters the lung and connects with the heart, the retention of fluid, which is due to kidney-asthenia, may attack the lung or heart; and because the Heart Channel of Hand-*shaoyin* runs along the posterior border of the medial aspect of the upper arm, angina pectoris often radiates to the region④.

2. Helping Diagnose Diseases

As the channels differs in their running courses and pertaining organs, during the diagnosis an inference about the channel or organ where pathological changes take place can be drawn from the analysis of where symptoms and signs are located. For example, pains in the hypochondrium probably indicate that the trouble lies in the liver or gall bladder because the hypochondrium is the region where travel Liver Channel of Foot-*jueyin* and the Gallbladder Channel of Foot-*shaoyang*;⑤ pains in the supraclavicular fossa are mostly caused by lung disease because the supraclavicular fossa is the place where the Lung Channel of Hand-*taiyin* passes.⑥ Another example, headache may be diagnosed in the light of the distributing law of the channels on the head because the pain in the forehead is most probably caused by *yangming* Channel disturbance; migraine by *shaoyang* Channel disturbance and pain of the top of the head by *jueyin* Channel disturbance. In recent years, people have also found that tenderness may occur at Point *zhongfu*(L1) in case of lung disease, at Point *lanwei*(Extra 37) in case of acute appendicitis, etc. All these discoveries are helpful in diagnosis.

3. Directing Clinical Treatment

The Theory of the channels and collaterals has long been widely applied to direct clinical treatment of all the departments of TCM, in particular, acupuncture, moxibustion, massage and herbal prescriptions. For instance, "the method of selecting points along the channels" is a good example.⑦ To be more specific, Point *zusanli*（S36）of the Stomach Channel of Foot-*yangming* should be selected for the treatment of stomachache; point *qimen*(Liv14) of the Liver Channel Foot-*jueyin* should be punctured for curing liver diseases. The selection of regions of massage is also based on the theory.

It is also through the channels and collaterals that the herbs exert influence on the pathological region and take effect as expected. Through protracted and repeated practice, TCM doctors have discovered that a certain herb possesses a selective effect for a certain disease of some channel and its pertaining organ, thus creatively formulating a theory of "classifying herbs according to their respective therapeutic effect on the disease of a specific channel and its pertaining organ"⑧. For example, through the work done by Chinese ephedra on the channels of the lung and urinary bladder, sweat is induced, asthma relieved, and diuresis promoted.⑨ Another example, thorowax root acts on the channels of the liver and gall bladder, so as to disperse the depressed energy of the liver and gall bladder, and regulate the vital energy by alleviation of mental depression. Zhang Jiegu and Li Gao, two of the four great physicians in the Jin and Yuan dynasties, formulated a theory of "medicinal guides" according to the theory of the channels and collaterals.⑩ For

Unit 6　The Channels and Collaterals

instance, in treating headache, notopterygium root should be prescribed if it is due to *taiyang* disturbance, or dahurian angelica root should be prescribed if due to disturbance of the *yangming*, or thorowax root prescribed if due to disturbance of the *shaoyang*. The above mentioned "medicinal guides" do not only work their way through the relative channel and its pertaining organ, but also direct other medicines to the right channel and organ in order to bring their therapeutic action into play.

In addition, the clinical applications of acupuncture anaesthesia, auricular needle are done under the guidance of the theory of the channels and collaterals, and will inevitably further prove and develop this theory.

(773 words)

New Words

bearing /ˈbeərɪŋ/ *n.*	关系,关联(on)
apt /æpt/ *a.*	易于……的,有……倾向的(to)
intrude /ɪnˈtruːd/ *v.*	侵入,闯入,把……强加(在)(on/upon)
exert /ɪɡˈzɜːt/ *vt.*	运用,行使,发挥,施加,用(力),尽(力)
selective /sɪˈlektɪv/ *a.*	有选择性的
formulate /ˈfɔːmjʊleɪt/ *vt.*	系统地阐述(或说明),配制
urinary /ˈjʊərɪnərɪ/ *a.*	尿的,泌尿的
induce /ɪnˈdjuːs/ *vt.*	引起,归纳
asthma /ˈæsmə/ *n.*	[医]气喘(病),哮喘
relieve /rɪˈliːv/ *vt.*	缓和,减轻,解除
promote /prəˈməʊt/ *vt.*	促进,发扬,提升,推销
disperse /dɪsˈpɜːs/ *v.*	驱散,解散,疏散,分散,散开
regulate /ˈreɡjʊleɪt/ *vt.*	管理,控制,为……制定规章
alleviation /əˌliːvɪˈeɪʃn/ *n.*	减轻,缓解,缓和,镇痛物
medicinal /məˈdɪsɪnl/ *a.*	医学的,药用的,有药效的
prescribe /prɪˈskraɪb/ *v.*	开(药方),为……开(药方),嘱咐(for),规定,指定
therapeutic /ˌθerəˈpjuːtɪk/ *a.*	治疗的,治疗学的,有疗效的
inevitably /ɪnˈevɪtəblɪ/ *ad.*	不可避免地,必然地

Expressions

be apt to	有……倾向的
owing to	由于,归咎于
take place	发生,出现
lie in	在于
in the light of	鉴于,由于,按照,根据
under the guidance of...	在……的指导下

Notes

① The channels and collaterals have a direct bearing on the occurrence and progress of diseases. 经络与疾病的发生、转变密切相关。

② If a channel is in functional disorder, it is apt to be attacked by exogenous factors; then the exogenous factors will further intrude into the internal organs along the channels. 某一经络功能异常,就容易遭受外邪的侵袭。既病之后,外邪又可沿着经络进一步内传脏腑。

③ The channels and collaterals are not only the route along which exogenous factors intrude into the internal organs from the body surface, but also the way through which the pathological changes between the viscera, and between the internal organs and tissues of the body surface affect one another. 经络不仅是外邪由表入里的途径,而且也是内脏之间、内脏与体表组织之间病变相互影响的途径。

④ ... and because the Heart Channel of Hand-*shaoyin* runs along the posterior border of the medial aspect of the upper arm, angina pectoris often radiates to the region. 手少阴心经行于上肢内侧后缘,所以真心痛常放射至这些部位。

⑤ For example, pains in the hypochondrium probably indicate that the trouble lies in the liver or gall bladder because the hypochondrium is the region where travel Liver Channel of Foot-Jueyin and the Gallbladder Channel of Foot-*shaoyang*:例如,胁部疼痛,多病在肝胆,因为胁部是足厥阴肝经和足少阳胆经的行径之处。胁部,主要指腰以上,肋骨的位置,又称"胁肋部"。

⑥ ... pains in the supraclavicular fossa are mostly caused by lung disease because the supraclavicular fossa is the place where the Lung Channel of Hand-*taiyin* passes. 缺盆中痛,多病变在肺,因为缺盆是手太阴肺经所过之处。缺盆,即指锁骨上窝。

⑦ For instance, "the method of selecting points along the channels" is a good example. 如针灸中的"循经取穴法",就是经络学说的具体应用。

⑧ ... thus creatively formulating a theory of "classifying herbs according to their respective therapeutic effect on the disease of a specific channel and its pertaining organ". 从而创立了"药物归经"理论。

⑨ For example, through the work done by Chinese ephedra on the channels of the lung and urinary bladder, sweat is induced, asthma relieved, and diuresis promoted. 如麻黄入肺、膀胱经,故能发汗、平喘和利尿。文章在这里用了一个动宾结构的排比:sweat is induced, asthma relieved, and diuresis promoted,学习时要注意动名词的搭配。

⑩ Zhang Jiegu and Li Gao, two of the four great physicians in the Jin and Yuan dynasties, formulated a theory of "medicinal guides" according to the theory of the channels and collaterals. "金元四大家"中的张洁古、李杲还根据经络学说,创立了"引经报使药"理论。

Unit 6 The Channels and Collaterals

Exercises

Ⅰ. Fill in the blanks with the words given below. Change the form when necessary.

bearing	apt	intrude	exert
selective	formulate	induce	relieve
promote	disperse	regulate	medicinal

1. Such food is _____ to deteriorate in summer.
2. The hospital has been _____ pressure on me to get another doctor qualification.
3. Antibiotics are somewhat _____ in their antibacterial actions.
4. Recent events had no _____ on the fame of our hospital.
5. Certain plants have _____ properties.
6. No longer is it necessary to _____ physically upon the intended victim's turf.
7. The government is trying to _____ a new policy on the nation's health service.
8. The two heart disease still _____ serious complication.
9. Painkilling drugs were not enough to _____ her suffering.
10. This publication is made to _____ healthy blood sugar levels.
11. Police fired tear gas to _____ the demonstrators.
12. There are strict rules _____ the uses of chemicals in food.

Ⅱ. Choose the best answer to each of the following questions or unfinished statements.

1. When are the exogenous factors likely to attack a channel or collateral?
   A. When one is catching a cold.
   B. When a channel doesn't function well.
   C. When a serious disease takes place.
   D. When an organ is broken.
2. Which of the following sentences is right?
   A. Liver Channel of Foot-*jueyin* runs by the liver and pours into the lung.
   B. The Heart Channel of Hand-*shaoyin* runs along the front border of the medical aspect of the upper arm.
   C. Pains in the hypochondrium may indicate that there is something wrong with the liver or gall bladder.
   D. *Yangming* Channel disturbance can cause pain in stomachache.
3. The theory of the channels and collaterals has long been applied to the treatment of all the departments of TCM, in particular _____.
   A. moxibustion
   B. nursing
   C. psychological treatment
   D. *qigong*
4. TCM doctors have discovered a certain herb possesses a selective effect for certain disease of some channel and its pertaining organs, thus the theory of _____ came into existence.

A. selecting the points along the channels
  B. medicinal guides
  C. classifying herbs according to their respective therapeutic effect on the disease of a specific channel and its pertaining organ
  D. treating the same disease with different methods
5. Which of the following treatment is NOT done under the guidance of the theory of the channels and collaterals?
  A. Acupuncture anaesthesia. B. Auricular needle.
  C. Massage. D. Overall analysis of signs and symptoms.

Ⅲ. Translate the following sentences into English or Chinese.

1. 经络与疾病的发生和转变密切相关。
2. 经络是外邪由表入里的途径。
3. 这些均有助于疾病的诊断。
4. 这一学说早被广泛应用于指导中医临床各科的治疗。
5. 为了发挥其治疗作用，别的药品也被引入这一经络。
6. This kind of disease is apt to spread.
7. The operation was delayed owing to technical reasons.
8. Headache may be diagnosed in the light of the distributing law of the channels on the head.
9. Their marking strategy is based on a study of consumer spending.
10. All the activities take place under the guidance of an experienced doctor.

Urinary System（泌尿系统）

Root	Meaning	Examples
urino- uro- -uria	urine, micturition 尿	urination 排尿 uricolysis 尿酸分解 genitourinary 生殖泌尿的 uremia 尿毒症 urokinase 尿激酶 urolithiasis 尿石病，尿石形成 dysuria 排尿困难 pyuria 脓尿

续表

Root	Meaning	Examples
reno- nephro-	kidney 肾	renin 肾素 adrenalin 肾上腺素 suprarenopathy 肾上腺（机能障碍）病 nephron 肾单位 nephrotic syndrome 肾病综合征 nephremia 肾充血
pelvo- pyelo-	renal pelvis 肾盂	pelvioplasty 肾盂成形术 pelviostomy 肾盂造口术 ureteropelvic 输尿管肾盂的 pyelonephritis 肾盂肾炎 pyelography 肾盂造影术 pyelolithotomy 肾盂切开取石术
uretero-	ureter 输尿管	ureterocystoscope 输尿管膀胱镜 nephroureterectomy 肾输尿管切除术 ureteritis 输尿管炎 ureterostenosis 输尿管狭窄 ureterocele 输尿管脱垂, 输尿管囊肿 ureterodialysis 输尿管破裂
vescio- cysto-	bladder 膀胱	vesicostomy 膀胱造口术 vesicocele 膀胱膨出 cystitis 膀胱炎 cystalgia 膀胱痛 cystine 胱氨酸 cystometry 膀胱测压
meato- urethro-	urethra 尿道	meatal 尿道的 meatorrhaphy 尿道口缝合术 meatotomy 尿道口切开术 urethral meatoplasty 尿道成形术 urethropexy 尿道固定术 urethrometry 尿道测量 urethritis 尿道炎 urethral meatus 尿道

Root	Meaning	Examples
calculo- litho-	stone, calculus 结石	urinary calculus 尿路结石 calculus pyelitis 结石性肾盂炎 calciuria 钙尿 vesical calculus 膀胱结石 cystolith 膀胱结石 lithiasis 结石病 lithopedion 石胎 nephrolithiasis 肾结石 cholelithiasis 胆结石

Unit 7　An Overview of TCM Etiology

 Text A

Fire (Heat)

Fire comes into being when *yang* becomes predominant. Fire includes warm and heat. Heat is the extreme of warm, and fire is the extreme of heat.① Heat mainly acts as an exogenous evil existing in different forms;② for example, wind-heat, summer-heat and damp-heat, while fire mostly acts as an endogenous evil causing many kinds of syndromes③, such as flaming up of the heart-fire, ascending of the liver-fire, and running wild of the gallbladder-fire.

The syndromes caused by fire and heat can also be divided into exogenous and endogenous. The exogenous is primarily produced by the direct invasion of warm-heat evils, and the endogenous is mainly due to the failure of the coordination of *zang*-viscera and *fu*-viscera, *yin* and *yang*, *qi* and blood, and to the predominating of the *yang-qi*. Chapter 62 in *Su Wen* (*Plain Questions*) says, "The endogenous heat comes into being when *yin* becomes deficient; the exogenous heat comes into being when *yang* becomes predominant." Dr. Zhu Danxi also said, "Fire comes from an excess of *qi*." In addition, wind, cold, summer-heat, dampness, dryness, or emotional stimulation coming from a condition where "the five emotions become extreme", all can produce fire, from which comes out the terms "fire-transformation of the five climatic factors" and "fire-transformation of the five emotions".

The characteristics and pathogenic features of the fire-heat evil are as follows:

(1) Pathogenic fire-heat is one of the *yang* evils and it flames upwards. Chapter 5 in *Su Wen* says, "Heat will come into being when *yang* becomes predominant."

Yang is characterized by restlessness and upwardness; so fire-heat belongs to *yang* evils since it "burns and flames" upwards. On attacking the human body, therefore, fire-heat mostly produces high fever, aversion to heat, thirst with restlessness, sweating, a full and rapid pulse, etc. When flaming upwards and disturbing the mind, this *yang* evil often produces vexation and insomnia, mental disarrangement and wild behavior, coma, delirium, and so on. Chapter 74 in *Su Wen* says, "All the symptoms characterized by restlessness and mania are related to fire."④ In clinical practice, it can be seen that the syndromes caused by fire-heat are mostly related with the upper part of the human body, for example, the head and face.

(2) Fire is likely to consume *qi* and impair the body fluid. The fire-heat evil is most likely to drive the body fluid out and to heat the *yin*-fluid, and leads to the consumption and impairment of the *yin*-fluid. The diseases caused by the fire-heat evil often produce thirst with desire for drinking, dry mouth, scanty urine in dark color, constipation, etc., which are related to the consumption and impairment of the body fluid.⑤ *Su Wen* points out, "Sthenic fire eats *qi*." The sthenic fire refers to the excessive fire caused by hyperactive *yang-heat*, which is most likely to impair the genuine-*qi*, causing general loss of the body fluid and *qi*.

(3) Fire may produce wind and stir up the blood. When fire-heat evil invades the human body, it will often heat the liver meridian and consume the *yin*-fluid; as a result, the tendons and vessels can not be nourished and moistened; and the syndrome of stirring-up of the liver-wind can appear, of which it is said, "The extreme of heat produces wind." In such a case, there will be symptoms like high fever, coma, delirium, convulsion, upwards staring, stiff neck, and opisthotonos.⑥ So Chapter 74 in *Su Wen* says, "Heat syndromes characterized by fainting and convulsion are related to fire." The fire-heat evil, at the same time, can speed up the blood flow and damage the blood vessels by heating them, and in critical cases, it can make the blood go out of its course, which leads to various kinds of bleeding such as hematemesis, nosebleed, stool with blood, urine with blood, purpura, profuse menstruation, metrorrhagia and metrostaxis.

(4) Fire is likely to cause sores and ulcers. On attacking the blood phase of the body, the fire-heat evil can stagnate at a particular site and erode the blood and flesh there, thus leading to sores and ulcers. Chapter 81 in *Ling Shu* says, "When high fever persists and becomes predominant, the flesh will erode and produce pus, which is termed carbuncle." Chapter 74 in *Su Wen* also says, "All kinds of painful and itchy sores are related to the heart," which means that all kinds of painful and itchy sores are caused by the fire-heat in the heart meridian. *The Golden Mirror of Medicine*⑦ also speaks on this subject. It says, "Carbuncles and gangrene are caused by the poisonous fire." In clinical practice, swollen sores and ulcers with a local fever are differentiated as *yang* and fire-problems.

In addition, it is held that fire and heat are related to the heart, which dominates the blood vessels and stores the mind. When it becomes predominant, fire can cause disturbance of the heart, producing symptoms of mental restlessness, dysphoria, delirium, wild behavior, coma⑧, in addition to the syndromes with symptoms related to the heat in the blood and stirring-up of the blood.

(849 words)

Unit 7 An Overview of TCM Etiology

New Words

exogenous /ekˈsɒdʒənəs/ a.   外生的,外成的,外因的
pathogenic /ˌpæθəˈdʒenɪk/ a.   引起疾病的
vexation /vekˈseɪʃn/ n.   烦恼,忧虑
insomnia /ɪnˈsɒmnɪə/ n.   失眠(症)
coma /ˈkəʊmə/ n.   昏迷
delirium /dɪˈlɪrɪəm/ n.   神志昏迷,说胡话
mania /ˈmeɪnɪə/ n.   狂躁症
sthenic /ˈsθenɪk/ a.   强壮的,亢奋的
convulsion /kənˈvʌlʃn/ n.   抽搐,惊厥
opisthotonos /ˌəʊpɪsθəʊˈtənəʊz/ n.   角弓反张
hematemesis /ˌhiːməˈteməsɪs/ n.   咯血,吐血
purpura /ˈpəpjʊrə/ n.   紫癜
metrorrhagia /ˌmətrəˈreɪdʒɪə/ n.   子宫出血
metrostaxis /ˌmetˈrɒstæksɪs/ n.   子宫渗血,漏下
ulcer /ˈʌlsə/ n.   溃疡
carbuncle /ˈkɑːbʌŋkl/ n.   [医]痈
gangrene /ˈɡæŋɡriːn/ n.   坏疽

Expressions

act as   担当…… 起……的作用
come into being   形成……局面,产生
as follows   如下所述
aversion to   对……讨厌
drive... out   逐出
in clinical practice   在临床实践中
stir up   引起,激起
desire for   渴望,要求
It is held that...   人们认为……

Notes

① Heat is the extreme of warm, and fire is the extreme of heat. 热是温的极致,而火是热的极致。

② Heat mainly acts as an exogenous evil existing in different forms. 热主要作为外邪以不同的形式存在。

③ ... while fire mostly acts as an endogenous evil causing many kinds of syndromes. 而火主要是内邪,它能导致各种综合征产生。

④ All the symptoms characterized by restlessness and mania are related to fire. 所有心神

不定和狂躁的症状都与火有关联。

⑤ The diseases caused by the fire-heat evil often produce thirst with desire for drinking, dry mouth, scanty urine in dark color, constipation, etc., which are related to the consumption and impairment of the body fluid. 由火热毒导致的疾病常会有口干舌燥想喝水的感觉,小便少,且呈深色,伴有便秘等。这些是与体液的消耗和损害相联系的。

⑥ In such a case, there will be symptoms like high fever, coma, delirium, convulsion, upwards staring, stiff neck, and opisthotonos. 在这种情况下,将有一些高烧、昏迷、说胡话、惊厥、眼向上翻、脖子僵硬和角弓反张等症状出现。

⑦ *The Golden Mirror of Medicine*:《医宗金鉴》。《医宗金鉴》是清乾隆四年由太医吴谦负责编修的一部医学教科书。《医宗金鉴》这个名字也是由乾隆皇帝钦定的。《医宗金鉴》被《四库全书》收入,在《四库全书总目提要》中对《医宗金鉴》有很高的评价。自成书以来,这部御制钦定的太医院教科书就被一再的翻刻重印。《医宗金鉴》全书共分 90 卷,是我国综合性中医医书中比较完善而又简要的一种。全书采集了上自春秋战国,下至明清时期历代医书的精华。图、说、方、论俱备,并附有歌诀,便于记诵,尤其切合临床实用。流传极为广泛。

⑧ ... fire can cause disturbance of the heart, producing symptoms of mental restlessness, dysphoria, delirium, wild behavior, coma:火能导致心乱,产生心神不定、焦躁不安、神志不清、行为粗暴、昏迷等症状。

Exercises

I. **Fill in the blanks with the words given below. Change the form when necessary.**

ulcer	scanty	mania	urine
stimulation	impair	aversion	restlessness
syndrome	clinical	insomnia	fluid

1. My father suffered from stomach _____ for a long time.
2. Smoking _____ our health.
3. I underwent _____ therapy for my addiction to smoking.
4. Kleptomania(盗窃癖) is a(n) _____ for stealing things.
5. He was afflicted always with a gnawing _____.
6. After the _____ examination, the consultant invited his students to put forward any suggestions they had kicked about the nature of the disease.
7. _____ (or sleeplessness) is most often defined by an individual's report of sleeping difficulties.
8. There is _____ evidence to support their accusations.
9. These wastes are finally eliminated from the body in the _____.

Unit 7　An Overview of TCM Etiology

10. The spots on his throat are part of a(n) _____.
11. What are the different types of body _____?
12. Electric _____ causes the regrowth of bones.

II. Choose the best answer to each of the following question or unfinished statements.

1. According to the text, fire comes into being when _____ becomes predominant.
   A. *yin*　　　　B. *yang*　　　　C. wind　　　　D. heat
2. According Dr. Zhu Danxi, _____.
   A. fire comes from an excess of *qi*
   B. all kinds of painful and itchy sores are related to the heart
   C. when high fever persists and becomes predominant, the flesh will erode and produce pus
   D. fire can cause disturbance of the heart
3. Which of the following statement is NOT true?
   A. Heat mainly acts as an exogenous evil existing in different forms.
   B. Fire mostly acts as an endogenous evil causing many kinds of syndromes.
   C. *Yang* is characterized by restlessness and upwardness.
   D. The extreme of wind produces heat.
4. It is held that _____, which dominates the blood vessels and stores the mind.
   A. fire and heat are related to the lung
   B. fire and heat are related to the heart
   C. fire and heat are related to the liver
   D. fire and heat are related to the kidney
5. The syndromes caused by fire and heat can also be divided into _____.
   A. exogenous　　　　　　　　　B. endogenous
   C. exogenous and endogenous　　D. upwardness and restlessness

III. Translate the following sentences into English or Chinese.

1. 在临床实践中,可以看出由火热所致的综合征主要与人身体的上部有关,如:头和脸。
2. 火可能导致疮和溃疡。
3. 当继续高烧不退时,肉会腐烂并且化脓,这就叫痈。
4. 极热导致风。
5. 当阳盛时,火就形成了。
6. Fire is likely to consume *qi* and impair the body fluid.
7. Fire may produce wind and stir up the blood.
8. Carbuncles and gangrene are caused by the poisonous fire.

9. In clinical practice, swollen sores and ulcers with a local fever are differentiated as *yang* and fire-problems.

10. It is held that fire and heat are related to the heart, which dominates the blood vessels and stores the mind.

Ⅳ. Write a 150-word composition about TCM etiology.

 Text B

The Six Climatic Evils①

The six climatic evils include wind, cold, summer-heat, dampness, dryness and fire. These are normally called "the six climatic factors", i.e., the six natural climatic variations. The six climatic factors represent the natural conditions within which all living things exist, and they do people no harm. Chapter 25 in *Su Wen* says, "People live on what is produced by the sky and earth, and grow and develop according to the law of the seasons.②" In other words, human beings depend on the air and nutrient essence existing between the sky and the earth, and live, grow and develop in accordance with the seasonal law of germinating, growing and maturing③. Moreover, human beings have learned how to deal with the seasonal changes through their living experiences and obtained certain adaptive abilities, so the six natural climatic factors generally can not cause people to suffer from disease. But the climate may become a pathogenic factor under certain circumstances; for example, when climates change abnormally, i.e., the energetic levels of the six climatic factors become too high or too low and do not correspond to their respective season (for example, an abnormally cool spring, or an abnormally warm autumn), or when climates change wildly. Then they will invade the human body and cause diseases if the body's energetic level of genuine-*qi*④ is low, and if its ability to resist disease is weak. Only under these circumstances are the six climatic factors termed "the six climatic evils". (They are also termed the "six *yin*".⑤ The Chinese word "*yin*" heft means overacting, penetrating and dispersing.) The six climatic evils belong to the category of exogenous pathogenic factors.⑥

The six climatic evils have the following pathogenic features.

(1) The diseases caused by the six climatic evils are mostly related with seasons and living or working environments. For example, generally, there are wind diseases in spring, summer-heat diseases in summer, damp diseases in late summer and early

Unit 7 An Overview of TCM Etiology

autumn, dry diseases in autumn and cold diseases in winter. In addition, "people who live for an extended period of time in a damp environment tend to be easily attacked by the damp evil, and those who work long in an environment of high temperature tend to be easily attacked by the dry-heat evil or fire evil."

(2) All of the six evils can act either alone or in a combination of two or more in attacking the human body. Such syndromes as common cold of wind-cold type, damp-heat diarrhea, wind-cold-damp blockage, etc., are examples of medical problems caused by the composite evils.⑦

(3) In the course of causing diseases, any one of the six climatic evils not only can be influenced by the others, but also can be transformed into another kind of evil under certain conditions. For example, the cold evil that enters the interior of the body can be transformed into the heat evil, and the long-persisting summer-heat with dampness can be transformed into dryness, causing *yin* consumption⑧.

(4) In most cases, the six climatic evils get into the body and cause diseases through the skin and muscle, or the mouth and nose, or through both ways; so they are also termed "the six exogenous evils"⑨.

(5) In today's clinical practice, the syndromes and diseases caused by the six climatic evils also include the pathological problems produced by biological factors (bacteria, virus, etc.), chemical factors, and so on. At a minimum, TCM's study of the cause and course of disease should take all the exogenous etiological factors which can be classified according to the clinical manifestation of the six climatic evils, and the body's pathological responses to them, into consideration.⑩

Although this concept needs refining, it is an acceptable beginning approach.

(621 words)

New Words

essence /ˈesns/ n.	本质，要素，(植物，药物等)精髓，精华，精油
germinate /ˈdʒɜːmɪneɪt/ v.	发芽，生长
heft /heft/ n.	重量，体积
v.	举起
overact /ˌəʊvərˈækt/ v.	活动过度
blockage /ˈblɒkɪdʒ/ n.	堵塞物
consumption /kənˈsʌmpʃn/ n.	消耗
manifestation /ˌmænɪfeˈsteɪʃn/ n.	显示，表明
refine /rɪˈfaɪn/ v.	精炼，使纯净
energetic /ˌenəˈdʒetɪk/ a.	精力充沛的
acceptable /əkˈseptəbl/ a.	值得接受的，可接受的
composite /ˈkɒmpəzɪt/ a.	复合的，综合成的

Expressions

do... no harm	对……无害
the law of...	……的法则
suffer from disease	患病
be influenced by	受……影响
take... into consideration	考虑
at a minimum	至少

Notes

① The Six Climatic Evils:六淫。所谓六淫,是风、寒、暑、湿、燥、火六种外感病邪的统称。阴阳相移、寒暑更作、气候变化都有一定的规律和限度。如果气候变化异常,六气发生太过或不及,或非其时而有其气,以及气候变化过于急骤,超过了一定的限度,使机体不能与之相适应的时候,就会导致疾病的发生。于是,六气由对人体无害而转化为对人体有害,成为致病的因素。

② People live on what is produced by the sky and earth, and grow and develop according to the law of the seasons. 人们依靠天地产出之物生活,随着四季规律成长、发展。

③ ... human beings depend on the air and nutrient essence existing between the sky and the earth, and live, grow and develop in accordance with the seasonal law of germinating, growing and maturing. 人类依靠存在于天地之间的空气及营养精华,依照四季的发芽、成长和成熟规律而生存、成长和发展。

④ genuine-*qi*:真气。由先天元气与后天水谷之精气结合而化生,为维持全身组织、器官生理功能的基本物质与原动力。

⑤ They are also termed the "six *yin*". 他们也被叫做"六淫"。

⑥ The six climatic evils belong to the category of exogenous pathogenic factors. 六淫属于外感病因。

⑦ Such syndromes as common cold of wind-cold type, damp-heat diarrhea, wind-cold-damp blockage, etc., are examples of medical problems caused by the composite evils. 像风寒型的普通感冒、湿热腹泻、风湿寒便秘等综合征都是由各种病邪综合引起的。

⑧ ... the long-persisting summer-heat with dampness can be transformed into dryness, causing *yin* consumption. 长期的暑热加上潮湿会转变成干燥,导致阴消。

⑨ ... they are also termed "the six exogenous evils". 它们也被称为"外感六邪"。

⑩ At a minimum, TCM's study of the cause and course of disease should take all the exogenous etiological factors which can be classified according to the clinical manifestation of the six climatic evils, and the body's pathological responses to them, into consideration. 至少,对于中医病因及病程的研究应该考虑外因,这些外部因素可根据六淫的临床表现和身体的相应病理反应进行划分。

Unit 7 An Overview of TCM Etiology

Exercises

I. Fill in the blanks with the words given below. Change the form when necessary.

essence	diarrhea	disperse	consumption
germinate	refine	manifestation	acceptable
pathogenic	syndrome	pathological	energetic

1. Her favorite _____ smells like gardenias.
2. Heat and moisture will _____ the seeds.
3. The police fired into the air in an attempt to _____ the crowd.
4. This is a clinical study on _____ fire in hemorrhage of upper digestive tract.
5. Three days later his _____ was checked.
6. The food was declared unfit for human _____.
7. Often Down _____ is associated with some impairment of cognitive ability and physical growth, and a particular set of facial characteristics.
8. The production sequence is hydrogenation deacidification → furfural refine → hydrotreating (refined) or clay _____.
9. She has a(n) _____ fear of spiders.
10. Fever is one _____ of cold.
11. I don't feel _____ enough to rush about, so I'll sit down.
12. Their behaviors on that day were _____.

II. Choose the best answer to each of the following unfinished statements.

1. The six climatic evils include wind, cold, summer-heat, dampness, dryness and _____.
   A. metal   B. earth   C. fire   D. water
2. How many pathogenic features of the six climatic evils have been mentioned in Text B? _____.
   A. 5   B. 6   C. 7   D. 4
3. The six climatic evils can be also termed as "_____" according to the text.
   A. *liu yin*   B. *six yin*   C. climatic *yin* D. six climatic
4. The six climatic evils belong to the category of _____ pathogenic factors.
   A. endogenous   B. common   C. exogenous   D. extra
5. Such syndromes as common cold of wind-cold type, damp-heat diarrhea, wind-cold-damp blockage, etc., are examples of medical problems caused by the _____.
   A. composite evils B. incomplete evils C. compete evils D. compose evils

III. Translate the following sentences into English or Chinese.

1. 六淫包括风、寒、暑、湿、燥、火。

2. 然后如果在身体的真气不足或是抵抗疾病的能力很弱时它们会侵入人的身体而致病。
3. 在致病的过程中,六淫中的任何一个不仅会受其他几个的影响,而且能在特定的情况下被转变成另一种病邪。
4. 在大多数情况下,这六淫会通过皮肤和肌肉或(和)嘴和鼻两者进入人体,导致疾病。
5. 尽管这个观念需要提炼,但它是一种可以接受的开始的方法。
6. These are normally called "the six climatic factors", i. e. , the six natural climatic variations.
7. The six climatic factors represent the natural conditions within which all living things exist, and they do people no harm.
8. All of the six evils can act either alone or in a combination of two or more in attacking the human body.
9. But the climate may become a pathogenic factor under certain circumstances.
10. In today's clinical practice, the syndromes and diseases caused by the six climatic evils also include the pathological problems produced by biological factors (bacteria, virus, etc.), chemical factors, and so on.

Text C

Etiology

    The etiological factors that cause the occurrence of disease are varied, and these factors may lead to diseases under certain conditions.

    The ancient Chinese doctors classified the etiological factors in different ways in order to explain their properties and manners for causing diseases.① For example, in *The Yellow Emperor's Classic of Medicine*, all the etiological factors were classified into two categories for the first time, namely *yin* and *yang*. Chapter 62 in *Su Wen* points out, "The pathogenic evils either originate in *yin* or originate in *yang*; those coming from *yang* are related to wind, rain, cold, and heat; those coming from *yin* are related to food and drink, living places, sexual life, and emotions such as joy and anger." In his book entitled *Synopsis of Prescriptions of the Golden Cabinet*②, Dr. Zhang Zhongjing of the Han Dynasty said that all diseases were caused by the evils in three ways, "All diseases and medical problems are exactly within three categories: the meridians are first attacked by the evils, then the viscera are affected; and there is an endogenous cause for this; the

Unit 7　An Overview of TCM Etiology

vessels and blood circulation that maintain and connect the four limbs and the nine body orifices are blocked, and this is caused by the evils attacking the skin externally; and there are medical problems related to the factors such as sexual activities, injuries by sharp metal things, bites by insect or beast. From this point of view, it can be said that all the etiological causes are included here." Dr. Tao Hongjing③ of the Jin Dynasty, in his book entitled *A Pocketbook of 100 Recipes*, divided all etiological causes into "the endogenous, the exogenous, and others". Dr. Chen Wuze④, of the Song Dynasty, extended Dr. Zhang Zhongjing's idea of that "all diseases and medical problems are exactly within three categories", and put forward his "three-factors theory", saying, "The six climatic evils are related to the natural climatic changes;⑤ when they overact, they first get into the meridians and collaterals, then into the viscera, so they are exogenous etiological factors. The seven emotions are natural feelings of the human beings;⑥ when they⑦ arise up, they first affect the viscera, then the exterior of the body, so they are endogenous etiological factors. The others, like hunger, overeating, impairment of *qi* by yelling, traumatic injuries by metal things, incomplete fracture, infectious pathogens, evil spirit, fright, crushing, drowning, etc., are all beyond the natural scope⑧, so they are neither endogenous nor exogenous factors." It can be seen that the method used by ancient Chinese physicians to classify etiological factors according to their ways of causing disease possesses a guiding significance for clinical syndrome differentiation.

According to TCM, there is no symptom without any cause, and any kind of symptoms certainly is a reflection of the body being affected and influenced by some pathogenic factors⑨. To understand the causes of diseases, TCM examines the clinical manifestations of diseases and studies the possible pathogenic factors. The procedure of finding the cause of disease through an analysis of the symptoms and clinical signs is termed "finding the cause of disease by syndrome differentiation". The TCM etiology, therefore, studies not only the properties and pathogenic characteristics of etiological factors, but also the clinical manifestations of the syndromes and diseases caused by various etiological factors, in order to direct clinical diagnosis and treatment.

(557 words)

New Words

occurrence /əˈkʌrəns/ *n.*	发生,出现
etiological /ˌiːtɪəʊˈlɒdʒɪkl/ *a.*	病因学的,病原学的
orifice /ˈɒrəfɪs/ *n.*	孔,洞口
traumatic /trɔːˈmætɪk/ *a.*	外伤的
infectious /ɪnˈfekʃəs/ *a.*	传染的
maintain /meɪnˈteɪn/ *v.*	保持,维持
pathogen /ˈpæθədʒən/ *n.*	病原体,病菌

Expressions

in different ways	以不同的方法
blood circulation	血液循环
from this point of view	从这方面来看
It can be said that …	可以说……
syndrome differentiation	辨证

Notes

① The ancient Chinese doctors classified the etiological factors in different ways in order to explain their properties and manners for causing diseases. 古代中医将病因按不同方式进行分类，主要目的是解释它们致病的特点与方式。

② *Synopsis of Prescriptions of the Golden Cabinet*：《金匮要略》。东汉张仲景著述的《金匮要略》是中医经典古籍之一，撰于 3 世纪初。作者原撰《伤寒杂病论》十六卷中的"杂病"部分。经晋王叔和整理后，其古传本之一名《金匮玉函要略方》，共 3 卷上卷为辨伤寒，中卷则论杂病，下卷记载药方。后北宋校正医书局林艺等人根据当时所存的蠹简文字重新编校，取其中以杂病为主的内容，仍厘定为 3 卷，改名《金匮要略方论》。全书共 25 篇，方剂 262 首，列举病症六十余种。所述病证以内科杂病为主，兼有部分外科妇产科等病证。

③ Tao Hongjing：陶弘景（456～536），南北朝道教学家、中药学家，撰《神农本草经集注》等。

④ Chen Wuze：陈无择（1131～1189），名言，以字行，原籍宋青田鹤溪（今景宁县鹤溪镇）人。长期居住温州，行医济世。他精于方脉，医德高尚，医技精良，学术造诣深邃，除从事医学理论研究之外，多著书立说。因此，不但求医者众，而且受业者更是纷至沓来。由于他的名著《三因方》为永嘉医派奠定了学术基础，因此，陈无择也就成了永嘉医派的创始人。

⑤ The six climatic evils are related to the natural climatic changes. 六淫与自然气候变化相关。

⑥ The seven emotions are natural feelings of the human beings. 七情是人类的自然情感。

⑦ they：此处指的是前文中提到的 the seven emotions。

⑧ beyond the natural scope：超越了自然的界限。

⑨ … any kind of symptoms certainly is a reflection of the body being affected and influenced by some pathogenic factors. 任何症状显然都是身体受到一些致病因素的影响而产生的反应。

Unit 7　An Overview of TCM Etiology

Exercises

I. **Fill in the blanks with the words given below. Change the form when necessary.**

etiological	limb	orifice	symptom
viscera	traumatic	occurrence	infectious
differentiation	maintain	pathogen	syndrome

1. The _____ of storms delayed our trip.
2. This is a 80-case report of _____ analysis of obstruction of hilar bile duct.
3. Even the ugliest human exterior may contain the most beautiful _____.
4. He was very tall with long _____.
5. If this process is unilateral, then the problem originates from the ureteral _____ up to the pelvis.
6. The onset of depression often follows a(n) _____ event.
7. What is the _____ and relation between the two?
8. Influenza is a(n) _____ disease.
9. Food is necessary to _____ life.
10. The causative _____ is influenza virus.
11. Lemon juice can help to prevent economy-class _____ by improving blood circulation.
12. The doctor told her to watch out for _____ of measles.

II. **Choose the best answer to each of the following question or unfinished statements.**

1. Who's the writer of *A Pocketbook of 100 Recipes*?
   A. Dr. Tao Hongjing.　　　B. Dr. Zhang Zhongjing.
   C. Dr. Li Shizhen.　　　D. Dr. Chen Wuze.
2. In _____, all the etiological factors were classified into two categories for the first time.
   A. *A Pocketbook of 100 Recipes*
   B. *The Yellow Emperor's Classic* of Medicine
   C. *Synopsis of Prescriptions of the Golden Cabinet*
   D. None of the above.
3. The etiological factors that cause the occurrence of disease are _____.
   A. same　　　B. varied　　　C. not important　　　D. necessary
4. All diseases and medical problems are exactly within _____ categories according to Zhang Zhongjing.
   A. 6　　　B. 5　　　C. 4　　　D. 3
5. According to TCM, there is no symptom without any cause, and any kind of symptoms

certainly is a(n) _____ of the body being affected and influenced by some pathogenic factors.

A. presupposition B. reflection C. answer D. example

Ⅲ. **Translate the following sentences into English or Chinese.**

1. 病邪要么源于阴，要么源于阳。
2. 所有的疾病或健康问题都包含在三个范畴当中。
3. 根据中医，没有无因之症状。
4. 为了理解病因，中医检查各类疾病的临床表现，研究各种可能的病因。
5. 有些健康问题是和性行为、金属器物割伤和兽虫叮咬等相关的。
6. The etiological factors that cause the occurrence of disease are varied, and these factors may lead to diseases under certain conditions.
7. In *The Yellow Emperor's Classic of Medicine*, all the etiological factors were classified into two categories for the first time, namely *yin* and *yang*.
8. When the six climatic evils overact, they first get into the meridians and collaterals, then into the viscera, so they are exogenous etiological factors.
9. The procedure of finding the cause of disease through an analysis of the symptoms and clinical signs is termed "finding the cause of disease by syndrome differentiation".
10. The TCM etiology, therefore, studies not only the properties and pathogenic characteristics of etiological factors, but also the clinical manifestations of the syndromes and diseases caused by various etiological factors, in order to direct clinical diagnosis and treatment.

Reproductive System （生殖系统）

Root	Meaning	Examples
genitor- germino-	reproduction 生殖	genital 生殖的 genitalia 生殖器 urogenital 泌尿生殖的 genital tract 生殖道 germinoma 生殖细胞瘤 germ cell 生殖细胞，胚细胞

Unit 7　An Overview of TCM Etiology

续表

Root	Meaning	Examples
femino- gyneco- estro-	woman, female 女性	feminize 使女性化 gynecology 妇科学 gynecological surgery 妇科手术 estrogen 雌激素 estradiol 雌二醇
ovario- oophoro-	ovary, ovarium 卵巢	ovariectomy 卵巢切除术 ovarian 卵巢的 oophoritis 卵巢炎
salpingo-	oviduct, salpinx 输卵管	salpingitis 输卵管炎 salpingo oophorectomy 输卵管卵巢切除术
utero- hystero- metro-	womb, uterus 子宫	uterine 子宫的 uteroplacental 子宫胎盘的 hysterectomy 子宫切除术 endometrial 子宫内膜的 metrorrhagia 子宫出血
vagino-	vagina 阴道	vaginitis 阴道炎 vaginal bleeding 阴道出血
ovo- oo-	egg, ovum 卵	ovalbumin 卵白蛋白 oocyte 卵母细胞 oval cell 卵细胞
meno-	menses, menstruation 月经	menopause 绝经 dysmenorrheal 痛经
pregno-	pregnancy, gravidity 妊娠	pregnant 妊娠的 pregnenolone 孕烯醇酮
amnio-	amnion 羊膜	amniocentesis 羊膜穿刺 amniotic fluid 羊水
chorio-	chorion 绒毛膜	chorioamnionitis 绒毛膜羊膜炎 chorionic gonadotropin 绒毛膜促性腺激素

Root	Meaning	Examples
embryo- -derm	embryo 胚胎	embryogenesis 胚胎发生 embryonic 胚胎的 mesoderm 中胚层
-para toco-	delivery, childbirth labour 分娩	primipara 初产妇 tocopherol 生育酚 tocolytic agent 保胎药物
-didymus -pagus	conjoined twin 联胎	thoracodidymus 胸部联胎 craniopagus 颅部联胎
andro-	man, male, virility 男性	androgen 雄激素 androgenic steroid 雄激素类固醇
scroto-	scrotum 阴囊	scrotoplasty 阴囊成形术 scrotal elephantiasis 阴囊象皮病
testo- orchio-	testis, testicle 睾丸	testosterone 睾酮 orchiectomy 睾丸切除术 cryptorchidism 隐睾症
semino- spermato-	sperm, spermatozoon 精子	seminoma 精原细胞瘤 insemination 授精 spermatogenesis 精子发生 spermatic cord 精索
prostato-	prostate 前列腺	prostaglandin 前列腺素 prostatic hyperplasia 前列腺增生

Unit 8　Disease Mechanism in TCM

 Text A

Mechanism of Pathological Changes(1)

Mechanism of pathological changes① includes the nature of disease and its transmitting principles. The occurrence of disease results from the struggle between pathogenic factors and healthy *qi* which exists in the whole course of disease. In the struggle between pathogenic factors and healthy *qi*, various general or local pathological changes will be caused if healthy *qi* is impaired, the balance between *yin* and *yang* is damaged, the functions of meridians are in disorder and the flow of *qi* and blood is disturbed. Though complicated, pathological changes generally can be classified into such categories as predomination and decline of pathogenic factors and healthy *qi*, imbalance of *yin* and *yang* as well as disorder of *qi*, blood and body fluid②.

Predomination and decline of pathogenic factors and healthy *qi* refer to changes of pathogenic factors and healthy *qi* due to struggle between them. The result of predomination and decline of pathogenic factors and healthy *qi* affects the nature and transmission of disease.

The occurrence of disease is due to two factors, deficiency of healthy *qi* and attack of pathogenic factors. However, these two factors play different roles in a specific disease. Sometimes disease is caused by deficiency of healthy *qi*, and sometimes by attack of pathogenic factors, resulting in either deficiency syndrome or excess syndrome. *Huangdi Neijing* says, "Excess means predomination of pathogenic factors while deficiency means exhaustion of essence." That is to say, that "excess" is related to pathogenic factors while "deficiency" is related to healthy *qi*.

Excess Syndrome③

Excess syndrome is characterized by predomination of pathogenic factors and abundance or certain degree impairment of healthy *qi*. Violent struggle between pathogenic factors and healthy *qi* leads to a series of excess symptoms. That is why it is a syndrome of excess nature.④ Excess syndrome is often seen at the early and medium stages of diseases caused by six abnormal climatic factors or diseases caused by phlegm, rheum, stagnant blood, retention of food and accumulation of dampness and water in the body.⑤

Clinically, excess syndrome includes superabundance of phlegm, internal blockage of stagnant blood, indigestion and abnormal flow of water and dampness as well as the manifestations of high fever, mania, sonorous voice and hoarse breath, impalpable abdominal pain, constipation, anuria and powerful pulse, etc.

Deficiency Syndrome⑥

Deficiency syndrome is marked by deficiency of healthy *qi*. Though pathogenic factors are not totally eliminated, they are not strong enough to damage healthy *qi*. So the struggle between pathogenic factors and healthy *qi* is mild with symptoms of deficiency of healthy *qi* and hypofunction⑦ of the viscera. That is why this kind of syndrome is termed deficiency syndrome. Deficiency syndrome is often seen at the advanced stage of exogenous diseases. It usually results from non-restoration of healthy *qi*, or frequent weakness of the body, or exhaustion of essence due to serious disease, protracted disease and chronic disease, or damage of *qi*, blood and body fluid due to profuse sweating, violent vomiting and diarrhea and massive hemorrhage, etc. Clinically, the manifestations of deficiency syndrome include dispiritedness, sallow complexion, palpitation and shortness of breath, spontaneous sweating, night sweating, or feverish sensation in the five centers (palms, soles and chest), or aversion to cold and cold limbs as well as weak pulse, etc.⑧

During the course of a disease, the predomination and decline of pathogenic factors and healthy *qi* may lead to either simple deficiency syndrome and excess syndrome or mixture of deficiency syndrome and excess syndrome. Mixture of deficiency syndrome and excess syndrome may be caused by delayed or improper treatment of excess syndrome that leads to prolonged retention of pathogenic factors in the body and impairment of healthy *qi*, or by coagulation of pathological substances like dampness, water and stagnant blood due to deficiency of healthy *qi*.⑨

Mixture of deficiency syndrome and excess syndrome is characterized by either deficiency complicated by excess or excess complicated by deficiency. The former is marked by domination of deficiency syndrome accompanied by excess of pathogenic factors, such as edema due to inactivation of spleen-*yang*. The latter is marked by domination of excess syndrome accompanied by deficiency manifestations, such as excess-heat consuming *yin*-fluid at the medium stage of febrile diseases⑩.

(708 words)

New Words

impair /ɪmˈpeə/ *vt.*		损害，削弱
deficiency /dɪˈfɪʃnsɪ/ *n.*		缺乏，不足，短缺
excess /ɪkˈses/ *n.*		过分，过量
exhaustion /ɪgˈzɔːstʃən/ *n.*		精疲力竭，用光，耗尽
abundance /əˈbʌndəns/ *n.*		大量，充足

Unit 8　Disease Mechanism in TCM

retention /rɪˈtenʃn/ *n.*	保持,保留
stagnant /ˈstæɡnənt/ *a.*	不流动的,停滞的
sonorous /ˈsɒnərəs/ *a.*	圆润低沉的,响亮的,洪亮的
hoarse /hɔːs/ *a.*	沙哑的
palpitation /ˌpælpɪˈteɪʃən/ *n.*	心悸
spontaneous /spɒnˈteɪnɪəs/ *a.*	自发的,自动的,一时冲动的
aversion /əˈvɜːʃn/ *n.*	厌恶,讨厌,反感
edema /ɪˈdiːmə/ *n.*	水肿,浮肿,瘤腺体

Expressions

in disorder	混乱,无秩序
the former... the latter...	前者……后者……

Notes

① mechanism of pathological changes:病变机制。

② ... predomination and decline of pathogenic factors and healthy *qi*, imbalance of *yin* and *yang* as well as disorder of *qi*, blood and body fluid. pathogenic factors:病邪,邪气;healthy *qi*:正气;imbalance of *yin* and *yang*:阴阳失调;disorder of *qi*, blood and body fluid:气血紊乱。

③ Excess Syndrome:实证。

④ That is why it is a syndrome of excess nature. 这句中 that 引起下文,指代前一句话。

⑤ Excess syndrome is often seen at the early and medium stages of diseases caused by six abnormal climatic factors or diseases caused by phlegm, rheum, stagnant blood, retention of food and accumulation of dampness and water in the body. phlegm:痰;rheum:感冒;stagnant blood:瘀血;retention of food:积食。

⑥ Deficiency Syndrome:虚证。

⑦ hypofunction:hypo-（术语）低于正常的,过少的。例如:dying of hypothermia 死于体温过低。

⑧ Clinically, the manifestations of deficiency syndrome include dispiritedness, sallow complexion, palpitation and shortness of breath, spontaneous sweating, night sweating, or feverish sensation in the five centers (palms, soles and chest), or aversion to cold and cold limbs as well as weak pulse, etc. dispiritedness:灰心,沮丧;swallow complexion:面虚无力;shortness of breath:气短;spontaneous sweating:自汗;aversion to cold:恶寒。

⑨ Mixture of deficiency syndrome and excess syndrome may be caused by delayed or improper treatment of excess syndrome that leads to prolonged retention of pathogenic factors in the body and impairment of healthy *qi*, or by coagulation of pathological substances like dampness, water and stagnant blood due to deficiency of healthy *qi*. 此

句是一个复合句,其中 that 引导了一个定语从句,or by 与 caused by 保持并列,省略了 caused。coagulation:凝结。

⑩ febrile disease:热病,泛指一切外感引起的热性病。

Exercises

Ⅰ. **Fill in the blanks with the words given below. Change the form when necessary.**

transmit	deficiency	impair	retention
eliminate	exhaustion	stagnant	hoarse
essence	abundance	spontaneous	manifestation

1. Under the agreement, all trade barriers will be _____.
2. His voice was _____ from laughing.
3. The infection is _____ by mosquitoes.
4. Committee members voted for the _____ of the existing voting system.
5. _____ of the disease often doesn't occur until middle age.
6. The disease is caused by a vitamin _____.
7. Smoking _____ our health.
8. If you have been very worried, you will have nervous _____.
9. Wild flowers grow in _____ on the hillsides.
10. In his paintings Picasso tries to capture the _____ of his subjects.
11. Industrial output has remained _____.
12. The crowd gave a(n) _____ cheer when the result was announced.

Ⅱ. **Choose the best answer to each of the following questions or unfinished statement.**

1. What will cause pathological changes?
   A. The imbalance between *yin* and *yang*.
   B. The impairment of healthy *qi*.
   C. The disturbance of the flow of *qi* and blood.
   D. All of the above.
2. When will the disease occur?
   A. Healthy *qi* is deficient.
   B. Pathogenic factors are not attacked.
   C. Healthy *qi* is not deficient and pathogenic factors are not attacked.
   D. Healthy *qi* is deficient and pathogenic factors are attacked.
3. "The five centers" mentioned in the passage include the following ones EXCEPT _____.

Unit 8 Disease Mechanism in TCM

    A. soles   B. liver   C. palms   D. chest

4. What is the feature of mixture of deficiency syndrome and excess syndrome?

    A. Excess of pathogenic factors.

    B. Domination of excess syndrome.

    C. Deficiency complicated by excess or excess complicated by deficiency.

    D. Domination of deficiency syndrome.

5. According to the passage, which of the following statements is NOT true?

    A. Disorder of *qi* belongs to pathological changes.

    B. At the beginning of the disease excess syndrome is often seen.

    C. Struggle between pathogenic factors and healthy *qi* cannot transform deficiency syndrome into excess syndrome.

    D. Deficiency is connected with healthy *qi*.

Ⅲ. Translate the following sentences into English or Chinese.

1. 正邪相争会引起疾病。

2. 高烧是实证的临床表现。

3. 实与病邪有关，而虚与正气有关。

4. 温总理由官员们陪同参观了当地的企业。

5. 病变机制包括疾病的性质及其传播原理。

6. The predomination and decline of pathogenic factors and healthy *qi* may lead to mixture of deficiency syndrome and excess syndrome.

7. Mandala played a leading role in ending apartheid in South Africa.

8. A bad cold was brought on by going out in the rain.

9. Clinically, the manifestations of deficiency syndrome include dispiritedness, palpitation and night sweating, etc.

10. The figures in the left-hand column refer to our sales abroad.

Ⅳ. Write a 150-word composition about pathological changes.

Text B

Mechanism of Pathological Changes(2)

Deficiency syndrome and excess syndrome are not fixed, they often transform into each other due to struggle between pathogenic factors and healthy *qi*.

Such a mutual transformation is characterized by transformation either from excess into deficiency or from deficiency into excess. In excess syndrome, healthy *qi* is usually not deficient. However, delayed or improper treatment may prolong the course of duration, leading to impairment of healthy *qi* and the physiological functions of the viscera and resulting in transformation of excess into deficiency.① In deficiency syndrome, there is no invasion of pathogenic factors. However, deficiency of healthy *qi* and hypofunction of the viscera may lead to abnormal flow of *qi*, blood and body fluid and bring on *qi* stagnation, stagnant blood, phlegm and rheum as well as water and dampness, eventually resulting in deficiency complicated by excess. Though there is excess of pathogenic factors, healthy *qi* is still insufficient. Thus this morbid state is termed "excess caused by deficiency".

Relationship Between the Prognosis of Disease② and the State of Pathogenic Factors and Healthy *Qi*

In the course of struggle between pathogenic factors and healthy *qi*, healthy *qi* can eliminate pathogenic factors and pathogenic factors are also able to impair healthy *qi*. Thus, the struggle between pathogenic factors and healthy *qi* is marked by constant variation of both sides. Such a variation decides the development of disease that manifests in two ways: recovery or death.③ If healthy *qi* becomes dominant, pathogenic factors will be reduced and disease will be improved and gradually cured; if pathogenic factors become dominant, healthy *qi* will be weakened and disease will become worsened or death will be caused.

Domination of Healthy *Qi* and Decline of Pathogenic Factors

Domination of healthy *qi* and decline of pathogenic factors are the necessary conditions for improvement and cure of disease. If healthy *qi* is sufficient, it will be powerful in resisting pathogenic factors and pathogenic factors will gradually be eliminated. If timely treatment is resorted to, pathogenic factors will be eliminated or reduced and healthy *qi* will be gradually restored. In both cases the functions of the viscera are improved, pathogenic factors are eliminated and eventually disease is cured.

The course of domination of healthy *qi* and decline of pathogenic factors may be long or short, depending on individual conditions. Generally speaking, the duration of exogenous disease and excess syndrome is short because pathogenic factors have not penetrated deep into the body and healthy *qi* is not seriously impaired. So exogenous disease and excess syndrome are easy to improve and cure. However, the duration of endogenous disease④ and deficiency syndrome is long because pathogenic factors have penetrated deep into the body and healthy *qi* is seriously impaired. So endogenous disease and deficiency syndrome are difficult to improve and cure. Usually correct and timely treatment can shorten the course of domination of healthy *qi* and decline of pathogenic factors. Incorrect and delayed treatment will certainly prolong the course of such a development.

Domination of Pathogenic Factors and Decline of Healthy *Qi*

Domination of pathogenic factors and decline of healthy *qi* are the basic causes of aggravation of disease or death. Such a variation results either from frequent deficiency of healthy *qi* that fails to restrict the development of pathogenic factors, or from exuberance⑤ of pathogenic factors that go beyond the body resistance, or from wrong or delayed treatment that impairs healthy *qi* and strengthens pathogenic factors, resulting in declination of visceral functions and separation of *yin* and *yang*, and eventually leading to death.⑥

In the course of the variation of healthy *qi* and pathogenic factors, if healthy *qi* is not strong enough to eliminate pathogenic factors and pathogenic factors are not strong enough to further develop, it will bring on such a condition in which healthy *qi* and pathogenic factors are at a stalemate or healthy *qi* is deficient and pathogenic factors are still lingering⑦. In this case healthy *qi* is difficult to restore, disease may change from an acute one into a chronic one⑧ or become obstinate, or certain sequelae may be caused.

(673 words)

New Words

characterize /ˈkærəktəraɪz/ *vt.*	是……的特征,以……为特征
duration /djʊˈreɪʃn/ *n.*	持续,持续的时间,期间
invasion /ɪnˈveɪʒn/ *n.*	侵犯,侵入,闯入
sufficient /səˈfɪʃnt/ *a.*	足够的,充足的
prognosis /prɒgˈnəʊsɪs/ *n.*	[医]预后(指医生对疾病结果的预测)
eventually /ɪˈventʃʊəlɪ/ *ad.*	终于,最后
individual /ˌɪndɪˈvɪdʒʊəl/ *a.*	个别的,单独的,个人的
penetrate /ˈpenɪtreɪt/ *v.*	穿过,刺入,渗入
aggravation /ˌægrəˈveɪʃn/ *n.*	加重,更恶化
frequent /ˈfriːkwənt/ *a.*	时常发生的,常见的
stalemate /ˈsteɪlmeɪt/ *n.*	僵持,僵局
linger /ˈlɪŋgə/ *vi.*	逗留,徘徊
obstinate /ˈɒbstɪnət/ *a.*	难克服的,不易去除的

Expressions

in this case	在这种情况下
bring on	引来，导致
be able to	能够做
be marked by	具有……特征
resort to	采取，诉诸
generally speaking	总的来说

Notes

① However, delayed or improper treatment may prolong the course of duration, leading to impairment of healthy *qi* and the physiological functions of the viscera and resulting in transformation of excess into deficiency. leading to 和 resulting in 是并列关系的现在分词短语，作句子的结果状语。

② the prognosis of disease：疾病的预测。prognosis：（术语）预后，预断（医生对于病情如何发展的预测）。

③ Such a variation decides the development of disease that manifests in two ways: recovery or death. such a variation 指代前面提到的变化，that 引导了一个定语从句。

④ endogenous disease：由内因引起的疾病。endogenous 和 exogenous 是反义词。

⑤ exuberance：茂盛，丰富。

⑥ Such a variation results either from frequent deficiency of healthy *qi* that fails to restrict the development of pathogenic factors, or from exuberance of pathogenic factors that go beyond the body resistance, or from wrong or delayed treatment that impairs healthy qi and strengthens pathogenic factors, resulting in declination of visceral functions and separation of *yin* and *yang*, and eventually leading to death. 此句话的主要动词是 result from，由 either... or... 连接，其中三个 that 都引导定语从句，resulting in 和 leading to 作结果状语。

⑦ ...it will bring on such a condition in which healthy *qi* and pathogenic factors are at a stalemate or healthy qi is deficient and pathogenic factors are still lingering. in which 引导了一个定语从句。

⑧ a chronic one：慢性病，相对应的是 an acute disease：急性病。

Unit 8 Disease Mechanism in TCM

Exercises

I. Fill in the blanks with the words given below. Change the form when necessary.

penetrate	linger	pathogenic	mutual
characterize	frequent	sufficient	variation
physiological	stalemate	eventually	individual

1. The taste _____ in your mouth.
2. There are many _____ species.
3. We discovered a(n) _____ interest in gardening.
4. He worked so hard that _____ he made himself ill.
5. Bright colours _____ his paintings.
6. Each _____ leaf on the tree is different.
7. Prices are subject to _____.
8. Explorers _____ into unknown regions.
9. The doctors could find no _____ cause for his illness.
10. Her headaches are becoming less _____.
11. His income is _____ to keep him comfortable.
12. The discussions with miners' union ended in _____.

II. Choose the best answer to each of the following question or unfinished statements.

1. The viscera refers to _____.
   A. hand   B. heart   C. feet   D. mouth
2. In excess syndrome, healthy *qi* is _____.
   A. deficient   B. insufficient   C. sufficient   D. a little
3. Recovery or death is caused by _____.
   A. healthy *qi*
   B. pathogenic factors
   C. the struggle between pathogenic factors and healthy *qi*
   D. All of the above.
4. What is necessary to cure disease?
   A. Healthy *qi*.   B. Decline of pathogenic factors.
   C. Domination of healthy *qi*. D. Both B and C.
5. From the passage we can learn _____.
   A. if pathogenic factors are dominant, disease will become worse
   B. death is just caused by decline of decline of healthy *qi*
   C. mutual transformation between excess syndrome and deficiency syndrome is very difficult

D. the variation of healthy *qi* and pathogenic factors can't cure disease

III. Translate the following sentences into English or Chinese.

1. 这种变化可以决定疾病的发展。
2. 虚证与实证通常可以互相转化。
3. 在我们交谈中得知鲍勃已经入狱了。
4. 客气的请求不起作用时,我们便采取了威胁手段。
5. 很多外国人一直想学会讲汉语。

6. This morbid state is termed excess caused by deficiency.
7. Deficiency of healthy *qi* fails to restrict the development of pathogenic factors.
8. She's too obstinate to let anyone help her.
9. If timely treatment is resorted to, pathogenic factors will be eliminated or reduced.
10. Don't boil the sauce as this can impair the flavor.

Text C

Imbalance Between *Yin* and *Yang*

Normally *yin* and *yang* in the body maintain a dynamic balance through the interactions of inter-opposition, inter-dependence, inter-restriction and inter-transformation①. If such a dynamic balance is impaired by six exogenous abnormal climatic factors, endogenous impairment by abnormal changes of emotions, improper diet or overwork and over-rest, the normal relationships between the viscera, the meridians, *qi* and blood will be affected, leading to various complicated pathological changes.

The main pathological changes caused by imbalance between *yin* and *yang* are predomination and decline of *yin* and *yang*, mutual impairment of *yin* and *yang*, mutual rejection of *yin* and *yang*, mutual transformation of *yin* and *yang* as well as the loss of *yin* and *yang*.② Here we focus on the last two aspects.

Inter-transformation of *yin* and *yang* means that *yang*-heat syndrome may change into *yin*-cold syndrome and *yin*-cold syndrome may turn into *yang*-heat syndrome in the course of a disease.

Transformation of *Yang* into *Yin*

The nature of the disease originally pertains to *yang*-heat. But when *yang*-heat

Unit 8 Disease Mechanism in TCM

develops to a certain degree, it will turn into *yin*-cold. For example, some febrile diseases show a series of heat symptoms at the early stage, such as high fever, thirst, reddish tongue, yellowish tongue coating③ and rapid pulse, indicating that the syndrome is obviously of *yang*-heat. However, improper treatment or extreme exuberance of pathogenic factors may suddenly lead to such critical signs of *yin*-cold as low body temperature, cold limbs, cold profuse sweating and indistinct pulse④. This shows that the nature of the disease has been changed. Such a change is quite different from true-heat and false-cold syndrome in *yang* syndrome appearing like *yin* syndrome.

Transformation of *Yin* into *Yang*

The nature of the disease originally pertains to *yin*-cold. But when *yin*-cold develops to a certain degree, it will turn into *yang*-heat. For example, attack of exogenous pathogenic cold leads to a series of wind-cold symptoms at the early stage, such as serious aversion to cold and light fever, headache, body pain, thin and whitish tongue coating, and floating-tense pulse, indicating wind-cold affecting the superficies⑤. Eventually it develops into a *yang* heat syndrome marked by high fever, sweating, thirst, reddish tongue, yellowish tongue coating and rapid pulse. This shows that *yin* syndrome has been transformed into *yang* syndrome and cold syndrome has been turned into heat syndrome. Such a change is quite different from true-cold and false-heat syndrome in *yin* syndrome appearing like *yang* syndrome.⑥

Loss of *yin* and *yang* refers to a critical pathological state caused by sudden loss of great quantity of *yin*-fluid or *yang-qi*. Loss of *yin* or *yang* also pertains to relative predomination and relative decline of *yin* and *yang*⑦, quite different from relative predomination and decline of *yin* or *yang* in the occurrence and severity of disease.

Loss of *Yang*

Loss of *yang* is usually caused by predomination of pathogenic factors and weakness of healthy *qi* to control pathogenic factors, frequent deficiency of *yang* and overstrain⑧, wrong application of diaphoresis and profuse sweating that result in sudden loss of *yang-qi*, leading to the symptoms of profuse sweating, cold sensation in the skin, feet and hands, lying with the knees drawn up, spiritual lassitude and indistinct pulse, etc.

Loss of *Yin*

Loss of *yin* is usually caused by exuberant pathogenic heat⑨, violent vomiting, profuse sweating and diarrhea that result in loss of great quantity of body fluid with the symptoms of emaciation, curled skin, sunken ocular orbit, scanty and sticky sweating, irascibility and very weak pulse, etc.

Though loss of *yin* and loss of *yang* may appear solitarily, the loss of one side often leads to immediate exhaustion of the other because *yin* and *yang* depend on each other to exist. Thus untimely treatment of loss of *yin* or loss of *yang* may lead to death because "separation of *yin* and *yang* exhausts essence"⑩.

(632 words)

New Words

various /ˈveərɪəs/ a.	各种不同的，各种各样的
originally /əˈrɪdʒənlɪ/ ad.	起初，原来
indicate /ˈɪndɪkeɪt/ vt.	标示，指示，指出
improper /ɪmˈprɒpə/ a.	不合适的，不适当的
indistinct /ˌɪndɪˈstɪŋkt/ a.	不清楚的，模糊的
superficies /ˌsuːpəˈfɪʃɪːz/ n.	表面，表层
severity /sɪˈverɪtɪ/ n.	严重，剧烈
overstrain /ˌəʊvəˈstreɪn/ n.	过度紧张，过劳
sensation /senˈseɪʃn/ n.	感觉，感受
lassitude /ˈlæsɪtjuːd/ n.	无精打采
violent /ˈvaɪələnt/ a.	剧烈的，强烈的，猛烈的
emaciation /ɪˌmeɪsɪˈeɪʃn/ n.	消瘦，憔悴，衰弱
untimely /ʌnˈtaɪmlɪ/ a.	不适时的，不合时宜的

Expressions

change into	变成
to a certain degree	在某种程度下
turn into	变成，把……变成
a series of	一系列
be different from	与……不同
aversion to	讨厌，反感
develop into	发展，成长
draw up your knees	蜷起双腿
quantity of	大量，许多

Notes

① ... through the interactions of inter-opposition, inter-dependence, inter-restriction and inter-transformation. inter-：前缀，表示交互，互相。interaction：相互影响，相互作用；inter-opposition：互相排斥；inter-dependence：互相依赖；inter-restriction：相互限制；inter-transformation：相互转化。

② The main pathological changes caused by imbalance between *yin* and *yang* are predomination and decline of *yin* and *yang*, mutual impairment of *yin* and *yang*, mutual rejection of *yin* and *yang*, mutual transformation of *yin* and *yang* as well as loss of *yin* and *yang*. 阴阳失调可以导致病变，而这种病变主要包括阴阳消长、阴阳互损、阴阳互相排斥、阴阳互相转化和阴阳的流失。

③ yellowish tongue coating：淡黄舌苔。

④ ... such critical signs of *yin*-cold as low body temperature, cold limbs, cold profuse

Unit 8　Disease Mechanism in TCM

sweating and indistinct pulse:体温低、手足厥冷、冷汗、脉搏微弱等阴寒特征。cold limbs:手足厥冷;cold profuse sweating:冒冷汗;indistinct pulse:脉搏微弱。

⑤ ... a series of wind-cold symptoms at the early stage, such as serious aversion to cold and light fever, headache, body pain, thin and whitish tongue coating, and floating-tense pulse, indicating wind-cold affecting the superficies. wind-cold symptoms:风寒症;aversion to cold and light fever, headache, body pain, thin and whitish tongue coating, and floating-tense pulse:恶寒发热、头痛、身痛、舌苔薄白、浮脉紧。

⑥ Such a change is quite different from true-cold and false-heat syndrome in *yin* syndrome appearing like *yang* syndrome. 这种变化不同于阴证似阳中的真寒假热证。本句中such 指代前面的内容,appearing like 是分词短语作状语。

⑦ Loss of *yin* or *yang* also pertains to relative predomination and relative decline of *yin* and *yang*. 阴阳的流失也与阴阳的偏盛和偏衰有关。

⑧ over-:前缀,表示过多,过头,过分。例如本文中的 overwork:过度工作,over-rest:过度休息。

⑨ exuberant pathogenic heat:邪热盛。

⑩ ... because "separation of *yin* and *yang* exhausts essence". 因为阴阳分离会耗尽精气。

Exercises

Ⅰ. Fill in the blanks with the words given below. Change the form when necessary.

violent	maintain	originally	improper
various	pertain	scanty	obviously
sensation	indicate	severity	indistinct

1. The disease ranges widely in _____.
2. She _____ where I should go.
3. We're _____ going to need more help.
4. Britain wants to _____ its position as a world power.
5. She thought what I had done _____.
6. The _____ winds buried the village in sand.
7. The inspector was interested in everything _____ to the school.
8. The products we sell are _____.
9. She muttered something _____.
10. The book was _____ conceived as an autobiography, but it became a novel.
11. There is _____ evidence to support their accusations.
12. Seeing him again after so many years was a strange _____.

Ⅱ. Choose the best answer to each of the following questions or unfinished statements.

1. What will impair the balance between *yin* and *yang*?
   A. Proper diet.　　B. Overwork.　　C. Emotions.　　D. Climate.
2. Manifestations of *yang*-heat include the following EXCEPT _____.
   A. thirst　　　　B. slow pulse　　C. reddish tongue　D. high fever
3. Originally, disease is connected with _____.
   A. *yang*-heat　　　　　　　　　B. *yin*-cold
   C. *yin*-cold and *yang*-heat　　D. None of the above.
4. The word solitarily can mean _____.
   A. together　　　B. mutually　　C. only one　　D. each other
5. Which of the following statements is true according to the passage?
   A. *Yang*-heat and *yin*-cold cannot transform each other.
   B. If *yang* is lost, *yin* will be exhausted.
   C. High fever in *yin* syndrome is true-heat syndrome.
   D. Healthy *qi* can cause loss of *yang*.

Ⅲ. Translate the following sentences into English or Chinese.

1. 疾病的性质最初与阴寒有关。
2. 阴阳分离会耗尽精气。
3. 阳气与阴气的流失可以单独出现。
4. 你无法使铁变成金。
5. 卡车上发现了大量的武器。
6. The nature of the disease originally pertains to *yang*-heat.
7. Normally, *yin* and *yang* in the body maintain a dynamic balance.
8. I have an aversion to housework.
9. James has developed into a charming young man.
10. Our two sons are very different from each other.

Endocrine System（内分泌系统）

Root	Meaning	Examples
crin(o)- secret(o)-	secretion 分泌	endocrinology 内分泌学 endocrinid 内分泌性皮病 autocrine 自分泌 endocrinopathic 内分泌病的
thyr(o)-	thyroid 甲状腺	thyrotoxic 甲状腺毒性的 thyroxine 甲状腺素 thyroxinic 甲状腺素的 thyrotroph 促甲状腺细胞
pineal(o)-	pineal 松果体	pinealopathy 松果体病 pinealectomy 松果体切除术 pinealoma 松果体瘤 pinealocyte 松果体细胞
adren(o)-	adrenal 肾上腺	adrenochrome 肾上腺素红 adrenotoxin 肾上腺毒素 adrenotrophic 促肾上腺的 adrenopathy 肾上腺病
cortic(o)-	cortex 皮质	corticosterone 皮质酮 corticosteriod 皮质类固醇 corticotensin 皮质加压素 corticopontine 皮质脑桥的
thym(o)-	thymus 胸腺	thymin 胸腺激素 thymocyte 胸腺细胞 thymitis 胸腺炎 thymocrescin 胸腺生长激素
pitui- hypophys-	pituitary 垂体	pituitectomy 垂体切除术 pituicyte 垂体后叶细胞 hypophysitis 垂体炎 hypopituitarism 垂体机能减退
aden(o)-	gland 腺	adenosine 腺苷 adenous 腺的 adenyl 腺嘌呤 adenovirus 腺病毒
hypothalam(o)-	hypothalamus 下丘脑	hypothalamotomy 下丘脑切开术 hypothalamic 下丘脑的

续表

Root	Meaning	Examples
gonad(-)	gonad 性腺	gonadial 生殖腺的 gonadogenesis 性腺发育 gonadopathy 性腺病 gonadotrophin 促性腺激素

Unit 9 Four Diagnostic Techniques

Text A

Diagnostics of Traditional Chinese Medicine①

The basics of TCM diagnostics are: inspection, auscultation and olfaction, inquiry, pulse-taking and palpation.② Then a diagnosis is made using a system to classify the symptoms.

A modern cross that is not formal but in China TCM diagnosis is being very heavily influenced by and integrated with Western diagnostic thought moving towards total integration of the two systems.③ Modern practitioners often use the systems in combination to understand what is happening with the patient.

Because traditional Chinese medicine predates the more invasive④ medical testing used in conventional Western medicine, TCM requires skill in a range of diagnostic systems not commonly used outside of TCM. Much of this diagnostic skill involves developing the abilities to observe subtle appearances; to observe which is right in front of us, but escapes the observation of most people.

Diagnostic techniques contain the following aspects:
* Palpation of the patient's radial artery pulse in six positions⑤;
* Observation of the appearance of the patient's tongue;
* Observation of the patient's face;
* Palpation of the patient's body (especially the abdomen) for tenderness;
* Observation of the sound of the patient's voice;
* Observation of the surface of the ear;
* Observation of the vein on the index finger on young children⑥;
* Comparisons of the relative warmth or coolness of different parts of the body;
* Anything else that can be observed without instruments and without harming the patient.

The traditional treatment in Chinese medicine consists of six major methods: *tuina*, acupuncture, moxibustion, cupping, herbology, exercise like *qigong*, tai chi chuan, kung fu and other Chinese martial arts. *Dieda* practitioners specialize in healing trauma injury such as bone fractures, sprains, bruises, etc.⑦ Some of these specialists may also use or recommend other disciplines of Chinese medical therapies (or Western medicine in modern times) if serious injury is involved. These practices are also seen as health maintenance regimes as well as interventions.⑧

Traditional Chinese medicine uses herbs and other drugs as the last resort to fight health problems. This conforms to its basic belief: a human body has a sophisticated system to find illness, allocate resources and energy and heal the problems by itself.⑨ The goal of external efforts should carefully focus on assisting the normal self-healing function of human body, not interfering with it. There is a Chinese saying which reflects the same idea,"Any medicine has 30% poison ingredients."

The modern practice of traditional Chinese medicine is increasingly incorporating techniques and theories of Western medicine in its praxis.⑩

Since the founding of New China, Chinese government has attached great importance to traditional Chinese medicine and laid down a series of principles, policies and measures, aiming to develop traditional Chinese medicine, integrate it with Western medicine and modernize the traditional Chinese medicine. Quite a number of Chinese medical workers have carried out studies on traditional Chinese medicine with modern scientific knowledge and methods. They have also used combined Chinese and Western medical means in the treatment of a number of difficult and complicated cases, which have all shown satisfactory results. At the same time, many researchers have studied the basic theories of traditional Chinese medicine such as *yin* and *yang*, theory of *zang-fu*, channels and collaterals, *qi* and blood, the four diagnostic methods, the principles of *qigong* etc., with experimental research methods resulting in considerable progress.

In recent years, more and more people are interested in traditional Chinese medicine. They would like to accept its treatment. They are interested in learning its knowledge and technique to treat patients and studying why it works. Traditional Chinese medicine as a subject has been added into teaching plan in different famous medical colleges. Traditional Chinese medicine clinics and schools are everywhere in the world and increased continuously every year. With the present development of traditional Chinese medicine, its integration with modern science and technology will surely enhance its contribution to human health.

(679 words)

New Words

diagnostics /ˌdaɪəɡˈnɒstɪks/ n.   诊断学
classify /ˈklæsɪfaɪ/ vt.   把……分类,分为同一等级,说明,
       把……列为密件
symptom /ˈsɪmptəm/ n.   症状,表现,征兆,征候
predate /priːˈdeɪt/ v.   在日期上早于,提前日期

Unit 9 Four Diagnostic Techniques

invasive /ɪnˈveɪsɪv/ a.	侵入的,侵略性的,攻击性的
tenderness /ˈtendənɪs/ n.	触痛,压痛,对触摸或施压的异常敏感
artery /ˈɑːtəri/ n.	动脉,干线,要道,中枢
moxibustion /ˌmɒksɪˈbʌstʃən/ n.	艾灸,艾灼
trauma /ˈtrɔːmə/ n.	外伤,精神创伤
sprain /spreɪn/ n.	扭伤,(过度用力引起的)肿胀、炎症
bruise /bruːz/ n.	青肿,伤痕,擦伤(感情等方面的)创伤
discipline /ˈdɪsəplɪn/ n.	纪律,风纪,规定,训练,锻炼,修养,教养
regime /reɪˈʒiːm/ n.	政权,政治制度,食物疗法,养生法
resort /rɪˈzɔːt/ vi.	求助,依赖,诉诸,采取(某种手段等)
conform /kənˈfɔːm/ vi.	遵守,符合(to, with)
praxis /ˈpræksɪs/ n.	习惯,常规,实习,应用

Expressions

integrate with	与……结合
a range of	一系列,一类、批、组
resort to	求助,凭借,采取(手段等)
conform to	使一致,符合,适应
focus on	焦点,集中
attach importance to	认为……有(重要性等),把……归于
lay down	规定,制定(计划,规划,原则等)
a series of	一系列
carry out	实施,执行

Notes

① Diagnostics of Traditional Chinese Medicine:中医诊断学。
② The basics of TCM diagnostics are: inspection, auscultation and olfaction, inquiry, pulse-taking and palpation. 最基本的中医诊断有望、闻、问、切。
③ A modern cross that is not formal but in China TCM diagnosis is being very heavily influenced by and integrated with Western diagnostic thought moving towards total integration of the two systems. 这是一个现代化的跨越,不是正式的,但在我国,中医诊断深受西方诊断思想的影响,并与西方诊断观点渐趋完全融合。
④ invasive 可表示"扩散的""侵略的"。an invasive carcinoma:扩散性癌症;invasive war:侵略战争;invasive cancer cells:扩散了的癌细胞。
⑤ Palpation of the patient's radial artery pulse in six positions. 触诊患者的桡动脉脉搏的6个位置。radial artery:桡动脉。先经肱桡肌与旋前圆肌之间,继而在肱桡肌腱与桡侧腕屈肌腱之间下行,绕桡骨茎突至手背,穿第1掌骨间隙到手掌,与尺动脉掌深支吻合构成掌深弓。桡动脉下段仅被皮肤和筋膜遮盖,是临床触摸脉搏的部位。桡动脉在行

程中除发分支参与肘关节网和营养前臂肌外，主要分支是：①掌浅支，与尺动脉末端吻合成掌前弓。②拇主要动脉，分为3支，分布于拇指掌面两侧缘和示指桡侧缘。经过桡动脉的经络有"手太阴肺经"。本经共有11个穴位，其中9个穴位分布在上肢掌面桡侧，2个穴位在前胸上部，首穴中府、云门、天府、侠白、尺泽、孔最、列缺、经渠、太渊、鱼际、末穴少商。本经腧穴可主治呼吸系统和本经脉所经过部位的病症。例如，咳嗽、喘息、咯血、胸闷胸痛、咽喉肿痛、外感风寒及上肢内侧前缘疼痛等。

⑥ Observation of the vein on the index finger on young children. 观察小儿食指上的静脉脉象。

⑦ *Dieda* practitioners who specialize in healing trauma injury such as bone fractures, sprains, bruises, etc. 跌打医生擅长外伤治疗，如骨折、扭伤、淤伤等。

⑧ These practices are also seen as health maintenance regimes as well as interventions. 这些做法也被视为健康维护和干预。

⑨ This conforms to its basic belief: a human body has a sophisticated system to find illness, allocate resources and energy and heal the problems by itself. 这符合它的基本理念：人体是一个复杂的系统，它能自己发现疾病，分配资源和能量，并自我治疗。

⑩ The modern practice of traditional Chinese medicine is increasingly incorporating techniques and theories of Western medicine in its praxis. 现代中医学越来越多地融入了西医实践中的技术和理论。

Exercises

Ⅰ. Fill in the blanks with the words given below. Change the form when necessary.

diagnostics	practitioner	resort	invasive
palpation	bruise	artery	moxibustion
trauma	sprain	therapy	praxis

1. _____ is the application of heat resulting from the burning of a small bundle of tightly bound herbs, or moxa, to targeted acupoints. It is sometimes used along with acupuncture.
2. Inspection is a(n) _____ method that doctors learn the state of disease through visually observing relevant parts of the patients and their excrements and secretions.
3. They hope to create allies to unleash against diseases, pests, and _____ species.
4. She was a medical _____ before she entered politics.
5. He _____ his finger with a hammer.
6. The heart pumps blood out through one main _____ called the dorsal aorta.
7. The doctor said she should be given a physical _____.
8. Translation study undergoes a turning point from _____ philosophy to rational

Unit 9 Four Diagnostic Techniques

philosophy.
9. She _____ her ankle playing squash.
10. The phobia may have its root in a childhood _____.
11. _____ is a method of feeling with the fingers or hands during a physical examination. The health care provider touches and feels the patient's body to examine the size, consistency, texture, location, and tenderness of an organ or body part.
12. He couldn't have passed the exam without _____ to cheating.

II. Choose the best answer to each of the following questions or unfinished statements.

1. The basics of TCM diagnostics are _____.
   A. auscultation, olfaction, inquiry, pulse-taking and palpation
   B. inspection, auscultation and olfaction, inquiry, pulse-taking and palpation
   C. inspection, auscultation, olfaction, inquiry
   D. inspection, auscultation, pulse-taking and olfaction
2. Which of the following are NOT the traditional Chinese treatments?
   A. *Tuina*, moxibustion, cupping.
   B. Acupuncture, *qigong*, *tuina*.
   C. Surgery, injection, pharmacy.
   D. Acupuncture, cupping, herbology.
3. According to the passage, diagnostic techniques contain the following aspects EXCEPT _____.
   A. palpation of the patient's radial artery pulse in six positions
   B. observation of the patient's face
   C. observation of the surface of the ear
   D. observation of anything
4. Traditional Chinese medicine uses _____ as the last resort to fight health problems.
   A. herbs and needles   B. needles and other drugs
   C. herbs and other drugs   D. cupping and herbs
5. Which of the following statements is INCORRECT?
   A. *Yin* and *yang*, theory of *zang-fu*, channels and collaterals, *qi* and blood, the four diagnostic methods, the principles of *qigong* etc., are all basic theories of TCM.
   B. There is no need for TCM to integrate with modern science and technology to enhance its contribution to human health.
   C. A human body has a sophisticated system to find illness, allocate resources and energy and heal the problems by itself.
   D. Modern practitioners often use the modern systems in combination to understand what is happening with the patient.

Ⅲ. Translate the following sentences into English or Chinese.

1. 望、闻、问、切是最基本的传统中医诊断方法。
2. 应对健康问题时,不到万不得已,中医不主张使用草药和其他药物。
3. 中国有句谚语:"是药三分毒。"
4. 针对疑难病例,中西医结合的治疗方法取得了令人满意的疗效。
5. 繁重的工作安排使他不得不靠药物来维持精力。
6. Modern medicine has tended to focus too much on developing highly complicated surgical techniques.
7. The drug is effective against a range of bacteria.
8. The lamp conforms to new safety requirements.
9. Observation of the tongue is also known as tongue diagnosis, an important part of the observation.
10. Listening refers to the diagnostic method of identifying the sound of the voice, breathing, cough, etc.

Ⅳ. Write a 150-word composition on TCM diagnostics.

Text B

Diagnosis Methods in TCM

Diagnostic methods in traditional Chinese medicine include four basic methods: inspection, auscultation and olfaction, inquiry, pules-taking and palpation. The case history, symptoms, and signs gained through those four diagnostic methods are analyzed and generalized to find the causes, nature and interrelations of the disease, and to provide evidence for the further differentiation of syndromes.

Therapeutic Principles are the basis for guiding clinical practice. They include *biao* and *ben*, that is, the principle of treating a disease by analyzing both its root cause and symptoms.① Thus, factors such as climatic and seasonal conditions, geographic localities, and the patient's personal conditions must be considered in treatment, along with strengthening *zhengqi* and dispelling *xieqi*.

Unit 9　Four Diagnostic Techniques

1. The Principle of *Biao* and *Ben*

Biao and *ben* are contrasting concepts used to indicate the primary and secondary relationships of contradictory sides in various kinds of diseases and syndromes.② The principle of *biao* and *ben* is used in traditional Chinese medicine to treat the symptoms at the acute stage and to treat the root of disease at the chronic stage. If *biao* and *ben* have the same severity, treatment should then be applied to both *ben* (root cause) and *biao* (symptoms).

2. Strengthening *Zhengqi* and Dispelling *Xieqi*

Zhengqi is the ability of body resistance against disease. *Xieqi* are the pathogenic factors. Strengthening *zhengqi* and dispelling *xieqi* are two differing therapeutic principles. Generally, strengthening *zhengqi* is used where body resistance is weak and pathogenic factors are not strong; dispelling *xieqi* is applied to cases which have excessive pathogenic factors, and also an unweakened body resistance. Strengthening *zhengqi* and then dispelling *xieqi* are used in cases where *zhengqi* and *xieqi* are not weakened. The simultaneous strengthening of *zhengqi* and dispelling of *xieqi* is applied in cases of③ weak body resistance where pathogenic factors are in excess. When this principle is employed, one must differentiate between what is primary and what is secondary.④ In strengthening *zhengqi*, allowing for unforeseen pathogenic factors, and when dispelling pathogenic factors, do not influence the body resistance. It is necessary to make the principles of "strengthening body resistance" and "dispelling pathogenic factors" complement each other.

3. Principle of Treatment Based on Climatic and Seasonal Conditions, Geographic Localities, and Patient's Personal Conditions

Disease is the outcome of the struggle between body resistance and pathogenic factors. Therefore, in the treatment of a disease certain factors and conditions should be considered, that is⑤, time (seasonal and climatic conditions), place (geographical location and environment), and personal characteristics (living customs, age, sex and body constitution). In the clinical application of medicinal herbs these factors are also very important. This is an important therapeutic principle guiding clinical practice in traditional Chinese medicine.⑥ For example:

In summer, the surface pores on the body are open or loose, while in winter they are closed and tight. If the body is affected by the same exogenous pathogenic wind and cold both in summer and winter then pungent drugs having a warming property of relieving exterior syndromes should not be administrated in summer, but should be used in large dosage in winter. Because summer is humid, the pathogenic factors which cause diseases in this season always mix with damp. Therefore, medicinal herbs used for summer diseases should be combines with herbs having properties of dissolving or removing damp. The same disease, but with different sexes, different physiological characteristics, and different body constitutions should be treated accordingly.

Chinese medical theory, as a product of traditional Chinese culture, reflects an extraordinary sensitivity toward Nature. Throughout the world, traditional Chinese medicine is praised for its holistic attitude in the understanding and curing of disease. With a 2,000-year written tradition, Chinese medical culture has accumulated an impressive body of theoretical and practical experience.

(648 words)

New Words

generalize /ˈdʒenrəlaɪz/ v.	概括,归纳,推广,使一般化
locality /ləʊˈkælətɪ/ n.	地方,位置
contrasting /ˈkɒntrɑːstɪŋ/ a.	形成鲜明对比的,截然不同的
severity /sɪˈverətɪ/ n.	严格,严肃,严厉,猛烈
simultaneous /ˌsɪmlˈteɪnɪəs/ a.	同时的,同时发生的
differentiate /ˌdɪfəˈrenʃɪeɪt/ v.	区别,区分,鉴别
resistance /rɪˈzɪstəns/ n.	抵抗,反抗,抗性,抵抗力,耐性
pore /pɔː/ n.	毛孔,细孔
v.	注视,凝视,默想,沉思,钻研,熟读
pungent /ˈpʌdʒənt/ a.	苦痛的,严厉的,刺激性的
administrate /ədˈmɪnɪstreɪt/ v.	给予,经营,实施,掌管,料理
dissolving /dɪˈzɒlvɪŋ/ a.	消融的
sensitivity /ˌsensəˈtɪvətɪ/ n.	敏感,灵敏
accumulate /əˈkjuːmjəleɪt/ v.	积聚,累积,积攒

Expressions

provide for	提供
in excess	超出,超过
in the treatment of	在治疗……的过程中
be applied to	应用于,运用于
be affected by	受……的影响
be combined with	与……联合
be praised for	因……而受到表扬

Notes

① They include *biao* and *ben*, that is, the principle of treating a disease by analyzing both its root cause and symptoms. 它们包括标和本,即遵循通过分析疾病的根本原因和症状而进行治疗的原则。

② *Biao* and *ben* are contrasting concepts used to indicate the primary and secondary

Unit 9 Four Diagnostic Techniques

relationships of contradictory sides in various kinds of diseases and syndromes. 标和本是截然不同的概念，被用来表明各种疾病和症状方面的主次关系。

③ in cases of：在……的情况下。例如：The company only dismisses its employees in cases of gross misconduct. 公司仅在雇员严重失职的情形下才予以解雇。

④ When this principle is employed, one must differentiate between what is primary and what is secondary. 应用这一原则时，必须区分什么是主要的，什么是次要的。

⑤ that is：那就是，也就是说。例如：We'll meet you in a week, that is, on March 1st. 我们一星期后见，也就是3月1号那天见。

⑥ This is an important therapeutic principle guiding clinical practice in traditional Chinese medicine. 这是一个重要的指导中医临床实践的治疗原则。

Exercises

I. Fill in the blanks with the words given below. Change the form when necessary.

inspection	auscultation	olfaction	inquiry
locality	severity	simultaneous	differentiate
pore	sensitivity	administrate	dosage

1. A medical _____ is a thorough visual examination of the physical body. It is typically performed by a medical professional, like a physician or a nurse.
2. _____ is the act of listening to sounds arising within organs (as the lungs) as an aid to diagnosis and treatment.
3. The four diagnostic methods refer to inspection, auscultation and _____, inquiry and palpation.
4. The two _____ shots sounded like one.
5. Bioavailability is the proportion of a(n) _____ drug that reaches the systemic circulation and is therefore available for distribution to the intended site of action.
6. This is a matter of great _____.
7. It was the _____ of the crime.
8. The disease ranges widely in _____.
9. This facial wash cleans clogged _____ of dirt and oil that can cause blemishes.
10. The recommended _____ is one tablet every four hours.
11. Chief complaint and history of present illness are the main aspects included in _____ and are important for diagnosis, treatment and syndrome differentiation.
12. It's wrong to _____ between boys and girls.

Ⅱ. Choose the best answer to each of the following questions or unfinished statements.

1. What are analyzed and generalized to find the causes of the disease?
   A. *Biao* and *ben*.   B. The case history, symptoms and signs.
   C. The *zhengqi* and the *xieqi*.   D. The symptoms.

2. Which one of the following is not the factor considered in treatment?
   A. Climatic and seasonal conditions.   B. Pathogenic factors.
   C. Geographic localities.   D. The patient's personal conditions.

3. Which statement is NOT true?
   A. The principle of *biao* and *ben* is used to treat the symptoms at the acute stage.
   B. The principle of *biao* and *ben* is used to treat the root of disease at the chronic stage.
   C. Disease is the outcome of the struggle between body resistance and pathogenic factors.
   D. *Zhengqi* and *xieqi* are the pathogenic factors.

4. Medicinal herbs used for summer diseases should be combined with _____.
   A. herbs having a warming property of relieving exterior syndromes
   B. herbs strengthening *zhengqi*
   C. herbs having properties of dissolving or removing damp
   D. herbs dispelling *xieqi*

5. According to the passage, disease results from _____.
   A. the struggle between body resistance and pathogenic factors
   B. weak body resistance
   C. having excessive pathogenic factors
   D. bad climatic conditions

Ⅲ. Translate the following sentences into English or Chinese.

1. 通过对这四种方法得出的病史、症状、信息进行分析和总结，以发现疾病的原因、本质和内在联系。

2. 治疗准则是指导临床实践的基础。

3. 治疗过程中必须考虑到气候、季节条件、地理位置和病人的个人情况。

4. 疾病是身体抵抗力和致病因素之间斗争的结果。

5. 夏季，身体表面毛孔都处于张开或松散状态。

6. *Zhengqi* is the ability of body resistance against disease.

7. The principle of *biao* and *ben* is used in traditional Chinese medicine to treat the symptoms at the acute stage.

8. Medicinal herbs used for summer diseases should be combined with herbs having

Unit 9 Four Diagnostic Techniques

properties of removing damp.
9. Diagnosis by smelling includes smelling odor of the body, and the odor of the bodily secretions, including breath, sputum, nasal discharge, sweat, blood, urine and stools.
10. Inquiry is a way to interview the patient, his or her accompanies to know the history and condition of a disease.

 **Text C**

Listening to Sounds

Listening and olfaction means listening to various sounds and noises made by the patient and smelling the odor and excreta from the body of the patient so as to understand the pathological conditions of the patient. Since various sounds and noises as well as odor all come from the activities of the viscera, listening to sounds and smelling odors are helpful for examining the morbid conditions of the viscera. ①

Listening to Sounds

Voice is produced by vibration of air in the cavity and tube organs. ② The voice made in the mouth is in close relation to the lung, throat, epiglottis, tongue, teeth, lips and nose. All kinds of voice (sounds) are made by means of the activities of the lung and the lung governs *qi* and respiration. That is why the ancient people believed that "the lung is the governor of *qi* and the kidney is the root of *qi*③" "the lung is the door of voice" and "the kidney is the root of voice"④. Since the pathological changes of the other viscera may affect the functions of the lung and the kidney in producing sounds and because the other viscera are under the domination of the heart spirit, listening to sounds not only can examine the conditions of the organs directly related to voice, but also further diagnose visceral disease according to the changes of voice (sounds).

Speech

In listening to speech, cares should be made to detect whether the speech is strong or weak, whether the words are coherent and whether the expression is clear and fluent. ⑤ The speech of normal people is natural in pronunciation, smooth in tone, clear in expression and consistent in words. Since the viscera, constitution and physical building are different from person to person, the voice is either high or low, loud or small and clear or full. For example, male voice is low and full, female voice is high and clear, children's voice is sharp and melodious, and voice of the aged is low and deep. ⑥ Generally speaking, high and sonorous voice in healthy people is a manifestation of sufficiency of primordial *qi* and pulmonary *qi*.

There is close relation between speech and emotions. For example, the voice in joy is lively and cheerful, the voice in rage is stern and quick, the voice in sorrow is sad and disjointed. These are the normal changes of voice.

Voice

The abnormal changes of voice are either strong or weak, heavy or deep, hoarseness or aphonia.

Strong and weak voice: Generally speaking, sonorous voice with restlessness and polylogia indicates sthenia syndrome and heat syndrome⑦; low, weak and disjointed voice with quietness and oligologia indicates asthenia syndrome and cold syndrome.

Deep and heavy voice: Deep and heavy voice is usually caused by failure of pulmonary *qi* to disperse and obstruction of the nose due to exogenous pathogenic wind, cold and dampness, or by obstruction of the airway due to stagnation of dampness.

Hoarseness and aphonia: Hoarseness means harsh voice, while aphonia means complete loss of voice. Hoarseness is similar to aphonia in pathogenesis. If hoarseness is very serious, it will develop into aphonia. Hoarseness or aphonia in new disease pertains to sthenia syndrome due to exogenous pathogenic factors attacking on the lung or due to failure of the pulmonary *qi* to disperse resulting from stagnation of phlegm. Such a pathological condition is known as "a solid bell cannot ring (dysphonia or hoarseness due to sthenia syndrome of the lung)". Hoarseness or aphonia in a chronic disease pertains to asthenia syndrome due to exhaustion of fluid and impairment of the lung caused by asthenia of lung and kidney *yin* and asthenia-fire scorching metal (lung). Such a pathological condition is known as "a broken bell cannot ring (hoarseness due to impaired function of the lung)". Hoarseness or aphonia may be caused by prolonged speaking or singing or shouting with rage, which impairs beth *qi* and *yin* and deprives the throat of moisture. Hoarseness at the advanced stage of pregnancy is due to pressure of the fetus on the uterine collaterals which obstructs the kidney meridian and prevents kidney essence to be transported to the upper.⑧ It will heal automatically after delivery.

Delirium: Delirium means raving with high and sonorous voice in coma⑨. Such a morbid condition pertains to sthenia syndrome due to heat disturbing the mind seen in invasion of pathogenic factors into the pericardium in seasonal febrile disease or sthenia syndrome of *yangming fu*-organ.⑩

Slurred Speech

Slurred speech is marked by unclear and slow expression without fluency, usually seen in wind stroke or sequela of wind stroke. It is due to obstruction of the collaterals by wind-phlegm and malnutrition of the tongue musculature and vessels, which make the tongue inflexible. Slurred speech at the advanced stage of febrile disease is due to heat consuming *yin* and malnutrition of the tongue.

(803 words)

Unit 9 Four Diagnostic Techniques

New Words

odor /ˈəʊdə/ n.	（尤指不好的）气味,名声
fluent /ˈfluːənt/ a.	流利的,流畅的,液态的,畅流的
cavity /ˈkævətɪ/ n.	洞,穴,凹处
visceral /ˈvɪsərəl/ a.	内脏的,出于本能的,发自肺腑的,粗俗的
pregnancy /ˈpregnənsɪ/ n.	怀孕
detect /dɪˈtekt/ vt.	发现,察觉,查出,看穿
coherent /kəʊˈhɪərənt/ a.	一致的,协调的
aphonia /æˈfəʊnjə/ n.	（耳鼻喉）失音,不能发音
melodious /məˈləʊdɪəs/ a.	旋律优美的,悦耳动听的
consistent /kənˈsɪstənt/ a.	始终如一的,一致的
stern /stɜːn/ a.	严厉的,坚定的
deprive /dɪˈpraɪv/ vt.	使丧失,剥夺
uterin /ˈjuːtərɪn/ n.	子宫
restlessness /ˈrestləsnəs/ n.	坐立不安,心神不宁
febrile /ˈfiːbraɪl/ a.	[医]热病的,发烧的
inflexible /ɪnˈfleksəbl/ a.	不可改变的,不容变更的,不屈不挠的
sequela /sɪˈkwiːlə/ n.	[医]后遗症,结果,后继者

Expressions

so as to	以便
be helpful for	对……有益
by means of	借助于,通过
known as	被认为是,以……著称
attacking on	攻击
at the stage o f	在……阶段

Notes

① Since various sounds and noises as well as odor all come from the activities of the viscera, listening to sounds and smelling odors are helpful for examining the morbid conditions of the viscera. 由于各种声音和气味都源于脏腑的活动,所以听声音和闻气味对检查脏腑的状况很有用途。

② Voice is produced by vibration of air in the cavity and tube organs. 声音是空气在空腔性器官里的震动而产生的。

③ the lung is the governor of qi and the kidney is the root of *qi*: 肺为气之主,肾为气之根。

④ … "the lung is the door of voice" and "the kidney is the root of voice": 声音出于肺而根于肾。

⑤ In listening to speech, cares should be made to detect whether the speech is strong or weak, whether the words are coherent and whether the expression is clear and fluent. 听声音,应当注意语音的强弱,话语是否连贯,表达是否清晰、流利。

⑥ Male voice is low and full, female voice is high and clear, children's voice is sharp and melodious, and voice of the aged is low and deep. 男性声音低沉而充实,女性声音则高亢而清晰,孩子们的声音尖利又悦耳,老人的声音低沉且深邃。

⑦ Generally speaking, sonorous voice with restlessness and polylogia indicates sthenia syndrome and heat syndrome. 总的说来,患者若语声洪亮、言语过多则为实证和热证。

⑧ Hoarseness at the advanced stage of pregnancy is due to pressure of the fetus on the uterine collaterals which obstructs the kidney meridian and prevents kidney essence to be transported to the upper. 怀孕后期声音嘶哑是由于胎儿对胞脉形成的压力,阻塞了足少阴肾经,也阻碍了肾精向上传输。

⑨ Delirium means raving with high and sonorous voice in coma. 谵语指神志不清时声高有力且语无伦次。

⑩ Such a morbid condition pertains to sthenia syndrome due to heat disturbing the mind seen in invasion of pathogenic factors into the pericardium in seasonal febrile disease or sthenia syndrome of *yangming fu*-organ. 这种情况见于温病中实热扰乱心神或者阳明腑实证。

Exercises

Ⅰ. **Fill in the blanks with the words given below. Change the form when necessary.**

odor	detect	coherent	disperse
melodious	stern	deprive	inflexible
restlessness	visceral	consistent	delirium

1. She always makes _____ demands of herself.
2. In his _____ the man talked nonsense.
3. The flowers gave off a fragrant _____.
4. The leisurely and _____ music took us to fairyland.
5. Small quantities of alcohol were _____ in the driver's blood.
6. Door-to-door service is the _____ style of our shop.
7. The spread of television have considerably _____ us of our time for read.
8. These signals move our body parts, control our heartbeats and other _____ functions, and give us sensation.
9. Worshippers threw stones, bottles and trash and police fired stun grenades and tear gas to _____ the crowd.
10. These two paragraphs are not _____ enough.

11. A great man is always one who has a firm resolution and a(n) _____ spirit.
12. From the audience came increasing sounds of _____.

II. Choose the best answer to each of the following questions.

1. According to the passage, where are the various sound and odor of people from?
   A. Vibration of air in the cavity.　　B. Visceral activities.
   C. The activities of the lung.　　　　D. Sthenia syndrome.
2. What does the underlined word "sonorous" mean in Para. 9?
   A. Sorrowful.　　B. Hoarse.　　C. Ringing.　　D. Cheerful.
3. Which one of the following are NOT TCM thought?
   A. Lung governs "qi".　　　　　　　B. Qi takes root in kidney.
   C. The lung is the door of voice.　　D. Kidney originates from voice.
4. Which one of the following is INCORRECT?
   A. Weak and disjointed voice with oligologia indicates asthenia syndrome and cold syndrome.
   B. Normal people speak smoothly and clearly.
   C. Deep and heavy voice appears due to the failure of pulmonary qi to spread and prevention of the nose.
   D. Because we are healthy, the voice of us will keep constant.
5. What will NOT cause the hoarseness or aphonia?
   A. Prolonged speaking.　　　　　　B. The advanced stage of pregnancy.
   C. Singing or shouting with anger.　 D. Heat disturbing the mind.

III. Translate the following sentences into English or Chinese.

1. 闻诊之听声音，即听患者发出的各种声音。
2. 由于人与人之间的脏腑器官及体质各有不同，人的声音亦有高低、大小、清晰和饱满与否之差异。
3. 嘶哑意味着声音粗糙刺耳，而失音就意味着声音完全失去了。
4. 语言含糊的特点是表达不流利，不清晰，语速慢，这些在中风或者中风的后遗症中可见。
5. 这样的病态和实证有关。
6. The speech of normal people is natural in pronunciation, smooth in tone, clear in expression and consistent in words.
7. Generally speaking, high and sonorous voice in healthy people is a manifestation of sufficiency of primordial qi and pulmonary qi.
8. Hoarseness or aphonia in new disease pertains to sthenia syndrome due to exogenous pathogenic factors.

9. The sound of voice not only reflects the prosperity or decline of healthy *qi*, but also relates to the nature of pathogens.
10. Generally speaking, a loud and coarse voice together with talkativeness and irritability is indicative of a sthenia syndrome.

Nervous System（神经系统）

Root	Meaning	Examples
encephal(o)-	brain 脑	encephalauxe 脑肥大 encephalion 小脑 encephalitic 脑炎的 encephalitis 脑炎
cerebr(o)-	cerebrum 大脑	cerebropathy 脑病 cerebropontile 大脑桥的 cerebrosclerosis 脑硬化 cerebral 大脑的
mening(o)-	membrane 脑膜,脊膜	meningoma 脑(脊)膜瘤 meningomyelitis 脊髓脊膜炎 meningeal 脑(脊)膜的 meningocele 脑(脊)膜突出
ventricul(o)-	ventricle 脑室	ventriculomegaly 巨脑室 ventricular 脑室的 ventriculostomy 脑室切开术 ventriculostium 脑室瘘
spin(o)-	spine 脊柱	spinal 脊柱的 spinitis 脊髓炎 spinogram 脊柱 X 线照片 spinothalamic 脊髓丘脑的
cerebell(o)-	cerebellum 小脑	cerebello-olivary 小脑橄榄体的 cerebellar 小脑的 cerebellofugal 小脑传出的

续表

Root	Meaning	Examples
medull(o)-	marrow 髓质	medullary 骨髓的,髓质的 medullitis 骨髓炎 medulloencephalic 脑脊髓的 medullotherapy 脊髓疗法
ax(o)-	axon 轴突	axoaxonic 轴轴突触的 axolysis 神经轴分解 axolemma 轴膜 axopodia 轴伪足
dendr(o)-	dendrite 树突	axodendritic 轴树突触的 dendritic 树突的 dendrodendritic 树状树突触的 dendron 树突
neur(o)-	nerve	neurology 神经病学 neurokinin 神经激肽 neurotmesis 神经断伤 neuroscience 神经科学

Unit 10　Differentiation of Syndromes

Text A

TCM Differential Diagnosis

The traditional Chinese medical is featured by such treatment based on pathogenesis obtained through differentiation of symptoms and signs as its essence. It is necessary to differentiate disease and constitutes a special procedure of research and treatment in traditional Chinese diagnosis. Based on such treatment and diagnosis, a traditional Chinese medicine practitioner can prescribe drugs, identify and treat diseases. "*Zheng*" is a kind of pathology of the disease development of a body in a certain stage, including the disease wherefrom, the cause, the feature and the conflicts between healthy energy and evils.① It reflects the nature of pathological change at a certain stage, and reveals the intrinsic quality of disease more completely, profoundly, and accurately than symptoms, e. g. , excessive rising of liver-*yang*, damp invasion of lower energizer. Another "*zheng*" should be clarified and refers to symptoms, such as fever, headache, yellow tongue coat and pulse.②

The diagnosis is to differentiate a disease by analyzing and synthesizing the information, symptoms, patients' physical status collected through such four diagnostic methods as inspection, auscultation and olfaction, inquiry, puke-taking and palpation.③ In terms of "*zhi*" is to decide the treatment.④ The traditional Chinese medicine first focuses on the "*zheng*", not on differences of the disease. So, of a disease with different symptoms may be treated in different methods; while different diseases with the same symptom may be cured in the same way⑤, which is "Heterotherapy for Hoemopathy⑥, Homeotherapy for Heteropathy". Such different methods for the contradictions of different quality in the process of disease development is the essence of determination of treatment based in pathogenesis obtained through differentiation of symptoms and signs.

Differential diagnosis and treatment is to identify different "*zheng*" of the traditional Chinese medicine for flexible treatment according to different symptoms of patients. The traditional Chinese medicine can give prominence to "flexibility" with the differential diagnosis and treatment which requires the traditional Chinese medicine practitioners to keep dynamic human disease under control in the dynamic universe, and to use the theory

Unit 10　Differentiation of Syndromes

of harmony between man and the nature and the theory of differential diagnosis and treatment to accurately grasp the best balance point between human body and the nature, as well as to ingeniously balance *yin* and *yang* of the body to change the disease into nothing. With the flexibility and creativity, diseases can be treated through the differential diagnosis and treatment even if there is no accurate name. Therefore, as for known and unknown diseases, treatment programs can be worked out for timely curing as long as symptoms are available, which is the most significant feature of the traditional Chinese medicine.

Commonly-used clinical methods for differential diagnosis and treatment are as follows: syndrome-differentiation by eight principles, differentiation of *qi*-blood-body fluid, differentiation of *zang* and *fu*, syndrome-differentiation of the six meridians, differentiation of the development of a seasonal febrile disease by studying the four stages: *wei*, *qi*, *ying* and *xue*, syndrome differentiation of triple energizer, differentiation of syndromes of meridian.⑦

Yin and *yang* are the principles for categorizing diseases and also the leading ones in the eight principles.⑧ Syndrome differentiation of *yin* and *yang* are used in two aspects: differentiating *yin* syndrome and *yang* syndrome; differentiating *yin* asthenia and *yang* asthenia as well as *yin* sthenia and *yang* sthenia.⑨

The eight principles concentrate on specific syndromes respectively. However, they are inseparable and not static. Among the eight principles, *yin* and *yang* are the general principles which can be used to generalize the other six principles, i. e. external, heat and sthenia are of *yang*; while internal, cold and asthenia are of *yin*. The syndromes of the eight principles are often complicated, transformable and intermingled. Sometimes there're false manifestations.⑩ Therefore, clinical differentiation of syndromes should concentrate both on the difference of the syndromes related to the eight principle respectively and their close relationship so as to have a comprehensive cognition of the disease.

(719 words)

New Words

conflict /kɒnˈflɪkt/ *vi.* 　　　　　冲突,矛盾,斗争,争执
intrinsic /ɪnˈtrɪnsɪk/ *a.* 　　　　　本质的,固有的
timely /ˈtaɪmlɪ/ *a.* 　　　　　　　及时的,适时的
excessive /ɪkˈsesɪv/ *a.* 　　　　　过多的,极度的,过分的
static /ˈstætɪk/ *a.* 　　　　　　　静态的,[物]静电的,静力的
intermingle /ˌɪntəˈmɪŋgl/ *vt.* 　　使混合,使掺和
significant /sɪgˈnɪfɪkənt/ *a.* 　　重大的,有效的,有意义的,值得注意的
clarify /ˈklærəfaɪ/ *vt.* 　　　　　澄清,阐明

profoundly /prəˈfaʊndlɪ/ *ad.*	深刻地,深深地,极度地
synthesize /ˈsɪnθəsaɪz/ *vt.*	合成,综合
grasp /ɡrɑːsp/ *vt.*	抓住,领会
n.	抓住,理解,控制
internal /ɪnˈtɜːnl/ *a.*	内部的,内在的,国内的
categorize /ˈkætəɡəraɪz/ *vt.*	分类

Expressions

be featured by	以……为特点
in the process of	在……过程中
as for	至于
work out	解决,算出,实现
concentrate on	集中注意于
in terms of	就……而言

Notes

① "*Zheng*" is a kind of pathology of the disease development of a body in a certain stage, including the disease wherefrom, the cause, the feature and the conflicts between healthy energy and evils. "证"是疾病不同阶段和不同类型的病机概括,包括病源、病因、疾病特点、正邪相争情况。

② Another "*zheng*" should be clarified and refers to symptoms, such as fever, headache, yellow tongue coat and pulse. 另外一个"症"指的是症状,比如发热、头疼、舌苔黄及其相应的脉象。

③ The diagnosis is to differentiate a disease by analyzing and synthesizing the information, symptoms, patients' physical status collected through such four diagnostic methods as inspection, auscultation and olfaction, inquiry, pulse-taking and palpation. 通过四种诊断方法:望、闻、问、切了解到病人的身体状况,再加上分析整合信息,就可以诊断病情。

④ In terms of "*zhi*"(治) is to decide the treatment. "治"即治疗方法。

⑤ So, of a disease with different symptoms may be treated in different methods; while different diseases with the same symptom may be cured in the same way. 所以,不同症状的同一疾病其治疗方法未必相同,而相同症状的不同疾病却又可以用同一种治疗方法。

⑥ Homeopathy:顺势疗法,其理论基础是"同样的制剂治疗同类疾病",意思是为了治疗某种疾病,需要使用一种能够在健康人中产生相同症状的药剂。例如,毒性植物颠茄(也被称为莨菪)能够导致一种搏动性的头痛、高热和面部潮红。因此,顺势疗法药剂颠茄就用来治疗那些发热和存在突发性搏动性头痛的病人。

⑦ Commonly-used clinical methods for differential diagnosis and treatment are as follows: syndrome-differentiation by eight principles, differentiation of *qi*-blood-body fluid,

Unit 10　Differentiation of Syndromes

differentiation of *zang* and *fu*, syndrome-differentiation of the six meridians, differentiation of the development of a seasonal febrile disease by studying the four stages: *wei*, *qi*, *ying* and *xue*, syndrome differentiation of triple energizer, differentiation of syndromes of meridian. 通常所用的辨证方法有以下几种：八纲辨证、气血津液辩证、脏腑辨证、六经辨证、卫气营血辨证、三焦辨证和经络辨证。

⑧ *Yin* and *yang* are the principles for categorizing diseases and also the leading ones in the eight principles. 阴阳为八纲辨证之总纲。

⑨ Syndrome differentiation of *yin* and *yang* are used in two aspects: differentiating *yin* syndrome and *yang* syndrome; differentiating *yin* asthenia and *yang* asthenia as well as *yin* sthenia and *yang* sthenia. 阴阳辩证主要是辨别阴证和阳证，阴虚和阳虚，阴盛和阳盛。

⑩ The syndromes of the eight principles are often complicated, transformable and intermingled. Sometimes there're false manifestations. 疾病症状通常表现得错综复杂，甚至有假象存在。

Exercises

Ⅰ. Fill in the blanks with the words given below. Change the form when necessary.

synthesize	respectively	prescribe	dynamic
internal	static	grasp	clinical
intrinsic	excessive	clarify	profoundly

1. For medical student, diagnostic practice is the first step of _____ study.
2. Unfortunately, the resulting literature has done little to _____ the basic problem.
3. Within days, two of the G20 countries, Russia and India, raised tariffs on cars and steel _____.
4. What they manage to smoothly do is _____ it all into a formula that makes sense.
5. _____ noise can gradually destroy hearing.
6. Civilization does not remain _____, but changes constantly.
7. You have a natural and _____ talent and skill.
8. To do that, one must have a good _____ of the concepts.
9. Embracing globalization, London has become one of the most _____ cities in the world.
10. Please _____ some medicine for the burn.
11. We Chinese were opposed to be interfered with _____ affairs.
12. These difficulties are _____ to such a situation.

II. **Choose the best answer to each of the following questions or unfinished statements.**

1. Traditional Chinese medicine practitioner prescribes drugs based on _____.
   A. patients' complaint   B. patients' symptoms
   C. diagnosis   D. *yin* and *yang*

2. About the example "*zheng*"(证), which statement is NOT true?
   A. *Zheng* is a kind of pathology of the disease development of a body in a certain stage.
   B. *Zheng* reveals the intrinsic quality of disease.
   C. It reflects the nature of pathological change at a certain stage.
   D. *Zheng* includes the disease wherefrom, the cause, the feature and the conflicts between healthy energy and evils.

3. Which one of the following is INCORRECT?
   A. Analyzing and synthesizing the information is a necessary step in the diagnosis.
   B. Different diseases with the same symptom are always cured similarly.
   C. Traditional Chinese medicine don't emphasize on differences of the disease.
   D. The traditional Chinese medicine first focuses on the "*zhi*".

4. From the paragraph 3, we can know that _____.
   A. diseases can't be treated through the diagnosis and treatment if there is no accurate name
   B. the traditional Chinese medicine can stress "flexibility" with the differential diagnosis
   C. treatment programs must be worked out in time curing as long as symptoms are available
   D. differential diagnosis and treatment is to identify different "*zheng*" according to eight principles

5. Clinical differentiation of syndromes should concentrate on two aspects, because _____.
   A. we can't easily make a conclusion only in terms of one aspect
   B. eight principles concentrate on specific syndromes respectively
   C. syndromes may have false manifestation
   D. *yin* and *yang* are the principles for categorizing diseases

III. **Translate the following sentences into English or Chinese.**

1. 八纲中,阴和阳是总纲,可以用来指导其他六纲。
2. 虚证常常与慢性疾病有关。
3. 基于这样的辨证,中医可以进行对疾病作出诊断、治疗和开方。
4. 传统中医首先关注的是"证",而不是在于疾病的区别。
5. 在中医诊断中,辨证是非常必要的。
6. The more one understands disease mechanisms, the easier it is to accurately and

Unit 10   Differentiation of Syndromes

efficiently make syndrome differentations.

7. The symptoms of disease, though intricate, can be analyzed with the eight principles according to the category, location and nature of disease.

8. The differentiation of the asthenia and sthenia syndromes is relatively simple.

9. Among the eight principles, *yin* and *yang* are a generalization of the other six principles since the exterior, heat and sthenia are *yang* and the interior, cold and asthenia are *yin* in nature.

10. The exterior and interior are the principles that describe the location, serious condition and tendency of a disease.

IV. Write a 150-word composition to introduce the general history of syndrome differentiation with what you have learnt in TCM class.

 Text B

Syndrome Differentiation of Spleen Diseases[①]

Spleen diseases mainly marked by dysfunction of the spleen to transport, transform and govern blood. The clinical symptoms are usually poor appetite, abdominal distension or pain, loose stool, dropsy, heaviness of limbs, prolapse of the viscera and bleeding, etc.

Spleen disease is either asthenic or sthenic.[②] Asthenic spleen disease is mainly caused by improper diet, irregular daily life, excessive vomiting and diarrhea as well as other acute or chronic diseases which impair the spleen and lead to such problems like asthenia of splenic *qi*, asthenia of splenic yang, sinking of *qi* due to splenic asthenia and failure of the spleen to govern blood; sthenic spleen disease is caused by improper diet or intake of contaminated food or exogenous cold dampness or internal invasion of damp heat which leads to cold dampness encumbering the spleen and accumulation of damp heat in the spleen, etc.

Syndrome of Asthenia of Splenic *Qi*

Syndrome of asthenia of splenic *qi* refers to the syndrome due to asthenia of splenic *qi* and failure of transportation and transformation, usually caused by improper diet, overstrain and impairment of splenic *qi* by chronic and acute diseases.

Clinical manifestations: Poor appetite, abdominal distension, especially after meal, loose stool, or dry feces followed by loose stool, lack of *qi*, no desire to speak, lassitude of limbs, sallow complexion, emaciation, or dropsy, pale tongue with whitish fur, slow and weak pulse, usually seen in chronic gastritis, digestive ulceration, chronic enteritis and mal-absorption syndrome, etc.③

Analysis of Symptoms: Poor appetite and abdominal distension are due to asthenia of splenic *qi*④, failure of transportation and transformation, weakness to digest, absorb and transport cereal nutrient; aggravation of abdominal distension after meal is due to aggravation of stagnancy of splenic qi after meal; loose stool "or dry feces followed by loose stool are due to downward migration of dampness into the large intestine resulting from failure of the spleen to transform dampness; lack of *qi* and no desire to speak⑤ are due to failure of transportation and transformation resulting from asthenia as well as insufficiency of gastrosplenic *qi*⑥.

Syndrome of Asthenia of Splenic *Yang*

Syndrome of asthenia of splenic yang refers to the syndrome due to asthenia of splenic *yang* and internal exuberance of *yin* cold. This syndrome is caused by further development of the asthenia of splenic *qi*; or by excessive intake of uncooked or cold food; or by asthenia of splenic yang and failure of fire (heart) to generate (promote) earth (spleen).

Clinical Manifestations: Poor appetite, abdominal distension, lingering abdominal cold pain, preference for warmth and palpation, aversion to cold, cold sensation of four limbs, light whitish complexion, bland taste in the mouth without thirst, loose stool, or stool with indigested food, heaviness of limbs, or dropsy of limbs, dysuria, profuse and thin leukorrhagia⑦, pale, bulgy and tender tongue, or tongue with tooth prints, whitish slippery fur⑧, sunken, slow and weak pulse. Such manifestations are usually seen in chronic gastritis, digestive ulceration, chronic enteritis, mal-absorption syndrome.

Analysis of Symptoms: Poor appetite and abdominal distension are due to asthenia of splenic *yang* and failure of transportation and transformation; lingering abdominal cold pain, preference for warmth and palpation are due to asthenia of *yang* and exuberance of *yin*, internal generation of cold as well as cold coagulation and qi stagnation; bland taste in the mouth without thirst and loose stool, or even stool with indigested food are due to failure of splenic *yang* to warm and transport food because of asthenia; aversion to cold, cold sensation of limbs and light whitish complexion are due to failure of *yang* to warm because of asthenia; heaviness of limbs, even general edema and dysuria are due to inactivation of gastrosplenic *yang*, internal retention of dampness and extravasation of dampness; profuse and thin leukorrhagia is due to asthenia of splenic *yang*, weakness of belt vessel and downward migration of dampness; pale, bulgy and tender tongue, or tongue with tooth prints, whitish slippery pulse, as well as sunken, slow and weak pulse are signs of *yang* asthenia and internal exuberance of *yin* cold.

Syndrome of Sinking of Splenic *Qi*

Syndrome of sinking of splenic *qi* refers to the syndrome due to asthenia of splenic *qi*

Unit 10　Differentiation of Syndromes

and failure of splenic *qi* to rise. This syndrome is mainly caused by further development of asthenia of splenic *qi*; or by chronic diarrhea or dysentery, or overstrain; or by multiple delivery and improper nursing after labor which over consume splenic *qi*.

　　Clinical Manifestations: Prolapsing sensation and distension of epigastrium and abdomen②, especially after meal, frequent desire for defecation, prolapsing sensation of anus, or chronic diarrhea, or even prolapse of rectum, or prolapse of uterus, or turbid urine, accompanied by lack of *qi*, fatigue, lassitude of limbs, low voice or no desire to speak, dizziness, pale tongue with whitish fur and weak pulse. Such manifestations are usually seen in chronic gastritis, digestive ulceration, chronic enteritis③, malabsorption syndrome.

(813 words)

New Words

prolapse /prəʊˈlæps/ *vi.*	脱垂,下垂
n.	脱垂,下垂
dysuria /dɪsˈjʊərɪə/ *n.*	[泌尿]排尿困难
intake /ˈɪnteɪk/ *n.*	摄取量,通风口,引入口,引入的量
contaminated /kənˈtæmɪneɪtɪd/ *a.*	受污染的,弄脏的
encumber /ɪnˈkʌmbə/ *vt.*	阻塞,妨害,拖累
lassitude /ˈlæsɪtjuːd/ *n.*	疲乏,懒散,厌倦
sallow /ˈsæləʊ/ *a.*	气色不好的,灰黄色的
digestive /daɪˈdʒestɪv/ *a.*	消化的,助消化的
n.	助消化药
bland /blænd/ *a.*	乏味的,温和的,冷漠的
vt.	使……变得淡而无味,除掉……的特性
slippery /ˈslɪpərɪ/ *a.*	滑的,狡猾的,不稳定的
exuberance /ɪɡˈzjuːbərəns/ *n.*	丰富,茂盛,健康
gastrosplenic /ˌɡæstrəʊˈsplenɪk/ *a.*	[医]胃脾的

Expressions

lead to	导致,通向
caused by	由……造成
after meal	吃完饭后

Expressions

① Spleen Diseases: 脾病。脾病,泛指脾脏各种病证。《内经》曾载述脾风、脾热、脾疟、脾咳、太阴呕吐、泄泻、脾胀、脾疸、脾瘅、脾心痛、太阴腰痛、脾疝等多种病证,后世临床文献又

有较多的补充。脾为后天之本,职司运化,统血,主肌肉、四肢,开窍于口,受水谷之精气以充养五脏及人体各部,为生化之源。脾病的常见症状有:腹满作胀、脘腹痛、食少便溏、黄疸、身重乏力、肢冷,或见脱肛、阴挺(子宫脱垂)及内脏下垂,以及便血、崩漏、紫癜等症。

② Spleen disease is either asthenic or sthenic. 脾病有实有虚。

③ Clinical manifestations: Poor appetite, abdominal distension, especially after meal, loose stool, or dry feces followed by loose stool, lack of *qi*, no desire to speak, lassitude of limbs, sallow complexion, emaciation, or dropsy, pale tongue with whitish fur, slow and weak pulse, usually seen in chronic gastritis, digestive ulceration, chronic enteritis and mal-absorption syndrome, etc. 临床表现:食欲不振;腹胀,饭后加重;大便溏泄,或便溏后大便干燥;少气懒言;四肢倦怠;面色苍白;消瘦,或浮肿;舌苔白;脉搏缓慢而虚弱,这些经常出现在慢性胃炎、消化溃疡、慢性肠炎、消化综合症等中。

④ Poor appetite and abdominal distension are due to asthenia of splenic *qi*: 食欲低下、腹部胀满是由于脾气虚而引起。

⑤ lack of *qi* and no desire to speak: 少气懒言。

⑥ insufficiency of gastrosplenic *qi*: 脾胃气虚。

⑦ leukorrhagia: *n*. [妇产] 白带过多。

⑧ whitish slippery fur: 白滑舌苔。

⑨ Prolapsing sensation and distension of epigastrium and abdomen: 脘腹胀满下坠感。

⑩ chronic gastritis: 慢性胃炎; digestive ulceration: 消化性溃疡; chronic enteritis: 慢性肠炎。

Exercises

Ⅰ. **Fill in the blanks with the words given below. Change the form when necessary.**

intake	contaminated	turbid	exuberance
slippery	profuse	encumber	overstrain
lassitude	bland	sallow	digestive

1. She suffered from _____ trouble.
2. The river was _____ with waste from the factory.
3. The girl's long skirt _____ her while running.
4. The accident was caused by _____ roads.
5. After the window is opened outward, air _____ can be formed at the top of the window for ventilation.
6. There is a whiff of _____ around the world economy these days.
7. She is ill with a(n) _____ face.
8. The water in the river is _____ on one side and clear on the other.

Unit 10 Differentiation of Syndromes

9. Sometimes we feel _____ on a hot summer day.
10. You will make your eyes _____.
11. Why does airline food taste _____?
12. You're imaginative and _____ in a spirit of adventure.

II. Choose the best answer to each of the following questions or unfinished statements.

1. Spleen disease can NOT be caused by _____.
   A. improper diet   B. some acute or chronic diseases
   C. regular daily life   D. excessive vomiting
2. Sthenic spleen disease is caused by _____.
   A. incorrect diet or eating polluted food or exogenous cold dampness or internal invasion
   B. regular intake of contaminated food
   C. regular exercise
   D. failure of the spleen to govern blood
3. Which one of the following is NOT correct?
   A. Asthenia of splenic *qi* may be caused by improper diet, overstrain.
   B. Poor appetite, abdominal distension can be seen in the syndrome of asthenia of splenic yang.
   C. All clinical manifestations of syndrome of asthenia of splenic yang overlaps that of the splenic *qi*.
   D. Lack of *qi* and no desire to speak are due to failure of transportation and transformation.
4. What does the underlined word "retention" mean in Para. 8?
   A. Activity.   B. Retainment.
   C. Exchange.   D. Digest.
5. Through this passage, the writer intend to _____.
   A. tell us the about the different types of the spleen diseases
   B. let us pay attention to some medical knowledge
   C. tell us the various symptoms of spleen disease
   D. let us know how to prevent spleen disease

III. Translate the following sentences into English or Chinese.

1. 脾病的特点是脾的运化、统血功能低下。
2. 素体脾虚,湿邪内生。
3. 脾虚湿聚是因虚致实的一种表现。
4. 脾属土,主运化和统血。
5. 白带多而清稀是脾阳不足所致。
6. Preference for warmth and palpation are due to asthenia of *yang*.

7. Syndrome of sinking of splenic *qi* refers to the syndrome due to asthenia of splenic qi and failure of splenic *qi* to rise.
8. Lack of *qi* and no desire to speak are due to failure of transportation and transformation.
9. Asthenia and sthenia are the principles that describe the struggle between the body resistance and pathogenic factors.
10. Asthenia means insufficient of healthy *qi*, while sthenia indicates the presence of excessive pathogenic factors.

Text C

Syndrome Differentiation of Fluid Disorder

The disorders of body fluid① mainly include deficiency of body fluid as well as retention of phlegm and fluid and edema. The former is caused by insufficiency of the production of body fluid or excessive loss of body fluid, the latter is caused by dysfunction of the viscera and disturbance of the distribution and excretion of body fluid which leads to the retention and accumulation of fluid.

Insufficiency of Body Fluid

Insufficiency of body fluid refers to syndrome due to deficiency of body fluid which fails to nourish and moisten viscera, tissues and organs. This syndrome is mainly caused by excessive consumption of body fluid due to high fever, profuse sweating, excessive vomiting, excessive diarrhea and profuse urine or consumption of fluid by dryness and heat; or by insufficiency of body fluid due to scanty drinking of water and decline of visceral *qi*.

Clinical manifestations: Dry mouth and throat, dry or fissured lips, sunken orbit, dry skin, thirst with desire for water, scanty urine, retention of dry feces②, dry tongue with scanty saliva and thin and astringent pulse.

Key points for syndrome differentiation③: Dry mouth, lips, tongue, throat and skin as well as scanty urine and dry stool.

Phlegm Syndrome④

Phlegm syndrome refers to syndrome due to local retention of phlegm or migration of phlegm. Phlegm is produced by such factors like six exogenous pathogenic factors, emotional impairment, improper food⑤, overstrain and lack of necessary physical activities

Unit 10 Differentiation of Syndromes

which affect the transforming functions of the lung, spleen and kidney, leading to stoppage of fluid distribution and production of phlegm. The retention of phlegm in viscera, meridians and tissues results in phlegm syndrome.

Clinical manifestations: Cough with sticky sputum, chest oppression, dizziness, or epigastric mass, anorexia, nausea, vomiting, or coma with sputum rale, or mental derangement with mania, dementia and epilepsy, or numbness of limbs, hemiplegia, or scrofula, goiter, breast nodules, phlegm nodules, greasy fur and slippery pulse.

Key points for syndrome differentiation: This syndrome is marked by vomiting of sputum or dizziness, vomiting, or coma with sputum, or numbness of limbs, or phlegm nodules, greasy fur and slippery pulse⑥. Phlegm syndrome may be divided into cold phlegm, heat syndrome, damp phlegm, dry phlegm and stagnant phlegm according to the nature of phlegm and the complication which should be carefully differentiated.

Fluid-Retention Syndrome

Fluid-retention syndrome refers to syndrome caused by retention of fluid in the viscera and tissues, usually caused by stoppage of fluid and retention of fluid resulting from six exogenous pathogenic factors, or overstrain and weakness.

Clinical manifestations: Epigastric and abdominal fullness and distension, borborygmus, vomiting of clear fluid; or cough and asthma, profuse thin sputum, chest oppression and palpitation, even inability to lie flat on bed;⑦ or thoracic and hypochondriac fullness, distending pain, aggravation of pain after cough, spitting or rotating the body; or dizziness, dysuria, dropsy and aching heaviness of the limbs; whitish slippery fur and taut pulse.

Key points for syndrome differentiation: Phlegmatic fluid-retention is marked by epigastric and abdominal fullness and distension as well as borborygmus; suspended fluid-retention is marked by thoracic and hypochondriac fullness, distending pain, aggravation of pain due to spitting, cough or rotation of the body; sustained fluid-retention is marked by cough and asthma, profuse and thin sputum, chest oppression and palpitation.

Edema

Edema refers to dropsy of eyelid, face, four limbs, chest and abdomen or even the whole body due to accumulation of fluid in the muscles resulting from disturbance of the lung, spleen and kidney in distributing and excreting fluid. Clinically, edema is divided into *yang* edema and *yin* edema.⑧

Yang Edema

Yang edema, of sthenia in nature, is marked by swelling above the waist and short duration⑨ due to exogenous pathogenic wind or spreading of fluid and dampness.

Clinical manifestations: Dropsy of face and eyelids, eventually involving the whole body with rapid development, smooth and bright skin, scanty urine, accompanied by fever, aversion to wind and cold, aching pain of limbs, sore-throat, thin fur and floating pulse; or dropsy of the whole body with slow development, depression under pressure, heaviness of the limbs, epigastric and abdominal fullness and oppression, poor appetite, nausea and regurgitation, whitish greasy tongue fur as well as soft and slow pulse.

Key points for syndrome differentiation: This syndrome is marked by rapid onset and development of edema primarily involving the eyelids, face and head as well as severe edema of the upper part of the body.

***Yin* Edema**

Yin edema is marked by asthenia of spleen and kidney *qi*, severe edema of the part below the waist and long duration, usually caused by asthenia of the healthy *qi* due to prolonged illness, internal impairment due to overstrain and consumption of spleen and kidney *yang*.

Clinical manifestations: Repeated relapse of edema, severity below the waist, depression under pressure, epigastric and abdominal distension and oppression, poor appetite and loose stool, dispiritedness, fatigue of limbs, cold body and limbs, preference for warmth, or aching cold sensation of loins and knees, scanty urine, dull or pale complexion, pale and bulgy tongue with white and slippery fur as well as sunken, slow and weak pulse.

Key points for syndrome differentiation: Repeated relapse of edema, long duration, severity below the waist, accompanied by asthenia of spleen and kidney *yang*①.

(869 words)

New Words

relapse /rɪˈlæps/ *vi.*	故态复萌,旧病复发,再度堕落,再陷邪道
sweat /swet/ *vt.*	使出汗,流出,使干苦活,剥削,发酵
phlegm /flem/ *n.*	痰,黏液,黏液质
sticky /ˈstɪkɪ/ *a.*	黏的,黏性的
epilepsy /ˈepɪlepsɪ/ *n.*	[医]癫痫,癫痫症
greasy /ˈgriːsɪ/ *a.*	油腻的,含脂肪多的,谄媚的
numbness /ˈnʌmnəs/ *n.*	麻木,麻痹
distend /dɪˈstend/ *vt.*	使……膨胀,使……扩张
aching /ˈeɪkɪŋ/ *a.*	疼痛的,心痛的
v.	疼痛,渴望
rotate /rəʊˈteɪt/ *v.*	旋转,循环,轮流,交替
eyelid /ˈaɪlɪd/ *n.*	[解剖]眼睑,眼皮
bulgy /ˈbʌldʒɪ/ *a.*	凸出的,膨胀的,肿胀的
dispiritedness /dɪˈspɪrɪtɪdnəs/ *n.*	精神不振
fatigue /fəˈtiːg/ *n.*	疲劳,疲乏,杂役

Unit 10 Differentiation of Syndromes

Expressions

fail to	没能成功做
lack of	缺乏……
marked by	特点是……
lie on	躺在……上
accompanied by	连同,在……陪伴下
preference for	偏爱

Notes

① disorders of body fluid：体液代谢失常。
② ...fissured lips, sunken orbit, dry skin, thirst with desire for water, scanty urine, retention of dry feces：嘴唇干裂,眼眶凹陷,皮肤干燥,渴喜饮水,小便少,大便干燥。
③ Key points for syndrome differentiation：辨证要点。
④ Phlegm Syndrome：痰症,病症名。痰,古作"澹"或"淡",泛指痰浊之邪滞留于体内的病证,包含较广。痰与饮常兼并发病,《金匮要略》有专篇论述。《诸病源候论》则记述了寒痰、热痰等痰症。
⑤ six exogenous pathogenic factors, emotional impairment, improper food：外感六淫,情志内伤,饮食不节。
⑥ greasy fur and slippery pulse：舌苔腻,脉滑。
⑦ Epigastric and abdominal fullness and distension, borborygmus, vomiting of clear fluid; or cough and asthma, profuse thin sputum, chest oppression and palpitation, even inability to lie flat on bed. 脘腹胀痛,肠鸣音亢进,呕水,或者咳嗽,气喘,多淡痰,胸闷和心悸,甚至不能平卧。
⑧ Clinically, edema is divided into *yang* edema and *yin* edema. 临床上,水肿可分为阳水和阴水。
⑨ swelling above the waist and short duration：腰以上水肿,病程较短。
⑩ asthenia of spleen and kidney yang：脾肾阳虚。

Exercises

Ⅰ. Fill in the blanks with the words given below. Change the form when necessary.

rotate	dispiritedness	excrete	sticky
numbness	greasy	scanty	mania
relapse	sweat	distend	aching

1. The _____ food make her feel sick.

2. The _____ in your foot will soon pass off.
3. I have nothing to offer but blood, toil, tears and _____.
4. You can _____ the cube by the mouse.
5. The information available is _____.
6. The function of the kidneys is to _____ waste products.
7. This _____ tooth makes me feel wretched.
8. Some patients will _____.
9. He has a(n) _____ for driving fast cars.
10. It's much better than last week. It was so warm and _____ then.
11. When you get cold, _____ may affect you.
12. Don't let some negative feeling such as jealousy _____ in your pure heart.

II. Choose the best answer to each of the following questions or unfinished statements.

1. The disorders of body fluid mainly include _____.
   A. deficiency of body fluid
   B. retention of phlegm retention of fluid
   C. edema
   D. thirsty with desire to drink water

2. Which one of the following does NOT belong to the symptoms of *yang* edema according to the text?
   A. Dropsy of face and eyelids.
   B. Scanty urine.
   C. Aversion to wind and cold.
   D. Delirious speech.

3. _____ lead to stoppage of fluid distribution and production of phlegm.
   A. emotional impairment, improper food, overstrain
   B. six exogenous pathogenic factors
   C. asthenia of spleen and kidney yang
   D. All of the above.

4. What is NOT the different feature between the syndromes of *yang* and *yin* edema?
   A. Disease duration.
   B. Influencing position.
   C. Patients' complexion.
   D. Whether the patient sweats or not.

5. According to the passage, edema _____.
   A. is only limited in eyelid, face, four limbs, chest
   B. is due to accumulation of fluid
   C. is divided into three types
   D. can't influence whole body

III. Translate the following sentences into English or Chinese.

1. 前者是由津液不足或者水液的过度流失造成的。

Unit 10　Differentiation of Syndromes

2. 这种疾病多由外感六淫所致。
3. 水肿起自眼睑,迅速蔓延至四肢及全身。
4. 风为百病之长。
5. 在治疗水肿之前,需要先辨别阴水和阳水。
6. The treatment of edema based on syndrome differentiation also applies to some diseases in Western medicine that present with edema such as acute or chronic glomerulonephritis, nephritic syndrome, secondary glomerulopathy and general or localized edema due to cardiogenic, hepatogenic, malnutrition-related and endocrine factors.
7. This syndrome is marked by vomiting of sputum or dizziness.
8. The basic treatment principle for edema is to remove water retention through diaphoresis(发汗), diuresis(利尿) and catharsis(导泄).
9. Symptoms of *zang-fu* organs are the outer manifestations of them during the process of their pathogenic changes.
10. Since each organ has its own physiological features, each organ may display its particular syndrome.

Medical Physics (医用物理学)

Root	Meaning	Examples
physio-	physics 物理	physiotherapy 物理疗法
moto- kinesio- kinetio- cine-	movement, locomotion, motion 运动	motoneuron 运动神经元 kinesiology 运动学 kinetics 动力学 pharmacokinetics 药物动力学
scinti-	scintilla 闪烁	scintigraphy 闪烁扫描法
veloci-	speed, rate 速度	velocity 速度 velocimetry 速度测量学 velocity of wave 波速
tempo- chrono-	time 时间	temporospatial 时空的 chronological 年代学的

续表

Root	Meaning	Examples
longi-	length 长度	longitudinalis 纵的,纵肌 longitude 经度
hypso-	height, altitude 高度	hypsarrhythmia 高度节律失常
densito-	density 密度	densitometry 密度测量法
calori- thermo- pyro-	heat 热	calorimetry 测热法 thermometer 温度计 pyrogen 热原质
cryo-	cold 冷	cryosurgery 低温外科 cryoanalgesia 冷止痛 cryoanesthesia 冷冻麻醉
stereo-	solid 固体	stereoagnosis 实体觉缺失 stereopsis 立体影像
vaporo-	gas, vapor 气体	vaporizer 汽化器,喷雾器
aero- physo-	air 空气	aerosol 气溶胶,气雾剂 aerotitis 航空性耳炎 physostigmine 毒扁豆碱
photo- phos-	light, lumen 光	photosynthetic 光合作用 phosgene 光气
sono- phono-	voice, sound 声音	sonography 超声扫描术 phonetics 语音学
echo-	echo 回声	echocardiography 超声心动描记术 echocinesis 模仿运动 anechoic 无回声的 hypoechoic 低回声的
electro-	electricity 电	electrophysiology 电生理学 electroacupuncture 电针(刺)术 electrohemostasis 电止血法

Unit 10　Differentiation of Syndromes

续表

Root	Meaning	Examples
rheo-	current 流	rheology 流变学 rheotrope 电流变向器 rheoophthalmography 眼血流图描记术 gastrorrhea 胃液分泌过多
magneto-	magnet 磁	electromagnetic 电磁的 magnetology 磁学
radio- roentgeno-	ray 放射,射线	radioisotope 放射性核素 roentgenolucent 可透 X 线的
dynamo-	strength,force,power 力	pharmacodynamic 药效学的 cardiodynamics 心(脏)动力学 dynamogenesis 动力发生
baro-	pressure 压	baroreceptor 压力感受器 barometer 气压计
tenso-	tension 张力	tensor 张肌 extensor 伸肌
gravio-	weight,gravity 重力	gravimetric 比重测定的 ingravescent 渐重的
visco-	viscosity 黏	viscometer 黏度计

Unit 11　Chinese Materia Medica

 Text A

Medical Plants

The herbs and the natural medical plants are still proving very faithful.

Herbal medicine has come a long way since pioneer days①, and we now have institutes of phytotherapy or herbal medicine. In Europe, a great deal of research is being done every day and there are many institutes of phytotherapy.② The institute which I belong to, the National Institute of Medical Herbalists of Great Britain③, was established in 1864, and it is the oldest association of practicing herbalists in existence today④. It operates the School of Herbal Medicine in Sussex which conducts a four-year course and includes the study of the traditional medical subjects such as pathology, physiology, anatomy and biochemistry.⑤

In addition to that, plant remedies are studied in great detail including the pharmacological properties of the plants.⑥ Some plants contain over 170 different chemicals. These chemicals work together, and that is really the essence of the difference between allopathy and herbal medicine in its holistic approach.⑦

Many of us are under stress, which affects the body in many ways.⑧ We live in sealed buildings with no fresh air and we need to find ways of relieving the nervous system from the effects of this stress. Many of us suffer from lung problems. We suffer from problems caused by drinking water which has been polluted by steel mills and other industries. We get all sorts of pollution in our food as well. Chemicals enter our body which did not even exist before the 1940s. We put fungicides and pesticides on our soil and have very little control over what we are eating unless we are very careful and grow our own produce organically. What happens when our liver has to deal with these man-made chemicals? Our liver is the same organ we had as primitive man and there is no evidence that the liver is able to handle man-made molecules.

As a result, we have invented new diseases. Let's think about what we can actually do to help the liver. The first thing we must do is clean up our environment or we really won't survive this part of our history. In the meantime, to help us along, the herbs and

Unit 11 Chinese Materia Medica

the natural medical plants are still proving very faithful.⑨

(417 words)

New Words

phytotherapy /ˌfaɪtəʊˈθerəpɪ/	n.	植物治疗法,草本疗法
institute /ˈɪnstɪtjuːt/	n.	学会,学院,协会
	vt.	创立,开始,制定,任命
establish /ɪˈstæblɪʃ/	v.	建立,确立,制定,生长
herbalist /ˈhɜːbəlɪst/	n.	草药医生
pathology /pəˈθɒlədʒɪ/	n.	病理学,病理,病状,病变
anatomy /əˈnætəmɪ/	n.	剖析,解剖学,骨骼,结构
pharmacological /ˌfɑːməkəˈlɒdʒɪkl/	a.	药物学的,药理学的
allopathy /æˈlɒpəθɪ/	n.	对抗疗法
nervous /ˈnɜːvəs/	a.	神经紧张的,不安的,神经的
exist /ɪgˈzɪst/	vi.	存在,生存,发生
fungicide /ˈfʌndʒɪsaɪd/	n.	杀真菌剂
organically /ɔːˈgænɪklɪ/	ad.	有机性地,器官上地,有组织地
primitive /ˈprɪmətɪv/	n.	原始人,早期艺术家
	a.	原始的,上古的
evidence /ˈevɪdəns/	n.	根据,证据,迹象
environment /ɪnˈvaɪrənmənt/	n.	环境,外界,围绕

Expressions

a great number of	大量,许多
belong to	属于
in detail	详细地
in essence	实质上,本质上
under pressure/stress	处于压力之下
think sth. over	认真考虑某事
in the meantime	同时

Notes

① Herbal medicine has come a long way since pioneer days... 中药自最初使用以来已经经历了一个漫长的发展过程。

② In Europe, a great deal of research is being done every day and there are many institutes of phytotherapy. 在欧洲每天都要做大量的研究工作,并且成立了许多中草药研究所。a great deal of: 大量的,许多的(修饰不可数名词); institutes of phytotherapy：中草药研究所。

③ The institute which I belong to, the National Institute of Medical Herbalists of Great Britain... the National Institute of Medical Herbalists of Great Britain 是 the institute 的同位语，which I belong to 为定语从句，修饰先行词 the institute。

④ ...and it is the oldest association of practicing herbalists in existence today. 并且这是当今存在的最古老的执业中医组织。practicing herbalists：执业中医；in existence：存在。

⑤ It operates the School of Herbal Medicine in Sussex which conducts a four-year course and includes the study of the traditional medical subjects such as pathology, physiology, anatomy and biochemistry. 在这句里 which conducts...and biochemistry 为定语从句，修饰先行词 the School，在定语从句中有并列谓语 conducts...includes...

⑥ In addition to that, plant remedies are studied in great detail including the pharmacological properties of the plants. 此外，还对植物药物进行了非常详细的研究，其中包括对植物药理学特性的研究。including the pharmacological properties of the plants 是现在分词短语作状语。

⑦ These chemicals work together, and that is really the essence of the difference between allopathy and herbal medicine in its holistic approach. 这些化学成分共同起作用，这才是对抗疗法和中医整体疗法真正的本质区别。

⑧ Many of us are under stress, which affects the body in many ways. 我们许多人有压力，这样会在许多方面影响我们的身体。which affects the body in many ways 作非限制性定语从句。

⑨ In the meantime, to help us along, the herbs and the natural medical plants are still proving very faithful. 同时，中草药以及自然界的一些植物一直被我们证明在疗效方面是非常有效的。to help us along 是插入语。

Exercises

I. **Fill in the blanks with the words given below. Change the form when necessary.**

institute	establish	anatomy	relieve
nervous	exist	pesticide	primitive
evidence	environment	molecule	organ

1. _____ is the science of the structure of the (usually human) body, especially the study of the body by cutting up dead animal and human bodies.
2. My grandfather _____ the family business in 1938.
3. Inflammation will affect the internal _____.
4. The custom of arranged marriages still _____ in many countries.

Unit 11 Chinese Materia Medica

5. The house was _____, with an earthen floor and mud walls.
6. _____ is usually used to kill pests.
7. She was _____ about travelling by air.
8. There is a lecture at the Philosophical _____ tonight.
9. _____ is the smallest unit into which a substance can be divided without losing its basic nature or identity.
10. An unhappy home _____ may drive a teenager to crime.
11. Have you got enough _____ of her guilt to arrest her?
12. The doctor gave him some drugs to _____ the pain.

Ⅱ. Choose the best answer to each of the following question or unfinished statements.

1. In Europe, there are many institutes of _____.
   A. phytotherapy   B. research
   C. dandelion   D. important minerals
2. The National Institute of Medical Herbalists of Great Britain was built in _____.
   A. 1964   B. 1864   C. 1940s   D. 1970s
3. Among the following, the true one is _____.
   A. many of us are under stress and it is caused by drinking water
   B. stress only affects the body in some ways
   C. we get all sorts of pollution in our food but they don't cause new diseases
   D. our liver organ has not been proved to be able to handle man-made molecules(分子)
4. In order to survive, we human beings have to _____ according to the passage.
   A. grow more phytotherapy
   B. get rid of the pollutions in the environment
   C. clean up our environment and use herbs and the natural medical plants as well
   D. only use herbs and the natural medical plants
5. What does the underlined word "primitive" mean?
   A. Modern.   B. Ancient.   C. Old.   D. Mature.

Ⅲ. Translate the following sentences into English or Chinese.

1. 我所在的研究所成立于1864年。
2. 有些植物含有170多种化学成分。
3. 实质上，你已经告诉我如何解决那个问题。
4. 我们中许多人都有肺部毛病。
5. 我们的肝脏不得不应付这些人造的化学成分。
6. You should think it over, and then reply to me.
7. He read the contract in detail.

8. In modern society, a great number of people work under pressure.

9. We suffer from problems caused by drinking water which has been polluted by steel mills and other industries.

10. We get all sorts of pollution in our food as well.

Ⅳ. Write a 150-word composition about herbal medicine.

 Text B

Magic Chinese Herbs

As with many unexpected discoveries, bright new information is often happened upon by accident. Chinese medicine doctor Toni Balfour's focus on treating canine ailments was no exception.①

Balfour, whose Pacific Palisades practice is decidedly people-oriented, was in Florida visiting her parents when the idea occurred to turn her attention to dogs. "My parents' dog was walking on three legs, so I gave him some Chinese herbs and was surprised how quickly the dog responded." Balfour says, "In no time, he was walking on four legs and chasing after raccoons.②" In Balfour's eyes, a three-legged dog may be remarkably agile, but it doesn't have to be so hobbled. She believes that the principles of Chinese medicine apply equally to dogs.

Treating a disease in Chinese medicine means strengthening and protecting normal qi, which is the life force energy necessary for health and vitality. In ancient China, a physician was only paid while his patient was healthy, not while his patient was ill. The balance of *yin* and *yang* is maintained in the whole healthy body because the sum total of the *yin* and *yang* will be in a fluctuating balance③. Disease develops because normal qi is unable to resist the onslaught of the pathogenic qi; if pathogenic qi overwhelms normal qi then a functional disturbance④ of the body results.

The similarities between the physiology of human beings and dogs are closer than we think. Balfour says, "My goal was interpreting the common things that go on with dogs within a Chinese medicine framework." For example, dogs suffer from joint and muscle pain and arthritis as Balfour's parents' dog did. They also have digestive and bladder problems, and the aches and pains associated with old age.

Balfour spent a year researching what she calls wide patterns of disharmony in dogs and developed a line of herbal formulations⑤, qi Blends for dogs. That address eight different conditions. She will market them through veterinarians.⑥

Although most people associate Chinese medicine with acupuncture⑦, herb formulas are equally important. "I love herbs and I like to develop as precise a formula as I can." Balfour says, "The formula is based on the underlying problem. For example, there are two patterns that affect skin in dogs: one is flaky, itchy, irritated skin, and the other results in red, pussy skin lesions, what we call wet hot spots. We treat both internally and topically."

Balfour has developed two different programs to address a broad range of skin conditions. The Skin Repair for Hot Spots, Sores and More is a liquid tincture ingested, while the topical powder is applied to hot spots, open sores and moist sores. The second program—Skin Soothe Itch, both drops and powder—addresses itching with dry skin and flaky skin.

Because animals are likely to lick their skin, Balfour's herbal formulas are food-grade and organic. They contain no sulphur, preservatives or chemicals, and are mixed with filtered water.⑧ She purchases the herbs from a company in Northern California that has the Federal GMP certification. She makes her own tinctures and powders then seals and bottles them ready for shipping.

About 300 common herbs are used in day-to-day prescriptions.⑨ Balfour says, some are used to clear heat, others to extinguish wind and others to nourish the blood.

After working on her formulas for over a year, Balfour put out the word to friends and then friends of friends to find dogs to observe and to test her remedies.

(596 words)

New Words

herb /hɜːb/	n.	草本植物,药草,香草
agile /ˈædʒaɪl/	a.	灵巧的
maintain /meɪnˈteɪn/	vt.	保持,继续,保养,维护,坚持,主张,供给,赡养
onslaught /ˈɒnslɔːt/	n.	猛攻,攻击
fluctuate /ˈflʌktʃueɪt/	vi.	波动,涨落,起伏
overwhelm /ˌəʊvəˈwelm/	vt.	覆盖,淹没,压倒,制服,打败,使某人不知所措
arthritis /ɑːˈθraɪtɪs/	n.	关节炎
formulation /ˌfɔːmjʊˈleɪʃn/	n.	配方,构想,规划
flaky /ˈfleɪkɪ/	a.	薄片的,成片的,薄而易剥落的
itchy /ˈɪtʃɪ/	a.	使人发痒的
irritated /ˈɪrɪteɪtɪd/	a.	恼怒的,生气的
soothe /suːð/	vt.	安慰,抚慰,使舒服,使平静,减轻痛苦
federal /ˈfedərəl/	a.	联邦(制)的,联邦政府的
purchase /ˈpɜːtʃəs/	vt.	购买

	n.	购买,购置,买到的东西
tincture /ˈtɪŋktʃə/	*n.*	酊剂
extinguish /ɪkˈstɪŋgwɪʃ/	*vt.*	使熄灭,扑灭,使……不复存在

Expressions

happen upon/on	偶然碰上
by accident	意外地,偶然地
turn one's attention to	让某人注意
apply to	适用于
go on	发生
associate...with...	把……与……联系起来
as precise as I can	尽可能准确
be mixed with	与……混合

Notes

① Chinese medicine doctor Toni Balfour's focus on treating canine ailments was no exception. 中医托妮·巴弗尔专注于治疗犬科疾病也是如此。be no exception：不例外的。

② In no time, he was walking on four legs and chasing after raccoons. 此句表现小狗服用中草药后恢复很快,可以用四脚行走,并可以追赶浣熊,非常灵活。in no time：very soon 很快的。

③ ...the sum total of the *yin* and *yang* will be in a fluctuating balance. 人体内的阴阳是在波动中保持相对平衡。fluctuating balance：波动的平衡,不是静止的。

④ a functional disturbance：机能失调,紊乱。

⑤ Balfour spent a year researching what she calls wide patterns of disharmony in dogs and developed a line of herbal formulations. 巴弗尔花了一年的时间研究了犬科疾病的发病模式并研发了一系列的中药配方。

⑥ She will market them through veterinarians. 她研究了一些中药治疗模式和方法,将通过兽医推向市场。veterinarians：兽医。

⑦ ...most people associate Chinese medicine with acupuncture：大多数人提起中药就会联想到针灸。

⑧ They contain no sulphur, preservatives or chemicals, and are mixed with filtered water. 她的中药配方里不含硫磺,防腐剂和化学成分并用过滤水混合。filtered water：过滤水。

⑨ About 300 common herbs are used in day-to-day prescriptions. 大约有300种常见的中草药可以用于日常处方中。day-to-day：日常的。

Unit 11 Chinese Materia Medica

Exercises

I. Fill in the blanks with the words given below. Change the form when necessary.

maintain	onslaught	fluctuate	overwhelm
joint	flaky	itchy	irritated
soothe	purchase	extinguish	nourish

1. The beauty of the region has _____ the imagination of countless artists.
2. Carrie's pretty _____ but she is fun to be with.
3. He was confident his armies could withstand the Allied _____.
4. I _____ a new house.
5. She and her husband have a(n) _____ bank account.
6. She was _____ with work.
7. I feel _____ all over.
8. She was so upset that it took half an hour to _____ her.
9. The present output of oil _____ between 3 and 5 million gallons per week.
10. She _____ her car very well.
11. Please _____ your cigarettes.
12. John was _____ by the necessity for polite conversation.

II. Choose the best answer to each of the following questions or unfinished statements.

1. In the first paragraph, the example of the Chinese medicine doctor told us _____.
    A. if you want to cure disease, you need make a good effort
    B. canine ailments must be very dangerous
    C. as a doctor, you not only care about human beings, but also animals
    D. new important information may get by accident
2. In ancient China, when did you pay the physician?
    A. When he came home.   B. When you bought medicine.
    C. When his patient was healthy.   D. When his patient was ill.
3. Why did the disease develop according to the TCM?
    A. You eat something dirty.
    B. You disturb the balance of *yin* and *yang*.
    C. You have not enough *qi*.
    D. You didn't visit doctors.
4. Which of the following statements is NOT true according to the passage?
    A. We never think there are similarity between the physiology of human beings and dogs.
    B. Dogs would also suffer from joint and muscle pain just as we did.

C. There are two patterns that affect skin in dogs.

D. Animals like to lick their skin.

5. There are 300 common herbs in our day-to-day prescriptions, and they have many utilities EXCEPT _____.

   A. clean heat   B. extinguish wind
   C. nourish the blood   D. protect skin

Ⅲ. Translate the following sentences into English or Chinese.

1. 她花了 2 年的时间研发了一系列的中药配方。

2. 老年人缺乏精力可能是与健康问题有关。

3. 越来越多的人开始关注自身的健康。

4. 这个中药配方不含硫、防腐剂和化学成分。

5. 保持身心的平衡是健康的要素。

6. No pets are allowed inside, and your pet is no exception.

7. This medicine is to be taken after being mixed with boiling water.

8. He suffers from chronic digestive problems.

9. She believes that the principles of Chinese medicine apply equally to dogs.

10. The formula is based on the underlying problem.

Text C

The Magic Anti-Tumor Herb—Matrine

Matrine is one of the effective components from the alkaloids among the bean family, such as Sophora flavescens Ait, Sophora alopecuroides L and Euchresta japonica.① There have been a lot of reports researching the extraction, separation and purification② of Matrine from different angles and also dealing with its stability in a series of studies. The methods of extraction vary from the types of herbs. For example, due to the complexity of the Alkaloids among Sophora flavescens Ait and Sophora alopecuroides L, people often adopt the typical solvent extraction method③, while the simplicity of Euchresta Benn (Sophora tonkinensis gapnep) makes it possible to take easy methods to extract, separate and purify Matrine. The method is also easy to put into practice in large scales. Therefore, the experiments in the thesis take Euchresta Benn as the original medicinal

Unit 11 Chinese Materia Medica

herbs. There are many methods to extract and separate Matrine from Euchresta Benn, such as soaking, permeating (ion exchange column), boiling, trends of reflux and ultrasonic wave extraction.④ Supercritical Fluid Extraction (following short as SFE) is also another way being mentioned but without many details about the extraction technology.

Many modern pharmacological studies show that Matrine has various pharmacological effects, such as anti-tumor, anti-fibrosis, anti-virus, etc. It is safe without obvious harmful reactions.⑤ In the anti-tumor aspect, the outstanding advantages of Matrine are the lager scale of tumors, the stronger and continuous its effect, and the less harm to the healthy cells in the human beings. It can also increase the amount of white blood cells and enhance the organic immunity.⑥ At present, Matrine is clinically used to cure viral hepatitis. When used to treat chronic Hepatitis Type B, it has higher rate of turning into negative in HBV DNA and HBeAg, and has even better effect if used with other medicines. Matrine can also protect liver, has anti-fibrosis effect and decreases the level of enzymes.⑦ Further studies are made into other clinic uses of Matrine. In order to develop the level of clinic use of Matrine, conjoining principle of practical medical chemistry⑧ is adopted to embellish the structure of Matrine and other compounds which have definite biological activation⑨. The experiments composed Matrine with Vitamin C, Aspartic acid, Cinnamic acid, and Ferulic acid to get a series of structure-modified compounds. Taking the producing rate of synthesized compounds as the investigating index, different compounds' synthesizing process are focused on to analyze the influential factors of each compound by using TLC (thin layer chromatography). For example, orthogonal design is taken to study the influential factors on synthesizing Matrine and Vitamin C and the optimum preparation process is found as followed: the amount of Matrine is twice as much as Vitamin C. The reaction occurred at 45 degree centigrade for 5 hours, 100 ml sediment solvent is added to separate the crystal of extraction.⑩

(484 words)

New Words

anti-tumor /ˈæntɪtjuːmə/ a.　　　　　　抗肿瘤的
matrine /meɪtˈriːn/ n.　　　　　　苦参碱(抗肿瘤药,消炎镇痛药)
alkaloid /ˈælkəlɔɪd/ n.　　　　　　生物碱,植物碱基
solvent /ˈsɒlvənt/ n.　　　　　　溶剂
　　　　　　　　　a.　　　　　　有偿付能力的,有溶解力的
immunity /ɪˈmjuːnətɪ/ n.　　　　　　免疫,免疫性,免除
permeate /ˈpɜːmɪeɪt/ v.　　　　　　弥漫,渗透,充满,透入
ion /ˈaɪən/ n.　　　　　　离子
reflux /ˈriːflʌks/ n.　　　　　　回流,逆流,退潮

ultrasonic /ˌʌltrəˈsɒnɪk/	*n.*	超声波
	a.	超音速的
supercritical /ˌsjuːpəˈkrɪtɪkəl/	*a.*	超临界的
fibrosis /faɪˈbrəʊsɪs/	*n.*	纤维症
viral /ˈvaɪrəl/	*a.*	滤过性毒菌的,滤过性毒菌引起的
aspartic acid	*n.*	[化]天冬氨酸
cinnamic /sɪˈnæmɪk/	*a.*	苯乙烯的
ferulic acid		[医]阿魏酸

Expressions

from different angles	从不同的角度
vary from	因……而不同
put into practice	用于实践
in large scales	大规模地
in... aspect	在……方面
at present	目前
turn into negative	(实验结果)转阴

Notes

① Matrine is one of the effective components from the alkaloids among the bean family, such as Sophora flavescens Ait, Sophora alopecuroides L and Euchresta japonica. 苦参碱是中药苦参、苦豆子、山豆根等豆科植物中生物碱的主要有效成分之一。

② extraction, separation and purification：提取、分离、纯化。

③ The methods of extraction vary from the types of herbs. For example, due to the complexity of the Alkaloids among Sophora flavescens Ait and Sophora alopecuroides L, people often adopt the typical solvent extraction method：(溶剂提取法)从不同植物中提取苦参碱的方法不同，根据文献报道，中药苦参、苦豆子等植物中生物碱成分复杂，采用经典的溶剂提取法。

④ There are many methods to extract and separate Matrine from Euchresta Benn, such as soaking, permeating(ion exchange column), boiling, trends of reflux and ultrasonic wave extraction. 从山豆根中提取、分离苦参碱的方法很多，其中应用较多的是溶剂提取法，具体操作方法为浸渍法、渗漉法(离子交换柱法)、煎煮法、回流提取法，以及超声提取法等。

⑤ Many modern pharmacological studies show that Matrine has various pharmacological effects, such as anti-tumor, anti-fibrosis, anti-virus, etc. It is safe without obvious harmful reactions. 现代药理研究表明，苦参碱具有抗肿瘤、抗纤维化、抗病毒等多种药理作用，而且安全性好，没有明显的不良反应。

⑥ In the anti-tumor aspect, the outstanding advantages of Matrine are the lager scale of tumors, the stronger and continuous its effect, and the less harm to the healthy cells in

Unit 11 Chinese Materia Medica

the human beings. It can also increase the amount of white blood cells and enhance the organic immunity. 苦参碱在抗肿瘤方面，突出的优点在于抗肿瘤广谱、作用强且持久，对人体健康细胞损害很小，另外还可以提高白细胞数和机体免疫力。

⑦ When used to treat chronic Hepatitis Type B, it has higher rate of turning into negative in HBV DNA and HBeAg, and has even better effect if used with other medicines. Matrine can also protect liver, has anti-fibrosis effect and decreases the level of enzymes. 苦参碱治疗慢性乙型肝炎的 HBV DNA、HBeAg 转阴率较高，联合其他药物效果更佳，同时对保肝、抗肝纤维化及降酶都有较好的作用。

⑧ conjoining principle of practical medical chemistry：药物化学中的拼合原理。

⑨ ... to embellish the structure of Matrine and other compounds which have definite biological activation. 对苦参碱与具有已知生物活性的化合物进行结构修饰。

⑩ For example, orthogonal design is taken to study the influential factors on synthesizing Matrine and Vitamin C and the optimum preparation process is found as followed: the amount of Matrine is twice as much as Vitamin C. The reaction occurred at 45 degree centigrade for 5 hours; 100 ml sediment solvent is added to separate the crystal of extraction. 例如，用正交设计法研究苦参碱与维生素合成工艺的影响因素，优化出最佳的合成工艺如下：苦参碱物质的量是维生素 C 的 2 倍，温度为 45℃、反应时间为 5 小时、加 100ml 沉淀溶剂析晶。

Exercises

I. **Fill in the blanks with the words given below. Change the form when necessary.**

solvent	immunity	permeate	ion
viral	chronic	angle	scale
extraction	definite	outstanding	enhance

1. I have to wait until my paycheck arrives before I'm _____ again.
2. He's been suffering from _____ arthritis for years now.
3. She is of Greek _____.
4. _____ is an atom which has been given a positive or negative force by adding or taking away an electron.
5. I'll give you a(n) _____ answer later.
6. We need to look at the issue from a different _____.
7. This thermometer has two _____ marked on it, one in Fahrenheit and one in Centigrade.
8. She is suffering from _____ pneumonia.
9. They were granted _____ from prosecution.

10. The water had _____ into the soil.
11. You must pay all _____ bills.
12. The flavor of most foods can be _____ by good cooking.

II. Choose the best answer to each of the following questions or unfinished statement.

1. Which family does Sophora flavescens Ait belong to?
   A. Asteraceae family.
   B. Araliaceae family.
   C. Bean family.
   D. Podophyllaceae family.
2. Which method does people typically use when extracting Matrine from the complex Sophora alopecuroides L?
   A. Ion exchange column.
   B. Boiling.
   C. Soaking.
   D. Solvent extraction method.
3. As far as anti-tumor concerned, which statement about Matrine is true?
   A. It can only be used in a small scale of tumors.
   B. It can enhance the organic immunity.
   C. It increases the amount of red blood cells.
   D. Matrine produces obvious harmful reactions in clinic use.
4. Matrine has pharmacological effects, EXCEPT _____.
   A. anti-AIDS
   B. anti-tumor
   C. anti-fibrosis
   D. anti-virus
5. When Matrine is used to cure chronic Hepatitis Type B, which condition is IMPOSSIBLE to occur?
   A. It can also protect liver.
   B. It appears lower rate of turning into negative in HBV DNA and HBeAg.
   C. It decreased the level of enzymes.
   D. It has anti-fibrosis effect.

III. Translate the following sentences into English or Chinese.

1. 关于这个事件，记者已从不同的角度问了许多问题。
2. 此疗法简便易行，值得大规模推广使用。
3. 应该尽快实施这项法规。
4. 治疗组 HBV DNA 转阴率明显高于对照组。（治疗组：treatment group；对照组：control group）
5. 不同性别、年级、专业的大学生对这个问题看法都不一样。
6. This paper deals with the cultural barriers in communication.
7. This medicine can greatly increase the amount of white blood cells and enhance the organic immunity.

8. The research shows that the drug is safe without obvious harmful reactions (side effects).
9. The method is also easy to put into practice in large scales.
10. Supercritical Fluid Extraction (following short as SFE) is also another way being mentioned but without many details about the extraction technology.

Operative Surgery (外科手术学)

Root	Meaning	Examples
-tome	lancet(手术)刀	osteotome 骨凿 rheotome 电流断续器，断流器
-tomy	incision, section 切断术	laparotomy 剖腹术 anatomy 解剖学 cystotomy 膀胱切开术
-ectomy	excision, resection, removal 切除术	cholecystectomy 胆囊切除术 polysinusectomy 多鼻窦切除术 cordectomy 声带切除术 colpectomy 阴道切除术
-stomy	opening 造口术	gastrostomy 胃造口术 colostomy 结肠造口术 esophagostomy 食管造口术 gastrocolostomy 胃结肠吻合术
-plasty	shape 成形术	arthroplasty 关节成形术 conjunctivoplasty 结合膜成形术 angioplasty 血管成形术 cacoplastic 成形不良的 bronchoplasty 支气管成形术
-rraphy	sew, suture 缝合术	herniorrhaphy 疝缝合术 cardiorrhaphy 心脏(肌)缝合术 enterorrhaphy 肠缝合术 gastrorrhaphy 胃缝合术
-desis -pexy	fixation, immobilization 固定术	arthrodesis 关节固定术 mastopexy 乳房固定术 colpopexy 阴道固定术 lateral cordopexy 声带外移固定术

续表

Root	Meaning	Examples
-lysis	loosening 松解术	arthrolysis 关节松解术 ectolysis 外(胞)浆溶解 paralysis 麻痹,瘫痪 lympholysis 淋巴细胞溶解
ortho-	correction 矫正术	orthopedics 矫形外科学 orthopnea 端坐呼吸 orthoptics 视轴矫正术 orthokeratology 角膜矫正术
-centesis	puncture 穿刺术	thoracocentesis 胸腔穿刺术 abdominocentesis 腹腔穿刺术 enterocentesis 肠穿刺术 neurocentesis 神经穿刺术
trepo-	trapine 环钻	trepanation 环钻术 treponema pallidum 梅毒螺旋体
cryo-	cold 冷冻	cryosurgery 低温外科 cryofiltration 冷滤疗法 cryoextractor 冷冻摘出器 cryoablation 冷冻消融(术) cryobiology 低温生物学
planto-	plantation 植术	transplantation 移植术 implantation 种植,植入,植入法 xenotransplantation 异种移植 implantodontology 口腔种植学 replantation 再植入

Keys to Exercises

Unit 1

Keys to Text A

Ⅰ. 1. accustomed 2. representative 3. drafted 4. comprehensive 5. integrate
   6. eliminate 7. recovery 8. emphasis 9. extensive 10. exchanged 11. mutual
   12. respectively

Ⅱ. 1. A 2. B 3. C 4. A 5. D

Ⅲ. 1. To date, we have received more than a hundred applications.
   2. The association relies on member subscriptions for most of its income.
   3. Treat the head when the head hurts; treat the foot when the foot hurts.
   4. Western medicine treats the symptom; Chinese medicine treats the root.
   5. Representatives from several dozen countries jointly drafted the "Beijing Proclamation".
   6. 中医运用阴阳和五行理论，提倡"对症治疗"。
   7. 中医强调的是"天人合一"理论。
   8. 根据五行学说，肝和胆属木，心属火，脾和胃属土，肺和肠属金，肾和膀胱属水。
   9. 中医诊断通过望闻问切来了解全身的状况。
   10. 目前，中国已经在中医领域和100多个国家和地区展开了医疗、研究、教育的交流。

Ⅳ. Sample Writing:

Concept of holism and syndrome differentiation and treatment are the two basic characteristics of TCM in understanding human physiology and pathology as well as diagnosis, treatment and prevention of disease.

(1) Concept of holism: The concept of holism means that the human body is an organic whole and that human beings are interrelated with nature.

Organic wholeness of the body TCM believes that the human body is composed of various tissues and organs. These different tissues and organs are united into an organic whole because they are closely related to each other in structure, physiology and pathology.

(2) Syndrome differentiation and treatment:

Implication of syndrome differentiation and treatment Syndrome differentiation and treatment means to analyze, induce, synthesize, judge and summarize the clinical data of symptoms and signs collected with the four diagnostic methods (namely inspection, listening and smelling, inquiry, taking pulse and palpation) into certain syndrome. Then the therapeutic methods are decided according to the result of syndrome differentiation. Syndrome differentiation and treatment is a basic principle in TCM to understand and treat disease.

Keys to Text B

Ⅰ. 1. occurrence   2. concerned   3. correspond   4. bound   5. expand   6. overall
   7. surrounding   8. struggle   9. distinguish   10. penetrate   11. enrich
   12. symptom

Ⅱ. 1. B   2. C   3. D   4. D   5. A

Ⅲ. 1. The theories of TCM have been continually enriched and expanded through practice.
   2. Human ancestors created primitive medicine during their struggles against nature.
   3. The human body itself is an organic whole and has very close and inseparable relations with the external natural surroundings.
   4. The human body is made up of viscera, bowels, tissues and other organs.
   5. The component parts of the human body are inseparable from each other in structure.
   6. 五脏包括心脏、肝脏、脾、肺、和肾脏。
   7. 许多疾病的发生、发展和转变都具有季节性。
   8. 器官整体论为医药工作者在治病过程中提供了必要的思考方法。
   9. 最近这些年，科学家们发现人体周期性的变化规律和太阳黑子的周期有着某些联系。
   10. 中医的整体观体现了中医对人体以及人体和自然的关系的理解。

Keys to Text C

Ⅰ. 1. prevention   2. interdependent   3. stresses   4. composed   5. prosperity
   6. regarded   7. survival   8. heritage   9. attach   10. strengthen   11. inquiry
   12. identified

Ⅱ. 1. B   2. C   3. A   4. D   5. D

Ⅲ. 1. These symptoms may further develop into life-threatening illnesses.
   2. Will you please sum up your views in a few words?
   3. Everything had been done in accordance with the law.
   4. Not long ago did he put forward an applicable plan.
   5. This paper deals with basic concepts and therapy methodology of Traditional

Keys to Exercises

Chinese Medicine.

6. 这是一种由肌肉组织构成的瘤。
7. 中国不但不会对世界粮食安全构成威胁,还将为世界粮食发展做出更大的贡献。
8. 中医认为人体是一个有机整体。
9. 中医的整体观则意味着人体内部的和谐统一以及人体与外界的密切联系。
10. 中医对于人体的生理功能和病理变化的诊断和治疗都有着独特的理解。

Unit 2

Keys to Text A

Ⅰ. 1. evaluate 2. diagnosis 3. digestion 4. foundation 5. constant 6. superficial
7. immune 8. conversely 9. generate 10. significant 11. primary 12. nourished

Ⅱ. 1. D 2. D 3. B 4. C 5. A

Ⅲ. 1. Chinese Medical theory is built on a foundation of ancient philosophical thought.
2. *Yin-yang* represents the ancient Chinese understanding of how things work.
3. *Yin-yang* are bound together as parts of a mutual whole.
4. When a disease develops rapidly, it is in the acute or *yang* stage.
5. Acute diseases affect the surface or superficial aspects of the body.
6. 慢性疾病击破身体的防护并深入身体的内在。
7. 阴和阳的定义是通用的,并拓展到生活的各个方面。
8. 阴阳理论是理解自然现象的重要工具。
9. 阴阳理论的基本前提就是相信自然界中永恒不变的东西就是永远的变化。
10. 根据中医理论,疾病的产生是由于阴阳失衡。

Ⅳ. Sample Writing:

　　The theory of *yin-yang* originated in antiquity in China. It is a theory dealing with the origination of the universe as well as the motion and variation of all things in the natural world. It holds that the natural world is made up of materials and that the material world conceives, develops and constantly varies under the interaction of *yin* and *yang*. The philosophers and doctors in ancient China explained all the phenomena and the nature of the universe and life with the theory of *yin-yang*.

　　The *yin* and *yang* aspects within an object or phenomenon are not simply arbitrary divisions. In fact they are in constant and complicated interaction. Such interactions between *yin* and *yang* give rise to the origination, development and change of things. The interactions between *yin* and *yang* are various in manifestations. The following is a brief description of the major ones.

　　Since *yin* and *yang* are opposite to each other in nature, they constantly repel and restrain each other. If both *yin* and *yang* are quite powerful, such a mutual repelling and restraining activity will maintain general equilibrium of things. If one side is weak and the other side is strong, the strong side will restrain the weak side, consequently damaging the general balance of things. The so-called "contrary treatment", one of the basic therapeutic principles in TCM, is developed in the light of the opposition between *yin* and *yang*.

Keys to Text B

Ⅰ. 1. restriction 2. dynamic 3. inherent 4. manifestation 5. represents
  6. deficiency 7. principle 8. originate 9. analyze 10. outcome 11. opposite
  12. excess

Ⅱ. 1. A 2. C 3. B 4. D 5. D

Ⅲ. 1. According to TCM theory, the occurrence of diseases results from the imbalance between *yin* and *yang* and the treatment of diseases is the reestablishment of the equilibrium between them.
  2. *Yang* is the muscling principle in nature and *yin* is the opposite.
  3. *Yin* and *yang* are opposed to and yet, at the same time, depend on each other.
  4. *Yin* and *yang* are always in a state of dynamic balance, which is a state of relative balance rather than absolute balance.
  5. The *yin-yang* theory holds that the development and changes of everything in the universe result from the unity of opposites between *yin* and *yang*.
  6. 一旦阴阳失调，就一定会出现阴或阳的过盛或不足，人就会生病。
  7. 中医是一门关于人体生理、病理、诊断和疾病预防的科学。
  8. 阴阳理论作为一种辨证思想，可以被应用于医药的任何领域。
  9. 中医认为人体正常的生理功能是阴阳对立统一的结果。
  10. 阴阳互为对方存在的前提。

Keys to Text C

Ⅰ. 1. condensation 2. naive 3. cardinal 4. multiply 5. coexist 6. relative
  7. spontaneous 8. maintain 9. situate 10. transformed 11. profound 12. endanger

Ⅱ. 1. C 2. D 3. A 4. B 5. A

Ⅲ. 1. The theory of *yin-yang* and Five Elements believes that world is material.
  2. The five kinds of elements—metal, wood, water, fire and earth—are interdependent, situated in continuous movement and change.
  3. The theory of *yin-yang* exercises profound influence on ancient materialistic philosophy.

Keys to Exercises

4. The theory of *yin-yang* believes that world is a material whole including two aspects—*yin* and *yang*, which are interdependent and counterbalance each other.
5. *Yin-yang* has university, opposition and division.
6. 世界本身是阴阳两种气的对立和统一的产物。
7. 自然界中阴阳凝结成相互依存和相互对立的事物和现象。
8. 把了脉以后,医生对病人做出了感冒的诊断。
9. 从病理上说,阴阳的症状也有可能互相转换。
10. 阴阳相互转换也是有条件的,它包含了内部的和外部的条件。

Unit 3

Keys to Text A

Ⅰ. 1. component   2. motion   3. constitute   4. generations   5. deduce   6. descend
   7. moisten   8. respectively   9. restriction 10. complement   11. substance   12. purify

Ⅱ. 1. A   2. B   3. B   4. C   5. D

Ⅲ. 1. The Five-Element Theory resulted from the observations and studies of the natural world by the ancient Chinese people in the course of their lives.
2. Since ancient time, wood, fire, earth, metal and water have been considered as basic substances to constitute the universe.
3. The Five-Element Theory, like the theory of *yin-yang*, has become an important component of the theoretical system of TCM.
4. Wood has the nature of growing freely and unfolding.
5. Earth has the nature of giving birth to all things.
6. 五行的相生相克是相互依赖不可分离的。
7. 自古代以来,木、火、土、金、水就被认为是宇宙组成的基本物质,也是生命不可缺少的物质。
8. 金曰从革,可以净化和变化。
9. 水曰润下,可滋润万物,流动趋下。
10. 五行中任一都有两方面——克我,我克。

Ⅳ. Sample Writing:

According to the Five-Element theory of traditional Chinese medicine, there are five elements in the world, which are wood, fire, earth, metal, and water. The five elements have been considered as basic substances to make up the universe and they are closely related to each other. Their mutual relationship can be summarized as mutual generation and restriction.

Generation implies that one kind of thing can promote, aid or bring forth another, that is, wood generates fire, and fire generates earth; earth generates metal, and metal generates water, and water, in turn, generates wood. While restriction indicates that water extinguishes fire, but fire might evaporate water; wood breaks the ground (earth), but earth can bury wood too. Fire can melt metal, but metal might not melt before fire is extinguished. Earth can absorb water, but water can cover the land (earth). Metal can cut wood, but metal might become dull before breaking wood.

Similar to the theory of *yin-yang*, the theory of Five Elements is the one of the basic theories of the traditional Chinese medicine.

Keys to Text B

Ⅰ. 1. violate 2. encroach 3. surpass 4. moisture 5. philosophical 6. pathology
    7. interconnection 8. dynamic 9. emerge 10. tendon 11. kidney 12. pungent
Ⅱ. 1. D 2. C 3. B 4. A 5. B
Ⅲ. 1. Similar to the theory of *yin-yang*, the theory of Five Elements was an ancient philosophical concept used to explain the universe.
    2. In traditional Chinese medicine the theory of Five Elements is used to interpret the relationship between the physiology and pathology of the human body and the natural environment.
    3. The interdependence and mutual restraint of the five elements explain the complex connection between material objects as well as the unity between the human body and the natural world.
    4. In traditional Chinese medicine, the visceral organs, as well as other organs and tissues, have similar properties to the five elements.
    5. The movement and change of all things exist through their mutual promoting and restraining.
    6. 五个元素之间的相生的关系是木生火、火生土、土生金、金生水、水生木。
    7. 相互的侵蚀及违反是正常的相生相克关系的的病变。
    8. 五行中的任何一行都制约着另一行。
    9. 通过相互促进和抑制,各种系统的功能得以互相协调和稳态发展。
    10. 相互促进、相互制约的两个方面,不可分离。

Keys to Text C

Ⅰ. 1. female 2. destiny 3. evaporate 4. hostile 5. release 6. affinity
    7. complementary 8. contradictory 9. negative 10. dominant 11. unpredictable
    12. calendar
Ⅱ. 1. B 2. A 3. A 4. D 5. A

Keys to Exercises

Ⅲ. 1. There are two natural, complementary and contradictory forces in our universe.
2. *Yin* represents the female, negative, darkness, softness, moisture, night-time.
3. Ancient scholars treated this natural phenomenon as a natural universal law.
4. The "element" in Chinese also means movement, changeable and development.
5. These elements have their *yin* and *yang sides too*.
6. 这些学者也认为宇宙由五种基本元素构成,那就是:金属、水、木、火、和土。
7. 所有的一切,包括人,在宇宙里必然和这五种基本元素有关系。
8. 所以他们把这五种元素的理论不仅用于具体物质,还运用到颜色,方向,季节以及声音等方面。
9. 他们甚至把这种理论应用于农历的年、月、小时、分以及秒。
10. 如果你想做一个幸运的人,你就必须让自己的五行处于平衡状态。

Unit 4

Keys to Text A

Ⅰ. 1. transform 2. turbid 3. dominate 4. eliminate 5. vessel 6. extraordinary 7. intestine 8. discharge 9. absorb 10. harmony 11. correspond 12. emotion

Ⅱ. 1. B 2. D 3. D 4. C 5. A

Ⅲ. 1. TCM is greatly different from western medicine in method and viewing.
2. The visceral theory is based on *zang-fu* (viscera), a general term for internal organs.
3. Physiological function of heart is governing blood and the vessels, and giving motive power for blood circulation.
4. The heart governs spiritual activities.
5. The lungs are situated in the thorax.
6. 脾脏位于人体中部——焦。
6. 肝脏负责调整气的流畅流动、储存血液。
8. 胃的主要生理机能包括接收、消化食物和液体。
9. 中医将内部身体的器官分为三种:五藏、六府和一些特殊的器官,包括大脑、骨髓、骨、血管和子宫。
10. 大肠接受小肠排送的废物。

Ⅳ. Sample Writing:

The Relationship Between the Liver and the Kidney

The liver and the kidney share the same origin. There are two reasons to explain why "the liver and the kidney share the same origin". Essence and blood come from the same source. The liver stores blood and the kidney stores essence. Sufficient blood in the liver makes it possible for the kidney to store the essence and abundant essence in the kidney provides necessary nourishment for the liver. So blood and essence promote each other and transform into each other.

The kidney pertains to water and the liver to wood. Thus kidney-water nourishes liver-wood and liver-*yin* invigorates kidney-*yin*. The mutual promotion and transformation between liver-*yin* and kidney-*yin* maintain the coordination between them and the superabundance of them.

Pathologically, insufficiency of liver-blood may lead to deficiency of kidney-essence and deficiency of kidney-essence will, in turn, bring on insufficiency of liver-blood, consequently resulting in dizziness, tinnitus(耳鸣) and weakness of the waist. Besides, insufficiency of kidney-*yin* may lead to deficiency of liver-*yin* or prolonged deficiency of liver-*yin* may cause insufficiency of kidney-*yin*, usually resulting in deficiency of both liver-*yin* and kidney-*yin*.

Keys to Text B

Ⅰ. 1. complicated 2. surplus 3. appetite 4. bile 5. distention 6. dysphoria
   7. summarization 8. concise 9. dyspeptic 10. distress 11. intemperance
   12. stool

Ⅱ. 1. C 2. A 3. D 4. C 5. B

Ⅲ. 1. In TCM, the *zang* organs pertain to *yin* and are thought of as interior.
   2. The interior-exterior relationship between *zang* organs and *fu* organs is formed by the connections of their meridians.
   3. The heart and the small intestine are connected by the heart meridian and the small intestine meridian to form an exterior-interior relationship.
   4. When the lung functions normally, the large intestine does well.
   5. Conversely when the descending function of the lung *qi* does not work well, it will affect the function of the large intestine in transportation.
   6. 由于中医的简洁和高度概括,它很可能仅仅是一个大体上的轮廓。
   7. 在中医,藏器被认为是阴和内在的东西,而腑则被认为是阳和外部的东西。
   8. 胃控制着身体的接收,而脾控制着运输和转换。
   9. 当胆汁分泌正常时,肝脏就能够完全实现它调整气的通畅的功能。
   10. 膀胱负责储存和排泄尿液。

Keys to Text C

Ⅰ. 1. abdomen 2. scanty 3. attribute 4. transmit 5. nutrient 6. digest
   7. lucid 8. chime 9. sloppy 10. urine 11. diarrhea 12. anorexia

Keys to Exercises

Ⅱ. 1. C 2. C 3. A 4. A 5. C
Ⅲ. 1. The small intestine is located in the middle of the abdomen.
   2. The physiological function of the small intestine is to receive the chyle and separate the lucid from the turbid.
   3. The lucid refers to food nutrients and the turbid refers to the waste of food.
   4. The small intestine transmits the waste to the large intestine.
   5. The digesting function of the small intestine is attributed to the transporting and transforming function of the spleen.
   6. 经过进一步的消化和吸收的营养和部分水,小肠传输垃圾至大肠。
   7. 透明指的是食物营养部分,浑浊指的是食物的糟粕部分。
   8. 小肠吸收水分的功能决定了尿液的量。
   9. 如果小肠吸收过多的水,尿液变多,大便就会停留不动。
   10. 所有这些对话使得剧情节奏慢下来。

Unit 5

Keys to Text A

Ⅰ. 1. nourish 2. substance 3. moisten 4. transforms 5. supplements 6. participate
   7. dynamic 8. pathological 9. morbid 10. scanty 11. profuse 12. aggravated
Ⅱ. 1. C 2. B 3. A 4. C 5. B
Ⅲ. 1. Blood is made up of body fluid and the nutrient *qi*.
   2. Normally there is a dynamic balance maintained between the body fluid inside and outside the vessels.
   3. Sweat, transformed from body fluid, is closely related to blood.
   4. He explained that his lameness was due to an accident.
   5. On the other hand, natural gas is still cheaper than other energy sources.
   6. 她服用维生素片剂以补充营养。
   7. 血液和体液相互依赖和互相转化。
   8. 他因过早出院而病情恶化。
   9. 也就是说,如果自己问心无愧,那就没什么可以忧愁和恐惧的。
   10. 神经网络可以概括归纳,而且对噪音有抵抗力。
Ⅳ. Sample Writing:
   The body fluids (such as *jing*, *shen* and *jin-ye*), the *qi* and blood are the "fundamental substances" that are essential for life. They can be nourished by the use of herbs and are interrelated, e.g. herbs that nourish and notify blood—they also help to nourish *qi*.

The circulation of blood in the vessels provides nutrients and moisture to the organs. This maintains normal physiological activities. A glowing complexion, glossy hair and firm muscles indicate a healthy blood circulation. The reverse will be manifested in symptoms such as giddy spells, a sallow complexion, dry hair, dry skin, forgetfulness and unconsciousness. The body fluids comprise fluids from the various organs and normal body secretions. These fluids keep the internal organs moist and may also transform into blood. Hence, an excessive expenditure of body fluids will lead to weak *qi*, poor blood circulation and blood stagnation. Certain conditions like vomiting, diarrhea and profuse perspiration will also lead to the depletion of body fluids. At the same time, shortness of *qi*, a pallid complexion and heartburn may manifest.

Keys to Text B

Ⅰ. 1. derive 2. nutrient 3. stagnation 4. emaciated 5. propel 6. deficient
   7. disturbance 8. infiltrate 9. hemorrhage 10. cereal 11. Physiologically 12. purgation

Ⅱ. 1. D 2. B 3. D 4. B 5. C

Ⅲ. 1. Despite their differences in nature, form and function, *qi*, blood and body fluid have something in common with each other.
   2. They are the basic materials that constitute the human body and maintain life activities.
   3. Blood is formed from mutative *qi* and body fluid.
   4. Blood circulation depends on the propelling function of heart-*qi*.
   5. Blood provides adequate nutrients for *qi*.
   6. 气和体液之间的关系跟气和血之间的关系十分相似。
   7. 体液的形成、分布和排泄取依赖于所有气的运行。
   8. 血液和体液执行营养和滋润的职能。
   9. 另外,生长激素可以黏附结合蛋白质。
   10. 其发病原因主要可以归纳为内因和外因。

Keys to Text C

Ⅰ. 1. inhale 2. replenish 3. circulates 4. impairment 5. mobilization 6. primordial
   7. instability 8. Somatic 9. dizziness 10. category 11. accumulate 12. respiration

Ⅱ. 1. A 2. C 3. B 4. B 5. D

Ⅲ. 1. Similar to the theory of *yin-yang*, *qi* was derived from ancient Chinese philosophy.
   2. *Qi*'s movements explain various life processes.
   3. *Qi* is often called vital energy.

Keys to Exercises

4. A healthy body requires normal circulations of *qi*.
5. *Qi* plays an important role in the processes of the human body.
6. 气通常根据其作用的部位分类。
7. 医疗保健气功主要分为两大类。
8. 坐、站或躺都可以练气功。
9. 一些小动物通常在夏季储存坚果以备冬季食用。
10. 他们让你的孩子腿部用力以站起。

Unit 6

Keys to Text A

Ⅰ. 1. enhance　2. distribute　3. manifest　4. superficial　5. symmetrical　6. originate
　7. principal　8. circulation　9. muscle　10. feature　11. joint　12. extraordinary

Ⅱ. 1. C　2. B　3. A　4. D　5. A

Ⅲ. 1. The meridian (*jing-luo*) originated in TCM.
　2. The meridians are divided into 12 main meridians and 8 extraordinary meridians.
　3. The fine collaterals refer to numerous tiny collaterals.
　4. Twelve main meridians are symmetrically distributed on both sides of the body.
　5. The name of each main meridian includes three parts: hand or foot, *yin* or *yang*, and *zang* or *fu*.
　6. 十二经脉的走向以及连接是遵循一定规律的。
　7. 足阳经从脸部、头部一直到脚趾。
　8. 12个皮部是身体的表层区域,在那里12经脉的功能得以显现。
　9. 各弓状动脉进入宫壁后,即在宫壁内分支形成3个血管层：浆膜层、大血管层和粘肌层。
　10. 冲动和行动源于高级自我和低级自我。

Ⅳ. Sample Writing:

　　At present, each subject is high-speed developing in medical field. Only acupuncture and moxibustion is developing slowly relatively. As for the reason, we discover that all acupuncturists think the theory of channels and collaterals of *Huangdi Neijing* are perfect all along. In light of the theory of channels and collaterals, the channels and collaterals belong to the *zang-fu* organs interiorly and extend to the extremities and joints exteriorly, link the whole body, but as for limbs, there aren't channels and acupoints in some area. If symptom occurs in these area, what can we do? The points of organs are all from the back. In the 21 vertebrae, except for the back point of 12 channels, there is no corresponding back-*shu* and channel for the other back-*shu*. How to understand the completeness of back-*shu* and *zang-fu* organs, channels? Deeply studying and discussing, we think all acupuncturists should have the responsibility to develop the theory of channels and collaterals on the basis of the inheriting original theory, and make the level of acupuncture and moxibustion progress in all over the world. If we want to reach the target, we should begin from two ways as follows. At first, basing on the liberating thought, the theory of the meridians should be perfected; on the other side, the clinical differential diagnoses of acupuncture and moxibustion should make use of the modern technique and make differential diagnoses of acupuncture obtain objective data, we can superiorly improve the level of diagnoses and curative effect, like this, we can get the revolutionary breakthrough in acupuncture and moxibustion's field.

Keys to Text B

Ⅰ. 1. portion 2. tissue 3. divergent 4. extremity 5. organic 6. branch
 7. terminate 8. subsidiary 9. superficial 10. muscular 11. dominated 12. enhance
Ⅱ. 1. C 2. D 3. B 4. A 5. D
Ⅲ. 1. The meridian-collateral theory guides the clinical practice of TCM.
 2. The meridians are the major trunks of the meridian-collateral system.
 3. Collaterals are the branches of the meridians and are distributed over the whole body.
 4. Meridians and collaterals make all the body's organs and tissues an organic whole.
 5. The divergent collaterals are the larger and main collaterals.
 6. 十二别络是十二正经的拓展。
 7. 孙络指最小最细的络脉。
 8. 浮络运行于人体的表面。
 9. 指出可利用不同粒度的滤料颗粒组成滤层,使之接近理想滤层。
 10. 此外,早起对我们健康也有益处。

Keys to Text C

Ⅰ. 1. apt 2. exerting 3. selective 4. bearing 5. medicinal 6. Intrude
 7. formulate 8. Induce 9. relieve 10. promote 11. disperse 12. regulating
Ⅱ. 1. B 2. C 3. A 4. C 5. D
Ⅲ. 1. The channels and collaterals have a direct bearing on the occurrence and progress of diseases.
 2. The channels and collaterals are the route along which exogenous factors intrude into the internal organs from the body surface.
 3. All these discoveries are helpful in diagnosis.

Keys to Exercises

4. The theory has long been widely applied to direct clinical treatment of all the departments of TCM.
5. Other medicine has also been directed to the channel in order to bring the therapeutic action into play.
6. 这种疾病易被传染。
7. 这次手术由于技术原因被推迟。
8. 头痛可根据经络在头部的分部规律进行诊断。
9. 他们的销售策略是根据对消费者花钱的情况所作的研究而制定的。
10. 所有的活动都在一名经验丰富的医生指导下进行。

Unit 7

Keys to Text A

Ⅰ. 1. ulcer 2. impairs 3. aversion 4. mania 5. restlessness 6. clinical
 7. Insomnia 8. scanty 9. urine 10. syndrome 11. fluids 12. stimulation

Ⅱ. 1. B 2. A 3. D 4. B 5. C

Ⅲ. 1. In clinical practice, it can be seen that the syndromes caused by fire-heat are mostly related with the upper part of the human body, for example, the head and face.
 2. Fire is likely to cause sores and ulcers.
 3. When high fever persists and becomes predominant, the flesh will erode and produce pus, which is termed carbuncle.
 4. The extreme of heat produces wind.
 5. Fire comes into being when *yang* becomes predominant.
 6. 火很有可能耗气,并且还会损害体液。
 7. 火可以产生风并促进血流。
 8. 痈和坏疽都由毒热引起。
 9. 在临床实践中,有局热的肿起的疮和溃疡被区分为阳和上火。
 10. 人们认为火和热与心相关,因为心主血脉,主神明。

Ⅳ. Sample Writing:

Etiology

Traditional Chinese medicine posits a uniquely relative relationship between the *zang-fu* organs and tissues of the human body, as well as between the human body and the natural environment. All are in a relatively balanced state in order to maintain the body's normal physiological function. When this balance is destroyed disease results.

Through long term clinical practice, the ancient Chinese realized that there are many factors which may bring about imbalances in the human body and thus disease; climate abnormalities, pestilence, emotional stimulation, injury by irregular diet or overstrain, trauma, insect-bited, etc., plus pathological products of disease outcome, such as blood stasis, phlegm-humor, etc. All of these contribute to imbalances within the human system.

The etiology of traditional Chinese medicine used clinical manifestations as evidence, i.e., through the analysis of symptoms and signs of a disease, one can find its causative factors. This is technically termed "checking syndromes to find causative factors of a disease". For our study of etiology, we must concern ourselves with the properties of pathogenic factors and the characteristics of how and why they cause disease.

Keys to Text B

Ⅰ. 1. essence   2. germinate   3. disperse   4. pathogenic   5. diarrhea   6. consumption
7. syndrome   8. refine   9. pathological   10. manifestation   11. energetic
12. acceptable

Ⅱ. 1. C   2. A   3. B   4. C   5. A

Ⅲ. 1. The six climatic evils include wind, cold, summer-heat, dampness, dryness and fire.
2. Then they will invade the human body and cause diseases if the body's energetic level of genuine-*qi* is low, and if its ability to resist disease is weak.
3. In the course of causing diseases, any one of the six climatic evils not only can be influenced by the others, but also can be transformed into another kind of evil under certain conditions.
4. In most cases, the six climatic evils get into the body and cause diseases through the skin and muscle, or the mouth and nose, or through both ways.
5. Although this concept needs refining, it is an acceptable beginning approach.
6. 这些通常被叫做"六淫",也就是六种自然界的气候。
7. 六淫代表了不同的自然条件,其中包括了一切有生命的东西,他们对人没有害处。
8. 这六淫能单独或共同侵袭人体。
9. 但是气候也许会在特定情况下变成一种引起疾病的原因。
10. 在当今的临床实践中,因六淫导致的综合征或疾病也包括生物因素(细菌、病毒等)或化学因素等所导致的疾病问题。

Keys to Text C

Ⅰ. 1. occurrence   2. etiological   3. viscera   4. limbs   5. orifice   6. traumatic
7. differentiation   8. infectious   9. maintain   10. pathogen   11. syndrome
12. symptoms

Ⅱ. 1. A 2. B 3. B 4. D 5. B
Ⅲ. 1. The pathogenic evils either originate in *yin* or originate in *yang*.
   2. All diseases and medical problems are exactly within three categories.
   3. According to TCM, there is no symptom without any cause.
   4. To understand the causes of diseases, TCM examines the clinical manifestations of diseases and studies the possible pathogenic factors.
   5. There are medical problems related to the factors such as sexual activities, injuries by sharp metal things, bites by insect or beast.
   6. 导致发病的病因是多样的,而这些病因可能会在特定的情况下致病。
   7. 在《黄帝内经》中,所有的病因第一次被分为两类,也就是阴和阳。
   8. 当六淫作用过盛,它们就会侵入筋络,然后进入脏腑,所以它们属于致病外因。
   9. 通过分析症状和临床表现来需找病因的方法被称作"辩证法寻找病因"。
   10. 于是,中医病因学不仅研究病因的特点和致病特点,而且也研究因不同病因所产生的疾病和症状的临床表现。这样可以指导临床诊断和治疗。

Unit 8

Keys to Text A

Ⅰ. 1. eliminated 2. hoarse 3. transmitted 4. retention 5. Manifestation
   6. deficiency 7. impairs 8. exhaustion 9. abundance 10. essence
   11. stagnant 12. spontaneous
Ⅱ. 1. D 2. D 3. B 4. C 5. C
Ⅲ. 1. The occurrence of disease results from the struggle between pathogenic factors and healthy *qi*.
   2. Clinically excess syndrome manifests high fever.
   3. Excess is related to pathogenic factors while deficiency is related to healthy *qi*.
   4. Premier Wen, accompanied by officials, visited the local enterprises.
   5. Mechanism of pathological changes includes the nature of disease and its transmitting principles.
   6. 正邪消长有可能导致实证与虚证相混合。
   7. 曼德拉在结束南非种族隔离的运动中起了主要作用。
   8. 冒雨外出导致了重感冒。
   9. 虚症的临床表现有沮丧、心悸和盗汗等。
   10. 左栏里的数字是关于我们海外销售额的。
Ⅳ. Sample Writing:
   Inflammation is one of the most common mechanisms of disease. In medical terminology the suffix "it is" refers to inflammation. When you consider that the majority

of diseases have names ending in "it is" you have to be interested in inflammation, its causes and cures. Inflammation is manifest by pain, swelling, redness, and loss of function in the afflicted tissue. The process is created by immune cells invading the tissue like an army in full battle mode.

Inflammation is often triggered by circulating immune complexes that enter tissues. Immune complexes are found in rheumatoid arthritis in joints and as CICs in patients with systemic disease. Joint destruction begins as a vasculitis with increased capillary permeability, edema, followed by cell infiltrates that create and maintain inflammation. A constant supply of antigen is available from the food supply to maintain chronic inflammation and therefore is important to consider food causes of inflammation as in asthma, arthritis and other "autoimmune diseases".

Keys to Text B

Ⅰ. 1. lingers   2. pathogenic   3. mutual   4. eventually   5. characterize   6. individual
   7. variation   8. penetrated   9. physiological   10. frequent   11. sufficient
   12. stalemate

Ⅱ. 1. B   2. C   3. C   4. D   5. A

Ⅲ. 1. Such a variation decides the development of disease.
   2. Deficiency syndrome and excess syndrome often transform into each other.
   3. During the course of our conversation, it emerged that Bob had been in prison.
   4. When polite requests failed, we resorted to threats.
   5. Some foreigners have always wanted to be able to speak Chinese.
   6. 这种病理被称为由虚引起的实。
   7. 正气不足不能限制邪气的增长。
   8. 她太倔强了,不会让任何人帮她的。
   9. 如果采取适当的治疗,病邪可以消除或减少。
   10. 调味汁不要煮沸,否则会影响味道。

Keys to Text C

Ⅰ. 1. severity   2. indicated   3. obviously   4. maintain   5. improper   6. violent
   7. pertaining   8. various   9. indistinct   10. originally   11. scanty   12. sensation

Ⅱ. 1. B   2. B   3. C   4. C   5. B

Ⅲ. 1. The nature of the disease originally pertains to *yang*-cold.
   2. Separation of yin and yang exhausts essence.
   3. Loss of *yin* and loss of *yang* may appear solitarily.

4. You can't change iron into gold.

5. Quantities of arms were discovered hidden in the trucks.

6. 疾病的性质最初与阳热有关。

7. 人身体中的阴阳一般保持着动态的平衡。

8. 我讨厌做家务。

9. 詹姆斯已经长成为一个富有魅力的年轻人。

10. 我们的两个儿子一点也不像。

Unit 9

Keys to Text A

Ⅰ. 1. Moxibustion 2. diagnostic 3. invasive 4. practitioner 5. bruised 6. artery
  7. therapy 8. praxised 9. sprain 10. trauma 11. Palpation 12. resort

Ⅱ. 1. B 2. C 3. D 4. C 5. B

Ⅲ. 1. Inspection, auscultation and olfaction, inquiry, pulse-taking and palpation are the basics of TCM diagnostics.

2. Traditional Chinese medicine uses herbs and other drugs as the last resort to fight health problems.

3. There is a Chinese saying, "Any medicine has 30% poison ingredients."

4. In the treatment of a number of difficult and complicated cases, combined Chinese and western medical means have shown satisfactory results.

5. His punishing work schedule had made him resort to drugs.

6. 现代医学常趋向于过分注重发展高度复杂的外科技术。

7. 这种药品对这一类细菌有效。

8. 这种照明用具符合新的安全要求。

9. 望舌又称舌诊,是中医望诊中的重要部分。

10. 听声音,是凭听觉以觉察病人语言、呼吸、咳嗽等声音的异常变化。

Ⅳ. Sample Writing:

　　TCM diagnostics is a study of the theories, methods and diagnosis techniques. Some are unique to TCM while others are similar to those used in Western medicine. Its rich substantial content is the foundation of all branches of TCM.

　　A TCM doctor makes a diagnosis based on his sensory perceptions to gather clinical information and then analyses and interprets this data usually without resorting to any apparatus. The doctor can diagnose internal pathological (disease) changes through observation and analysis of external signs. The Chinese believe the human body is an organic whole, and all parts are connected with each other by channels and collaterals (otherwise known as meridians).

There are four examination methods: questioning/history taking, inspection, auscultation (listening) & olfaction (smelling), pulse-taking and palpation. The four methods have their unique clinical functions and cannot be replaced by one another. Sometimes, false manifestations of a disease occur which emphasize the importance of integrating all diagnostic methods.

Keys to Text B

Ⅰ. 1. inspection   2. Auscultation   3. olfaction   4. simultaneous   5. administrated
   6. sensitivity   7. locality   8. severity   9. pore   10. dosage   11. inquiry
   12. differentiate

Ⅱ. 1. B   2. B   3. D   4. C   5. A

Ⅲ. 1. The case history, symptoms, and signs gained through those four diagnostic methods are analyzed and generalized to find the causes, nature, and interrelations of the disease.
   2. Therapeutic Principles are the basis for guiding clinical practice.
   3. Factors such as climatic and seasonal conditions, geographic localities, and the patient's personal conditions must be considered in treatment.
   4. Disease is the outcome of the struggle between body resistance and pathogenic factors.
   5. In summer, the surface pores on the body are open or loose.
   6. 正气是身体抵抗疾病的能力。
   7. 中医上，表里原则应用于处理急性阶段的症状。
   8. 用来治疗夏季疾病的草药要与具有祛湿功效的草药结合。
   9. 嗅气味，主要是诊察病人的身体气味和排泄物气味，包括口气、痰、涕、汗、血、二便等。
   10. 问诊是医生询问病人或陪诊者，了解病情和病史的一种诊察疾病的方法。

Keys to Text C

Ⅰ. 1. stern   2. delirium   3. odor   4. melodious   5. detected   6. consistent
   7. deprived   8. visceral   9. disperse   10. coherent   11. inflexible   12. restlessness

Ⅱ. 1. B   2. C   3. D   4. D   5. D

Ⅲ. 1. Auscultation and olfaction means listening to various sounds and noises made by the patient.
   2. Since the viscera, constitution and physical building are different from person to person, the voice is high or low, loud or small and clear or full.
   3. Hoarseness means harsh voice, while aphonia means complete loss of voice.

Keys to Exercises

4. Slurred speech is marked by unclear and slow expression without fluency, usually seen in wind stroke or sequela of wind stroke.
5. Such a morbid condition pertains to sthenia syndrome.
6. 正常人说话发音自然,语气柔和,表达清晰,语意一致。
7. 一般来说,正常人又高又亮的声音是元气和肺气充足的一种表现。
8. 若声音嘶哑和失声在疾病初起时属于实证,是由外部致病因素引起的。
9. 病人说话声音的强与弱,一方面是反应正气的盛衰,同时也与邪气的性质有关。
10. 一般地说,语言高亢洪亮、多言而躁动的,属实证、热证。

Unit 10

Keys to Text A

Ⅰ. 1. clinical 2. clarify 3. respectively 4. synthesizing 5. Excessive 6. static 7. intrinsic 8. grasp 9. dynamic 10. prescribe 11. internal 12. intrinsic

Ⅱ. 1. C 2. A 3. B 4. D 5. C

Ⅲ. 1. Among the eight principles, *yin* and *yang* are the general principles which can be used to generalize the other six principles.
2. Sthenia syndromes are always associated with chronic diseases.
3. Based on such treatment and diagnosis, a traditional Chinese medicine practitioner can prescribe drugs, identify and treat diseases.
4. The traditional Chinese medicine first focuses on the "*zheng*"(证), not on differences of the disease.
5. It is necessary to differentiate disease and constitutes a special procedure of research and treatment in traditional Chinese diagnosis.
6. 掌握的病机越全面,越容易准确而有效地进行辨证。
7. 疾病的表现尽管错综复杂,但基本上都可以用八纲从疾病的类别、病变部位和病性进行分析。
8. 相对来说,辨别实证、虚证比较简单。
9. 其中阴阳又是八纲中的总纲,可以概括其它六纲,即表、热、实证属阳;里、寒、虚证属阴。
10. 表里是表示病变部位、病情轻重和病势趋向的两个纲领。

Ⅳ. Sample writing:

The content of the eight principles was discussed early in the *Huangdi Neijing* (*The Yellow Emperor's Classic of Medicine*). However it was not until the Ming Dynasty, that physicians used it regularly in diagnosis of patients. For example Zhang Sanxi wrote in the book *Yi Xue Liu Yao* (*Six Essence of Medicine*), "The ancient physicians treated on the basis of eight methods. These were *yin*, *yang*, exterior, interior, cold, heat, deficiency (sthenia) and excess (asthenia). In addition, *qi*, blood, phlegm and fire were also included within these." Wang Zhizhong, also from the Ming Dynasty, said in the book *Dong Yuan Xian Sheng Shang Han Zheng Mai*: *Juan Yi*, "If the doctor does not vary from the eight words (principles), then people will not be killed."

Today, TCM doctors still use the eight principles to understand the location and nature of pathological changes, the course of the disease and the strength of the evil and the vital energy (*qi*). It serves as the guiding rules for all syndrome identification.

Keys to Text B

Ⅰ. 1. digestive 2. contaminated 3. encumbered 4. slippery 5. intake 6. exuberance
   7. sallow 8. turbid 9. lassitude 10. overstrain 11. bland 12. profuse
Ⅱ. 1. C 2. A 3. C 4. B 5. A
Ⅲ. 1. Spleen disease is mainly marked by dysfunction of the spleen to transport, transform and govern blood.
   2. Dampness is generally triggered by pre-existing spleen asthenia.
   3. Fluid distention is a manifestation of spleen asthenia leading to sthenia.
   4. Spleen is associated with earth, and governs transformation and transportation.
   5. Profuse and thin leukorrhagia is due to asthenia of splenic *yang*.
   6. 喜温喜暗多由阳虚所致。
   7. 脾气下陷证指的是脾气虚或者脾气不能上升之证。
   8. 少气懒言是由于运化不足所致。
   9. 虚实是反映人体邪正盛衰的纲领。
   10. 虚指正气不足,实指邪气亢盛。

Keys to Text C

Ⅰ. 1. greasy 2. numbness 3. sweat 4. rotate 5. scanty 6. excrete
   7. aching 8. relapse 9. mania 10. sticky 11. dispiritedness 12. distend
Ⅱ. 1. C 2. D 3. D 4. D 5. B
Ⅲ. 1. The former is caused by insufficiency of the production of body fluid or excessive loss of body fluid.
   2. This disease is mainly due to six exogenous pathogenic factors.
   3. Edema starts from the eyelids, and then spreads to the four limbs and all over the body rapidly.
   4. Wind is regarded as the head among all the pathogenic factors.
   5. Before edema is treated, *yang* edema and *yin* edema should be distinguished first.

Keys to Exercises

6. 西医学中的急、慢性肾小球肾炎、肾病综合征、继发性肾小球疾病及心源性、肝源性、营养不良性、内分泌因素导致的全身性水肿，可参照本病辨证治疗。
7. 这种综合征的特点是呕吐、痰涎和头晕。
8. 水肿的治疗原则以发汗、利尿、导泄为基本原则。
9. 脏腑辨证是内在脏腑功能失调的反映。
10. 由于每一个脏腑的生理功能不同，所以它反映出的病症也有所不同。

Unit 11

Keys to Text A

Ⅰ. 1. Anatomy 2. established 3. organs 4. exists 5. primitive 6. Pesticide
   7. nervous 8. Institute 9. Molecule 10. environment 11. evidence 12. relieve

Ⅱ. 1. A 2. B 3. D 4. C 5. B

Ⅲ. 1. The institute which I belong to was established in 1864.
   2. Some plants contain over 170 different chemicals.
   3. In essence, you have told me how to settle the problem.
   4. Many of us suffer from lung problems.
   5. Our liver has to deal with these man-made chemicals.
   6. 你得认真考虑后再答复我。
   7. 他仔细地读了这份合同。
   8. 现代社会，很多人都在压力之下工作。
   9. 我们遭受到的问题是由于饮用水被钢铁厂和其他工业污染所造成的。
   10. 我们所食用的各种食物也遭受了污染。

Ⅳ. Sample Writing：

Herbal medicine has developed since pioneer days, and we now have institutes of phytotherapy or herbal medicine. It includes the study of the traditional medical subjects, such as pathology, physiology, anatomy and biochemistry. Besides, plant remedies are studied in great detail including the pharmacological properties of the plants. 170 chemicals contained in some plants work together, and that is really the essence of the difference between allopathy and herbal medicine in its holistic approach.

Stress affects the body in many ways. Many of us suffer from lung problems. We suffer from problems caused by pollution. Our liver is the same organ we had as primitive man and there is no evidence that the liver is able to handle man-made molecules. As a result, we have invented new diseases. To help us along, the herbs and the natural medical plants are still proving very faithful.

Keys to Text B

Ⅰ. 1. nourished   2. flaky   3. onslaught   4. purchased   5. joint   6. overwhelmed
   7. itchy   8. soothe   9. fluctuates   10. maintains   11. extinguish   12. irritated

Ⅱ. 1. D   2. C   3. B   4. A   5. D

Ⅲ. 1. She spent two years researching and developing a line of herbal formulations.
   2. Lack of energy in old age may be associated with health problems.
   3. More and more people turn their attention to their own health.
   4. This herbal formula doesn't contain any sulphur, preservations or chemicals.
   5. Maintaining a balance between the mind and the body is vital for health.
   6. 宠物不许入内，你的宠物也不例外。
   7. 开水冲化即可服用。
   8. 他有慢性消化系统疾病。
   9. 她相信中医的治疗原则同样可以运用在对狗类疾病的治疗上。
   10. 根据疾病隐藏的基本问题开方。

Keys to Text C

Ⅰ. 1. solvent   2. chronic   3. extraction   4. Ion   5. definite   6. angle
   7. scales   8. viral   9. immunity   10. permeated   11. outstanding   12. enhanced

Ⅱ. 1. C   2. D   3. B   4. A   5. B

Ⅲ. 1. Many questions have already been asked by the journalists from different angles.
   2. This therapy is simple and thus is worth of being applied in large scales.
   3. The law should be put into practice as soon as possible.
   4. The rate for HBV-DNA to turn into negative is much higher in treatment group.
   5. The views on this problem vary from different sex, grades and majors among college students.
   6. 本文论述了交际中的文化障碍。
   7. 这种药物可以大大增加白细胞数量和机体免疫力。
   8. 研究表明此药安全性好，没有明显的副作用。
   9. 这一方法也很容易在大范围内得以推广。
   10. 超临界溶剂提取法也被提及但是缺乏提取技术的诸多细节。

Glossary

A

abdomen	n.	腹部	U1
abnormal	a.	反常的,例外的,不规则的,变态的	U1
absorb	v.	吸收,使全神贯注,汲取,理解	U4
abundance	n.	大量,充足	U8
accumulate	vt.	积累,存储,蓄积(财产等),堆积	U5
aching	a.	疼痛的,心痛的	
	v.	疼痛,渴望	U10
accumulate	v.	积聚,累积,积攒	U9
acute	a.	尖锐的,剧烈的,激烈的,敏锐的,严重的	U2
administrate	v.	给予,经营,实施,掌管,料理	U9
affinity	n.	吸引力,姻亲关系,密切关系,类同	U3
aggravate	vt.	加重,加剧	U5
aggravation	n.	加重,恶化	U8
agile	a.	灵巧的	U11
alkaloid	n.	生物碱,植物碱基	U11
alleviation	n.	减轻,缓解,缓和,镇痛物	U6
allopathy	n.	对抗疗法	U11
analogize	v.	以类推来说明,类似	U3
analogy	n.	类似,相似,类推,类比,比拟,同功	U2
anatomy	n.	剖析,解剖学,骨骼,结构	U11
anorexia	n.	神经性厌食症	U4
anti-tumor	a.	抗肿瘤	U11
anus	n.	肛门	U4
aphonia	n.	(耳鼻喉)失音,不能发音	U9
appetite	n.	爱好,食欲,欲望	U4
apt	a.	易于……的,有……倾向的	U6
artery	n.	动脉,干线,要道,中枢	U9
arthritis	n.	关节炎	U11
ascendance	n.	上升,权势,支配地位	U3

aspartic acid	n.	[化]天冬氨酸	U11
asthma	n.	[医]气喘(病),哮喘	U6
astringency	n.	收敛性,严厉,严峻	U4
astronomy	n.	天文学	U2
attribute	vt.	把……归于,归属	U3
auscultation	n.	听诊	U1
aversion	n.	厌恶,讨厌,反感	U8

B

bearing	n.	关系,关联(+on)	U4
bile	n.	胆汁,愤怒,坏脾气	U4
bladder	n.	膀胱	U1
bland	a.	乏味的,温和的,冷漠的	
	vt.	使……变得淡而无味,除掉……的特性	U10
branch	n.	树枝,支流,分店	
	v.	分支,分割	U6
bruise	n.	青肿,伤痕,擦伤,(感情等方面的)创伤	U9
bulgy	a.	凸出的,膨胀的,肿胀的	U10

C

calendar	n.	日历,历法,日程表	U3
carbuncle	n.	[医]痈	U7
categorize	vt.	分类	U10
category	n.	种类,分类,范畴	U3
cavity	n.	洞,穴,凹处	U9
cereal	a.	谷类的	U5
characteristic	a.	特有的,典型的	U1
characterize	vt.	是……的特征,以……为特征	U4
chime	n.	一致,和谐	U4
chyme	n.	食糜	U4
cinnamic	a.	苯乙烯的	U11
circulate	vt.	使(血液等)循环,流通,散布,传播	U5
circulation	n.	循环	U5
clarify	vt.	澄清,阐明	U10
classify	vt.	把……分类,分为同一等级,说明,把……列为密件	U9
clinical	a.	临床的	U2
clinically	ad.	临床上地	U4

coherent	a.	一致的,协调的	U9
collateral	n.	络脉	
	a.	并行的,旁系的,附随的	U6
coma	n.	昏迷	U7
combination	n.	结合,化合,联合,组合	U3
complement	n.	补足物,余角,补语	
	v.	补助,补足	U3
complementary	a.	补足的,补充的	U3
complicated	a.	复杂的	U4
component	n.	组成整件部分的单件,构成要素,成分	U3
concise	a.	简洁的,简明的	U4
concrete	a.	实体的,有形的,确实的,明确的,确定的	U3
condensation	n.	凝结,缩合	U2
conflict	vi.	冲突,矛盾,斗争,争执	U10
conform	vi.	遵守,符合(to, with)	U9
connotation	n.	内涵意义,隐含意义	U2
consistent	a.	始终如一的,一致的	U9
constituent	n.	选民,成分,构成部分,要素	U1
constitute	v.	制定,组成,建立	U3
contaminated	a.	受污染的,弄脏的	U10
contradictory	a.	矛盾的,反驳的,反对的,抗辩的	U3
contrasting	a.	形成鲜明对比的,截然不同的	U9
convulsion	n.	抽搐,惊厥	U7
coordination	n.	同等,调和	U3
correlation	n.	相互关系,关联	U2
correspond	vi.	相符合,相一致,相当,相类似,通信	U2
corresponding	a.	相当的,对应的,符合的,一致的	U1
counterbalance	v.	对……起平衡作用,抵消	U2
crimson	n.	深红色	
	v.	变得绯红,成熟,染成深红色	U4

D

dampness	n.	潮湿,湿气	U1
deduce	v.	推论,演绎出	U3
deficiency	n.	缺乏,不足,短缺	U8
deficient	a.	缺乏,不足的	U5
delirium	n.	神志昏迷,说胡话	U7
deprive	vt.	使丧失,剥夺	U9

derive	vt.	获得,导出(from)	U5
descend	v.	下降,屈尊	U3
designation	n.	指定,命名,任命,称号	U2
destiny	n.	命运,定数,天命	U3
detect	vt.	发现,察觉,查出,看穿	U9
diagnostics	n.	诊断学	U9
dialectic	n.	论理的推论,辩证法	
	a.	辩证的,方言的,辩证法的	U1
dialectics	n.	辩证法	U2
diaphoresis	n.	发汗,出汗	U5
diaphoretics	n.	发汗剂	U5
diarrhea	n.	腹泻	U4
differentiate	v.	使有差异,区别,区分,鉴别	U9
digest	vt.	消化	U4
digestive	a.	消化的,助消化的	
	n.	助消化药	U10
discharge	n.	排泄	U4
discipline	n.	纪律,风纪,规定,训练,锻炼,修养,教养,方法,规律性	U9
disorder	n.	(身心、机能)失调	U1
dispense	v.	分发,分配,免除,省掉	U3
disperse	vt.	驱散,解散,疏散,分散,散开	U6
dispiritedness	n.	精神不振	U10
dissolving	a.	消融的	U9
distend	vt.	使……膨胀,使……扩张	U10
distention	n.	膨胀,扩张	U4
distress	n.	悲痛,不幸,穷困	
	v.	使悲痛,使苦恼,使贫困	U4
distributed	a.	分布式的	U6
disturbance	n.	障碍,失调	U5
divergent	a.	分歧的	U6
dizziness	n.	头昏眼花	U5
docile	a.	温顺的,驯服的,容易教的	U3
domain	n.	范围,领域	U2
dominant	a.	支配的,统治的,占优势的,显性的	U3
dominate	v.	支配,控制,统治	U4
draught	n.	气流,汇票,草稿	U3
duration	n.	持续,持续的时间,期间	U8
dynamic	a.	有活力的,强有力的	
	a.	[医]机能上的	U2

210

dysfunction	n.	[医]机能障碍,机能不良	U5
dyspeptic	n.	消化不良的人	
	a.	消化不良的,胃弱的	U4
dysphoria	n.	焦虑,烦躁不安	U4
dysuria	n.	排尿困难	U10

E

edema	n.	水肿,浮肿,瘤腺体	U8
emaciate	vt.	使憔悴,使瘦弱	U5
emaciation	n.	消瘦,憔悴,衰弱	U8
encroach	v.	(暗中或逐步)侵占,占用(on/upon),侵蚀,超越	U3
encumber	vt.	阻塞,妨害,拖累	U10
endogenous	a.	内长的,内生的	U1
enhance	v.	提高,增加,加强	U6
enmity	n.	敌意,憎恨	U3
environment	n.	环境,外界,围绕	U11
epilepsy	n.	[医]癫痫,癫痫症	U10
establish	v.	建立,确立,制定,生长	U11
etiological	n.	病因学的,病原学的	U7
evaluate	v.	评估,赋值,评价	U2
evaporate	vt.	使……蒸发,使……脱水,使……消失	U3
eventually	ad.	终于,最后	U8
evidence	n.	根据,证据,迹象	U11
excess	n.	过分,过量	U8
excessive	a.	过多的,极度的,过分的	U10
excreta	n.	排泄物,分泌物	U9
excrete	v.	排泄,分泌	U4
excretion	n.	排泄,分泌	U5
exert	vt.	运用,行使,发挥,施加,用(力),尽(力)	U6
exhalation	n.	呼气,散发,蒸发,散发物	U2
exhaustion	n.	精疲力竭,疲劳,用光,耗尽	U8
exist	vi.	存在,生存,发生	U11
exogenous	a.	外生的,外成的,外因的	U7
expel	vt.	驱逐,赶走	U1
expound	v.	解释,详细述说	U3
extinguish	vt.	使熄灭,扑灭,使……不复存在	U11
extraordinary	a.	非常的,特别的	U4
extravasate	vt.	使(血液等)由脉管中渗出	U5

extravasation	n.	[医]外渗（沉）		U6
extremity	n.	极端,困境,极点		U10
exuberance	n.	丰富,茂盛,健康		U10
eyelid	n.	眼睑,眼皮		U10

F

fatigue	n.	疲劳,疲乏,杂役		U10
febrile	a.	[医]热病的,发烧的		U9
federal	a.	联邦(制)的,联邦政府的		U11
female	a.	女性的,雌性的,柔弱的,柔和的		U3
ferulic acid		[医]阿魏酸		U11
fibrosis	n.	纤维症		U11
fine collaterals	n.	孙络		U6
flaky	a.	薄片的,成片的,薄而易剥落的		U11
flexible	a.	灵活的,柔韧的,易弯曲的		U10
fluctuate	v.	波动,涨落,起伏		U11
fluent	a.	流利的,流畅的,液态的,畅流的		U9
fluid	n.	液体,流体		U5
flux	n.	流量,流出,变迁,不稳定		U3
formulate	vt.	系统地阐述(或说明),配制		U6
formulation	n.	用公式表示,明确地表达,作简洁陈述		U11
frequent	a.	时常发生的,常见的		U8
fungicide	n.	杀真菌剂		U11

G

gall bladder	n.	胆囊		U1
gangrene	n.	坏疽		U7
gastric	a.	胃的		U4
gastrosplenic	a.	胃脾的		U10
generalize	v.	归纳,推广,泛论,推断		U9
generate	v.	产生,导致,发生		U2
generation	n.	一代,产生,一世		U3
genetically	ad.	基因地,遗传上地,从遗传学角度,从遗传方面地		U5
geographical	a.	地理(学)的		U1
germination	n.	发生,发芽,伟晶作用		U3
grasp	vt.	抓住,领会		
	n.	抓住,理解,控制		U10

| greasy | a. | 油腻的,含脂肪多的,谄媚的 | U10 |

H

harmony	n.	协调,融洽,调和,和睦	U3
hematemesis	n.	咯血,吐血	U7
hemorrhage	n.	[医]出血	U5
herb	n.	草本植物,药草,香草	U11
herbalist	n.	草药医生	U11
heritage	n.	遗产,继承物,传统	U1
hidrosis	n.	[医]汗病,多汗症	U5
hoarse	a.	沙哑的	U8
hostile	a.	敌对的,敌方的,怀敌意的	U3
humid	a.	潮湿的,湿气重的	U1
hypochondriac	a.	忧郁症的,患疑难症的	U5
hypochondrium	n.	忧郁症,疑病症,季肋部	U4

I

identification	n.	认出,鉴定,识别,确认	U2
ileocecal	a.	回盲肠的	U4
immunity	n.	免疫,免疫性,免除	U11
impair	vt.	损害,削弱	U8
impairment	n.	故障,缺陷,损害,损伤,减少,削减,恶化	U5
improper	a.	不合适的,不适当的	U8
indicate	vt.	标示,指示,指出	U8
indispensable	a.	不可缺少的,绝对必要的,不能避免的	U2
indistinct	a.	不清楚的,模糊的	U8
individual	a.	个别的,单独的,个人的	U8
induce	vt.	引起,导致	U6
infectious	a.	传染的	U7
infiltrate	vt.	渗(透,吸)入	U5
inflexible	a.	不可改变的,不容变更的,不屈不挠的	U9
influence	n.	影响,势力,权势,产生影响的人(事物)	
	vt.	影响,感化	U1
inhalation	n.	吸入,吸入物,吸入剂	U2
inhale	vt.	吸入(空气、水蒸气等),把……吸进肺里	U5
inquiry	n.	打听,询问,调查,查问	U1
inquiry	n.	质询,调查	U9

inseparable	a.	不可分的,分不开	U2
insomnia	n.	失眠(症)	U7
inspection	n.	检查,视察	U9
instability	n.	不稳定性,不坚决,反复无常,[化]不稳定度(性)	U5
institute	n.	学会,学院,协会	
	vt.	创立,开始,制定,任命	U11
intake	n.	摄取量,通风口,引入口,引入的量	U10
integral	a.	构成整体所必需的	U1
integrated	a.	综合的,完整的	U1
intemperance	n.	不节制,酗酒,过度	U4
interconnect	vi.	互相连接,互相联系	U1
interconnection	n.	互联联络,互连	U3
interdependence	n.	互相依赖	U2
interdependent	a.	互相依赖的,互相依存的	U2
intermingle	vt.	使混合,使掺和	U10
internal	a.	内部的,内在的,国内的	U10
interrelated	a.	相互关联的	U2
interrelation	n.	相互关系	U4
intestine	n.	肠	U1
intrinsic	a.	本质的,固有的	U10
intrude	v.	侵入,闯入,把……强加(在)(+on/upon)	U6
invasion	n.	侵犯,侵入,闯入	U8
invasive	a.	侵入的,侵略性的,攻击性的	U9
ion	n.	离子	U11
irritated	a.	恼怒的,生气的	U11
itchy	a.	使人发痒的	U11

J

joint	n.	关节	U6
jointly	ad.	共同地	U1
junction	n.	结合,连接	U4

L

lassitude	n.	疲乏,懒散,无精打采	U8
limb	n.	肢	U6
linger	vi.	逗留,徘徊	U8
locality	n.	地方,位置	U9

Glossary

longitudinally	ad.	经向地,纵向地,经度上地,长度上地	U6
lucid	a.	清楚的,透明的	U4
lumber	n.	腰	U4

M

maintain	v.	保持,维持	U7
mania	n.	狂躁症	U7
manifest	v.	清楚表示,显露	U6
materialism	n.	唯物主义,唯物论,实利主义,物质主义	U1
matrine	n.	苦参碱(抗肿瘤药,消炎镇痛药)	U11
medicinal	a.	药的,药用的,有药效的	U6
melodious	a.	旋律优美的,悦耳动听的	U9
meridian	n.	经络	U1
metabolic	a.	代谢作用的,新陈代谢的	U2
metabolism	n.	新陈代谢	U4
meteorology	n.	气象学	U2
metrorrhagia	n.	子宫不规则出血	U7
metrostaxis	n.	子宫渗血,漏下	U7
mobilization	n.	流通	U5
moisten	n./v.	润湿	U1
moisture	n.	潮湿,水分,降雨量,湿度	U3
morbid	a.	病态的,不健康的	U5
motion	n.	运动,动作	
	v.	向……摇头示意,打手势,摆动	U3
moxibustion	n.	艾灸,艾灼	U9
multiply	v.	使增加	U2
muscle	n.	肌肉	U6
muscular	a.	强壮的,有力的,肌肉发达的	U6
musculature	n.	肌肉组织	U6
mutative	a.	突变的	U5
mutual	a.	相互的,彼此的,共同的,共有的	U2

N

naive	a.	朴素的	U2
nausea	n.	反胃,恶心,晕船	U4
negative	a.	消极的,否定的,负的,阴性的	U3
nervous	a.	神经紧张的,不安的,神经的	U11

nourish	vt.	养育,滋养,使健壮	U3
numbness	n.	麻木,麻痹	U10
nutrient	n.	营养物	U4

O

obstinate	a.	难克服的,不易去除的	U8
obviously	a.	显然,明白地	U8
occurrence	n.	发生,出现	U7
odd	a.	奇数的,古怪的,临时的,剩余的,零散的	U3
odor	n.	气味,香气,臭气	U9
olfaction	n.	嗅,嗅觉	U1
oliguria	n.	尿过少,少尿(症)	U4
onslaught	n.	猛攻,攻击	U11
opisthotonos	n.	角弓反张	U7
opposition	n.	(强烈的)反对,反抗,对抗	U2
organ	n.	器官,元件,机构,机关	U2
organic	a.	器官的,器质性的,有机(体)的,有机物的	U1
organically	ad.	有机性地,器官上地,有组织地	U11
orifice	n.	孔,洞口	U7
originally	a.	起初,原来	U8
originate	v.	起源于,来自,创造,开创,发明	U2
overstrain	n.	过度紧张,过劳	U8
overwhelm	v.	战胜,压倒,征服,覆盖	U2

P

palpation	n.	触诊,扣诊	U1
palpitation	n.	心悸	U8
participate	vi.	参与,参加	U5
pathogen	n.	病原体,病菌	U7
pathogenesis	n.	发病机理	U1
pathogenic	a.	致病的,病原的,发病的	U7
pathological	a.	病理学的,病理上的	U2
pathology	n.	病理学,病理,病状,病变	U11
penetrate	v.	穿过,刺入,渗入	U8
pericardium	n.	心囊,心包膜	U4
permeate	v.	弥漫,充满,渗透,透入	U11
pertain	vi.	属于,附属(to)	U5

pharmacological	a.	药物学的,药理学的	U11
phenomena	n.	(phenomenon 的复数)现象,非凡的人,稀有的事,奇迹	U2
philosophical	a.	哲学的(等于 philosophic),冷静的	U3
philosophy	n.	哲学	U2
phlegm	n.	痰,黏液,黏液质	U10
physiological	a.	生理学的,生理学上的	U1
physiologically	ad.	生理学上地	U5
phytotherapy	n.	植物治疗法,草本疗法	U11
polyuria	n.	[医]多尿症	U5
pore	n.	毛孔,细孔	
	v.	注视,凝视,默想,沉思,钻研,熟读	U9
portion	n.	部分,一份,命运,定数	
	v.	把……分成多份	U6
praxis	n.	(pl. -xes)习惯,常规,实习,应用	U9
precisely	ad.	精确地,恰好,细心	U2
predate	vt.	在日期上早于,在日期上先,提前日期	U9
pregnancy	n.	怀孕	U9
preparation	n.	配制剂	U1
prerequisite	n.	先决条件,前提	U2
prescribe	v.	开(药方),为……开(药方),嘱咐(+for),规定,指定	U6
preventive	n.	预防,防止	
	a.	预防的,防止的	U1
primitive	n.	原始人,早期艺术家	
	a.	原始的,上古的	U11
primordial	a.	原始的,初生的,(从)原始时代存在的,基本的,根本的	U5
proclamation	n.	宣布,声明,公告	U1
profoundly	ad.	深刻地,深深地,极度地	U10
profuse	a.	极多的,充足的	U5
prognosis	n.	[医]预后(指医生对疾病结果的预测)	U8
prolapse	vi.	脱垂,下垂	
	n.	脱垂,下垂,脱出	U10
promote	vt.	促进,发扬,提升,推销	U6
propel	vt.	推动	U5
property	n.	财产,性质,性能,所有权	U3
prostration	n.	[医]虚脱,虚弱	U5
pulse	n.	脉搏,有节奏的跳动	
	v.	拍打,跳动,振动	U1
pungent	a.	苦痛的,严厉的,刺激性的	U9
purchase	vt.	购买	

	n.	购买,购置,买到的东西	U11
purify	v.	使纯净,提纯,净化	U3
purpura	n.	紫癜	U7
pylorus	n.	幽门	U4

R

reflux	n.	回流,逆流,退潮	U11
regime	n.	政权,政治制度,食物疗法,养生法	U9
regulate	vt.	管理,控制,为……制定规章	U6
relapse	vi.	故态复萌,旧病复发,再度堕落,再陷邪道	U10
release	vt.	释放,发射,让与,允许发表	U3
relieve	vt.	缓和,减轻,解除	U6
renew	v.	更新,恢复	U1
replenish	vt.	再斟(装)满(with),添足,加强,补充,再充电	U5
represent	vt.	表现,描绘,代表,象征,表示,作为……的代表	U2
requirement	n.	需求,要求,必要条件	U5
resistance	n.	抵抗,反抗,抗性,抵抗力,耐性	U9
resort	vi.	求助,依赖,诉诸,采取(某种手段等)	U9
respectively	ad.	分别地,各自地	U3
respiration	n.	呼吸,呼吸作用,植物的呼吸,生物的氧化作用	U5
restlessness	n.	坐立不安,心神不宁	U9
restrain	vt.	抑制,控制,制止,约束	U3
restriction	n.	约束,限制,管制,限定,法律,规章	U2
retention	n.	保持,保留	U8
rotate	v.	旋转,循环,转动,使轮流,交替	U10

S

sallow	a.	气色不好的,灰黄色的	U10
scanty	a.	数量不多的,稀少的	U4
scholar	n.	学者,奖学金获得者	U3
selective	a.	有选择性的	U6
sensation	n.	感觉,感受	U8
sensitivity	n.	敏感,灵敏	U9
sequela	n.	[医]后遗症,结果,后继者	U9
severity	n.	严重,剧烈	U8
significant	a.	重大的,有效的,有意义的,值得注意的	U10

simultaneous	a.	同时的,同时发生的	U9
situate	v.	使位于,使处于……地位(位置)	U2
skin regions		皮部	U6
slippery	a.	滑的,狡猾的,不稳定的	U10
sloppy	a.	稀薄	U4
solitary	a.	单独的,独居的,唯一的,人迹罕至的,幽静的	U2
solvent	n.	溶剂	
	a.	有偿付能力的,有溶解力的	U11
somatic	a.	身体的,肉体的	U5
sonorous	a.	圆润低沉的,响亮的,洪亮的	U8
soothe	vt.	安慰,抚慰,使舒服,使平静,减轻痛苦	U11
spleen	n.	脾脏,脾	U1
splenic	a.	脾脏的,脾的	U6
spontaneous	a.	自发的,自动的,一时冲动的	U8
sprain	n.	扭伤,(过度用力引起的)肿胀、炎症、出血和变色	U9
stagnant	a.	不流动的,停滞的	U8
stagnation	n.	淤滞,淤塞	U5
stalemate	n.	僵持,僵局	U8
static	a.	静态的,[物]静电的,静力的	U10
stern	a.	严厉的,坚定的	U9
sthenic	a.	强壮的,亢奋的	U7
sticky	a.	黏的,黏性的	U10
stool	n.	大便	U4
subjugation	n.	镇压,征服,平息	U3
subsidiary	n.	子公司,辅助者,附加物	
	a.	辅助的,附带的,隶属的	U1
substance	n.	物质	U5
substantial	a.	坚固的,结实的,大量的,可观的,重大的,重要的,实质的,基本的,大体上的	U2
sufficient	a.	足够的,充足的	U8
summarization	n.	摘要,概要	U4
summarize	vt.	总结,概述	U2
sunspot	n.	太阳的黑点,雀斑	U1
supercritical	a.	超临界的	U11
superficial	a.	表面的,浅薄的,肤浅的	U2
superficial collaterals		浮络	U6
superficies	n.	表面,表层	U8
supplement	vt.	补充,增补	U5
surpass	vt.	胜过,优于,超越,非……所能办到或理解	U3

surplus	n.	剩余,盈余	
	a.	过剩的	U4
sweat	vt.	使出汗,流出,使干苦活,剥削,发酵	U10
symmetrically	ad.	对称性地,对称地,平衡地	U6
symptom	n.	症状,表现,征兆,征候	U9
synthesize	vt.	合成,综合	U10

T

tenderness	n.	触痛,压痛,对触摸或施压的异常敏感	U9
tendon systems		经络	U6
tendon	n.	腱	U3
terminate	v.	使终止,使结束,结束,满期,终止	U6
theoretical	a.	理论上的	U3
therapeutic	a.	治疗的,治疗学的,有疗效的	U6
thorax	n.	胸,胸部,胸廓	U4
timely	a.	及时的,适时的	U10
tincture	n.	酊剂	U11
tissue	n.	组织,薄纸,棉纸,一套,一系列	U1
transform	vt.	转变,使变态,使改变性质	U5
trauma	n.	外伤,精神创伤	U9
traumatic	a.	外伤的	U7
turbid	a.	浑浊的,混乱的,泥水的	U4

U

ubiquity	n.	到处存在,普遍存在,无所不在	U2
ulcer	n.	溃疡	U7
ulceration	n.	溃疡,腐败	U4
ultrasonic	n.	超声波	
	a.	超音速的	U11
unpredictable	a.	出乎意料的,不可预知的,不定的	U11
untimely	a.	不适时的,不合时宜的	U8
urinary	a.	尿的,尿样的	U6
uterus	n.	子宫	U4

V

| variation | n. | 变化,变动(的程度),变奏(曲),变异,变种 | U2 |

Glossary

various	a.	各种不同的,各种各样的	U8
vein	n.	静脉,血管	U9
vessel	n.	容器,器皿,船,舰,脉管,血管	U3
vexation	n.	烦恼,忧虑	U7
vice versa	ad.	反之亦然	U2
violate	vt.	违反,侵犯,妨碍,亵渎	U3
violent	a.	剧烈的,强烈的,猛烈的	U8
viral	a.	滤过性毒菌的,滤过性毒菌引起的	U11
viscera	n.	内脏,内部的东西	U1
visceral	a.	内脏的,出于本能的,发自肺腑的,粗俗的	U9
vivid	a.	鲜艳的,生动的,栩栩如生的	U2
vomitive	n.	催吐剂	
	a.	呕吐的,使呕吐的	U4

W

wane	vi.	衰落,变小,亏缺,退潮,消逝	U3

12 branch meridians	十二经别	U6
12 main meridians	十二经脉	U6
8 extraordinary meridians	奇经八脉	U6